ECONOMICS OF RURAL LAND-USE CHANGE

Economics of Rural Land-Use Change

Edited by

KATHLEEN P. BELL
University of Maine, Orono, Maine, USA

KEVIN J. BOYLE
Virginia Polytechnic Institute and State University, USA

JONATHAN RUBIN
University of Maine, Orono, Maine, USA

Routledge
Taylor & Francis Group

LONDON AND NEW YORK

First published 2006 by Ashgate Publishing

2 Park Square, Milton Park, Abingdon, Oxon OX14 4RN
711 Third Avenue, New York, NY 10017, USA

Routledge is an imprint of the Taylor & Francis Group, an informa business

First issued in paperback 2016

British Library Cataloguing in Publication Data
Economics of rural land-use change. - (Ashgate studies in
    environmental and natural resource economics)
    1. Land use, Rural - United States - History 2. Land use,
    Rural - United States
    I. Bell, Kathleen P. II. Boyle, Kevin J. III. Rubin, Jonathan
    333.7'6'0973

Library of Congress Cataloging-in-Publication Data
Bell, Kathleen P.
    Economics of rural land-use change / by Kathleen P. Bell, Kevin J. Boyle and Jonathan Rubin.
        p. cm. -- (Ashgate studies in environmental and natural resource economics)
    Includes bibliographical references and index.

    1. Land use, Rural--United States. I. Boyle, Kevin J. II. Rubin, Jonathan. III. Title.
IV. Series.

HD256.B45 2005
333.76'0973--dc22

                                                                    2005021084

ISBN 978-0-7546-0983-4 (hbk)
ISBN 978-1-138-27237-8 (pbk)

Contents

List of Contributors

Mary Clare Ahearn is a Senior Economist with the United States Department of Agriculture's Economic Research Service. She received her Ph.D. in Economics from Oregon State University in 1984. Dr. Ahearn has worked on a variety of agricultural and natural resource policy issues, including farm structure and performance and the benefits of farm conservation practices and government programs. Dr. Ahearn has contributed extensively to the development of the Economic Research Service's program to study the public good benefits provided by farmland.

Ralph J. Alig is a Senior Economist with the United States Department of Agriculture's Forest Service. He received his Ph.D. in Land-Use Economics from Oregon State University in 1984. Dr. Alig has an established research program centered on the influence of economic and demographic factors on land-use changes involving forestry. For more than twenty years, he has researched these factors and applied models to policy analyses of timber supply, global change, and conservation programs. Dr. Alig is national coordinator for the Resource Planning Act Assessment and is a leader of the Forest Service's Land Use and Land Cover Dynamics team.

Kathleen P. Bell is an Assistant Professor of Resource Economics and Policy at the University of Maine. She received her Ph.D. in Economics from the University of Maryland in 1997. Her research interests include land-use change, the design of land conservation and management policies, the influence of government policies and natural amenities on household location decisions, spatial econometrics, and economic valuation of environmental goods and services.

Kevin J. Boyle is Department Head and Professor of Agricultural and Applied Economics at Virginia Polytechnic Institute and State University. He received his Ph.D. in Economics from the University of Wisconsin in 1985. Dr. Boyle's research is focused on understanding the publics' preferences for environmental and ecological resources, the effects of various methodologies on eliciting these preferences, and how people respond to environmental laws and regulations. His particular focus is on the estimation of economic values for environmental resources that are not expressed through the market.

Elena G. Irwin is an Associate Professor in the Department of Agricultural, Environmental, and Development Economics at the Ohio State University. She received her Ph.D. in Agricultural and Resource Economics from the University of Maryland in 1998. Her research interests include land use change, urbanization patterns in exurban and rural areas, the influence of government policies on household location decisions, and the relationship between urban sprawl and core urban decline.

J. Walter Milon is the Provost's Distinguished Research Professor of Economics at the University of Central Florida. He received his Ph.D. in Economics from Florida State University in 1978. Dr. Milon's research focuses on economic policy issues related to renewable resource management. He has conducted research on water quantity and quality management, fisheries, economic valuation of environmental goods, ecosystem management, and applications of benefit-cost analysis. His recent work has focused on economic issues related to restoration and protection of ecosystems, particularly the Everglades/South Florida region. He has served as a technical advisor to the Governor's Commission for a Sustainable South Florida and the U.S. Man and the Biosphere, Human Dominated Systems Directorate.

Raymond B. Palmquist is a Professor of Economics at North Carolina State University. He received his Ph.D. in Economics from the University of Washington in 1978. He specializes in measuring the benefits of environmental improvements using hedonic techniques in rural as well as urban settings. His research has dealt with air pollution, water pollution, the marine environment, forestry economics, noise, odor, erosion and drainage, and hazardous wastes.

Andrew J. Plantinga is an Associate Professor of Agricultural and Resource Economics at Oregon State University. He received his Ph.D. in Agricultural and Resource Economics from the University of California-Berkeley in 1995. His research focuses on empirical land-use modeling, climate change, the economics of forestry, and nonmarket valuation.

Stephen J. Polasky holds the Fesler-Lampert Chair in Ecological/Environmental Economics at the University of Minnesota. He received his Ph.D. in Economics from the Universiy of Michigan in 1986. He was senior staff economist for environment and resources for the President's Council of Economic Advisors 1998-1999. His research interests include biodiversity conservation and endangered species policy, integrating ecological and economic analysis, game theoretic analysis of natural resource use, common property resources, and environmental regulations.

Jonathan Rubin is the Interim Director of the Margaret Chase Smith Policy Center for Public Policy and Associate Professor of Resource Economics and Policy at the University of Maine. He received his Ph.D. in Economics from the University of California-Davis in 1993. Dr. Rubin's research focuses on market-based solutions to attain environmental goals. His current research addresses the potential economic and social impacts involved in the trading of pollution permits. and the economic and environmental impacts of alternative fuel vehicles.

Kathleen Segerson is Professor of Economics at the University of Connecticut. She also holds a joint appointment in the Department of Agricultural and Resource Economics. She received her Ph.D. in Economics from Cornell University in 1984. Dr. Segerson's research is primarily in the area of the economics of pollution control, with particular emphasis on the incentive effects of alternative policies. She specializes in the application of legal rules and principles to environmental problems and has worked extensively on environmental problems associated with agricultural land use.

Mario F. Teisl is an Associate Professor of Resource Economics and Policy at the University of Maine. He received his Ph.D. in Economics from the University of Maryland in 1997. Dr. Teisl's research is primarily in the area of the economics of information. His research interests include modeling demand under varying information states and measuring the effects of information on consumer welfare. He has made significant contributions in the development of conjoint analysis as a tool for nonmarket valuation.

JunJie Wu is an Associate Professor in the Department of Agricultural and Resource Economics at Oregon State University. He received his Ph.D. in Economics from the University of Connecticut in 1992. His major areas of research include the optimal design of conservation policy, the interactions between agricultural production and environmental quality, and the economics of land use.

List of Figures

List of Tables

Acknowledgements

The impetus for this book came from a workshop on the economics of land-use change held at the University in Maine in July 1999. Funding for the workshop was provided by the University of Maine College of Natural Sciences, Forestry, and Agriculture and the USDA Forest Service Pacific Northwest Research Station. The completion of this book would not have been possible without such support. Special thanks are due to Jessica Sargent-Michaud and Kelly Cobourn for providing much-needed technical and administrative support. Finally, we thank the editorial staff at Ashgate for their patience, guidance, and support.

PART I
INTRODUCTION AND
BACKGROUND

Chapter 1

Objectives and Perspectives

Kathleen P. Bell, Kevin J. Boyle, Andrew J. Plantinga,
Jonathan Rubin, and Mario F. Teisl

Introduction

Land is an input to the production of an array of private goods, including agricultural crops, forest products, and housing. Private decisions about the use of land, however, often give rise to significant external costs, such as non-point source pollution and changes to wildlife habitat, and external benefits, such as the provision of recreational opportunities. One role of land-use policies is to narrow the divergence between privately and socially desirable outcomes, either by altering the incentives faced by private agents or through direct government ownership and management of land.

The rural landscape of the United States underwent tremendous changes during the 20th century, and these changes have given rise to complex and pressing land-use policy issues. As shown in Figure 1.1, the share of the U.S. population living in rural areas has decreased steadily since 1900. In 2000, approximately 21 per cent of the U.S. population lived in rural areas. Much of the employment in rural areas has traditionally been in agriculture and forestry industries, for which land is an essential input. For example, in 1820 approximately 70 per cent of the U.S. population was engaged in farming, while in 2000 only two per cent of the U.S. population was engaged in farming (U.S. Department of Agriculture 2000). Labor-saving technology, which has reduced the labor requirements in these industries, accounts for some of this decrease. Other factors, such as an absolute decline in farm income, are also responsible. Figure 1.2 shows an almost 33 per cent decline in employment per $1,000 of real gross product in rural land-based industries since the 1950s. In addition, the relative importance of these industries to the U.S. economy has declined. Rural land-based employment and gross product, expressed as shares of U.S. totals, have declined steadily since the 1950s, although the rate of decline has diminished over time (Figure 1.2).

Paradoxically, while many rural areas struggle with problems of declining population and economic activity, other rural areas face problems with rapid population and economic growth. After World War II, there was a dramatic shift in population from traditional rural areas and urban centers to suburban areas. While many factors have contributed to suburbanization, including the availability of low-interest loans for new home construction provided to returning World War II

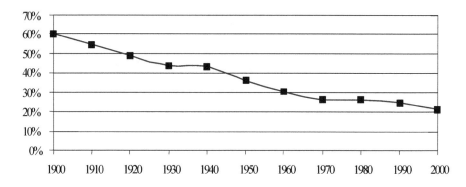

Figure 1.1 Percentage of the U.S. population living in rural areas, 1900–2000

Source: U.S. Department of Commerce, Bureau of the Census.

veterans by the Veterans Administration, it is difficult to overstate the importance of affordable private automobile transportation and public road construction. In 1950, the U.S. population (152 million people) used 43 million cars and trucks to drive 458 million miles. By 1997, the U.S. population (now 268 million people) used 201 million vehicles to drive 2.5 billion miles (Davis 1999). Vehicular transportation was made possible by extensive road construction, including the expansion of the Interstate Highway System, under the Federal Highway Aid Act of 1956, by 3.9 million miles (U.S. Department of Transportation 1999).

Suburbanization has resulted in the conversion of millions of acres of rural land near cities to developed uses (Vesterby, Heimlich, and Krupa 1994). According to the U.S. Bureau of the Census, the area of urban land, which by the Census definition includes suburban areas, increased by about 120 per cent between 1960 and 1990. At the national level, urbanization has outpaced population growth, which increased by only 40 per cent during this period. The post-war migration to suburban areas dramatically altered settlement patterns in the U.S., such that by the 1990s a majority of Americans lived in suburbia (Carlson 1995). These shifts in population have changed the rural landscape from one that provides simultaneous production, economic livelihood and residences for a large percentage of the population to one that provides opportunities for urban and suburban dwellers to relax and recreate.

The impacts of shifting populations and changing landscapes have been documented for many regions of the United States. The repercussions of these transitions are different in rural and urban areas, and across regions. In Maine, for example, a recent analysis revealed that the fastest growing communities (in terms of the rate of population growth between 1960 and 1990) were, in most cases, on the outskirts of traditional city centers (Maine State Planning Office 1997). Over

Figure 1.2 U.S. rural land-based employment and gross product*, 1948–1997

*The employment and gross product series are full-time equivalent employment and gross product (value added) for Standard Industrial Classification (SIC) 01–02 (farms), 07–09 (agricultural services, forestry, and fishing), 24 (lumber and wood products), and 26 (paper and allied products), and are expressed as a share of the U.S. total. The employment/real gross product series is the number of full-time equivalent employees per $1,000 of real (1982=100) gross product for rural land-based sectors.

Source: U.S. Department of Commerce, Bureau of Economic Analysis 2002.

the same period, many of these city centers experienced losses in population. Against this backdrop of suburban migration, the populations of more distant, rural parts of Maine have been declining. Between 1990 and 2000, four of Maine's sixteen counties, all located in the northernmost part of the state, experienced declines in population (U.S. Department of Commerce, Bureau of the Census 2000).

The changing function of rural lands is also the result of a fundamental shift in public preferences regarding land use and the environment. Following the proposed construction of the Hetch-Hetchy dam in Yosemite National Park in the early 1900s, public land management emerged as a matter of public concern and debate. During the 1960s, 1970s, and continuing today, the increased demand for non-commodity benefits from public lands has forced a reassessment of management practices by federal agencies, such as the U.S. Forest Service, who have traditionally placed a primary emphasis on commodity production (Bowes and Krutilla 1985). Public preferences for non-commodity benefits were central to the spotted owl controversy in the Pacific Northwest. While arguments focused on spotted owl habitat, underlying currents of the debate included the presumed right of forest industry firms and timber-dependent communities to harvest timber on national forest lands, public demand for forest recreation unaltered by timber harvesting, and existence values for old-growth forest ecosystems. Similar controversies have arisen on both coasts of the United States related to the protection and management of native salmon stocks. In recent decades, public expectations regarding rural land use have expanded to include activities that occur on privately owned lands as well, as evidenced by citizen-initiated efforts to regulate timber harvesting in Maine, Georgia, Alabama, and other eastern states. Another notable trend in recent decades is the willingness of citizens to support government land conservation programs. For example, in 2003, voters in 23 states passed 100 ballot measures, leveraging almost two billion dollars for land conservation (The Trust for Public Land and Land Trust Alliance 2004).

A confluence of demographic, economic, and social forces has stimulated conflicts over the use of public and private rural lands and policy actions at federal, state, and local levels of government aimed at resolving these conflicts. In response to changing preferences for outputs from public lands, federal land-management agencies have given greater weight to non-commodity benefits in the management of public lands for timber, agriculture, recreation, and environmental protection. Federal programs, such as the U.S. Department of Agriculture's Conservation Reserve Program, have put an increasing emphasis on achieving environmentally beneficial outcomes (Osborn, Llacuna, and Linsenbigler 1995). In some instances, federal policies regulating uses of private lands, such as the Endangered Species Act, have led to claims of government takings (Innes, Polasky, and Tschirhart 1998).

Another catalyst of conflict is declining economic activity in rural areas. In rural communities faced with declining population and economic activity, decisions to permit new land uses can prove controversial, especially when the facility is expected to generate economic activity but may also result in significant social and environmental costs. Examples of such facilities include waste disposal, gambling, or major industrial facilities. State legislation related to the siting of structures, such as large-scale confinement feeding operations for livestock and aquaculture pens, reflects a divergence of attitudes related to the use of lands and natural resources. Finally, there is evidence of conflict between long-term and newer residents in rural areas. For example, many states have passed 'right-to-farm' laws in response to conflicts arising from incompatibilities between residential and agricultural uses of land. In other instances, newer residents have pushed for rigid, local land-use controls to prevent further development and to preserve the amenities that initially attracted them to the area. In rural areas with limited local land-use control experience, these pushes can generate controversy, especially if they are viewed as infringing on private property rights and traditional uses.

Objectives of this Book

The broad objective of this book is to present an overview of economic analyses of rural land-use change. Earlier books on the economics of land use (e.g., Barlowe 1958; Alonso 1964; Van Kooten 1993) are rooted in the traditions of Ricardo and von Thünen and largely provide review and extensions of earlier concepts and models. Our point of departure is an emergent literature that uses modern economic methods to model land-use change and to investigate land-use policies in a cost-benefit framework. During the past decade, land use has been an active research area for economists. Theoretical models have been developed that explicitly consider the dynamic and potentially irreversible nature of land-use decisions. Moreover, procedures have been developed to estimate the external costs and benefits of changes in land use.

The book is divided into four parts. Part I offers an introduction to economic perspectives of rural land-use change and provides relevant background information on land-use trends. Following a discussion of recent land-use trends in Chapter 2 (Ahearn and Alig), Chapter 3 (Alig and Ahearn) provides an overview of the effects of policy and technological change on land use. Rubin offers a discussion of the interaction between land-use trends and transportation policies in Chapter 4. The introductory section of the book concludes with an overview of the demographic trends commensurate with recent land-use change, by Mageean and Bartlett (Chapter 5).

Part II focuses on theoretical and empirical models designed to gauge the determinants of rural land-use change. Segerson, Plantinga, and Irwin provide a synthesis of recent theoretical developments in characterizing land-use patterns and studying land-use decisions using an economic framework (Chapter 6). This summary is followed by a parallel synthesis of recent empirical developments. Irwin and Plantinga (Chapter 7) offer an overview of empirical methods employed to investigate the economic aspects of land-use change. The second part of the book concludes with two chapters that apply the empirical methods summarized in Chapter 7. Plantinga (Chapter 8) provides an example of an empirical application of a shares model of land-use change, and Irwin and Bell (Chapter 9) offer an empirical application of a spatially-explicit model of land-use change.

Changes in land use have implications for environmental quality and other outcomes of concern to policy makers. Part III considers these implications by featuring the consequences of land-use change. In Chapter 10, Milon chronicles the relationship between land-use change and ecosystem management using a South Florida case study. Polasky and Vossler (Chapter 11) focus on the interdependencies of land conservation and species conservation. In the final chapter of this part of the book, Wu presents an overview of land-use change and regulatory change in the western part of the United States (Chapter 12).

Part IV considers the role of economic valuation in assessing the welfare effects of land-use change. Applied welfare analysis of land-use issues strives to understand the services provided by land resources and to determine the relative values of different landscape components. Market and non-market valuation methods have been applied to estimate the benefits and costs of changes in land use. In Chapter 13, Boyle provides an overview of non-market economic valuation methods and their suitability for examining land-use issues. This part of the book concludes with two empirical studies that employ non-market economic valuation methods. Teisl and Boyle (Chapter 14) summarize an application of conjoint research methods to estimate attributes of forested landscapes. In Chapter 15, Palmquist presents a hedonic property value model designed to derive the impact of hog farms on residential property values in North Carolina.

Intended Readers

Land use is an extremely broad topic and, as a result, of interest to researchers, planners, and decision-makers from numerous disciplines. While acknowledging the many important contributions in this area from geographers, planners, and ecologists, the content of this text concentrates on economic approaches to analyzing land-use problems and, particularly, the application of modern economic methods. In addition, much of the content is geared to rural land uses, such as forest, agriculture, and wetlands. Urban or developed land uses are discussed in the context of how they affect rural land use, such as the conversion of rural land to developed uses at the urban fringe. Finally, there is little emphasis on local land management. Instead, land-use policy at the state and national level is featured. Although many of the drivers of land use change are local in nature, state and federal government policies arguably have broader implications for the rural landscape.

The intended audience of this book includes economists, decision-makers, policy analysts, and planners with some training in economic theory and econometrics. By design, the book is a reference for economists active in land-use research and for those seeking an introduction to this research area. It is designed to serve as a text for a graduate-level land economics course. Finally, the book is also intended to be a resource for land-use policy analysts and researchers from other relevant disciplines, including geography, landscape ecology, urban and regional planning, and transportation policy, who wish to find an overview of economic concepts and models related to land-use change.

References

Alonso, W. 1964. *Location and Land Use: Toward a General Theory of Land Rent.* Cambridge, Massachusetts: Harvard University Press.
Barlowe, R. 1958. *Land Resource Economics.* Englewood Cliffs, New Jersey: Prentice-Hall.
Bowes, M.D., and J.V. Krutilla. 1985. *Multiple-Use Management: The Economics of Public Forestlands.* Washington, District of Columbia: Resources for the Future.
Carlson, D., L. Wormser, and C. Ulberg. 1995. *At Road's End: Transportation and Land Use Choices for Communities.* Washington, District of Columbia: Island Press.

Davis, S.C. 1999. *Transportation Energy Data Book, Edition 19.* Prepared for the Oak Ridge National Laboratory, Center for Transportation Analysis. Oakridge, Tennessee.

Innes, R., S. Polasky, and J. Tschirhart. 1998. 'Takings, Compensation, and Endangered Species Protection on Private Lands.' *Journal of Economic Perspectives* 12(3): 35-52.

Maine State Planning Office. 1997. *The Cost of Sprawl.* Special report prepared by Evan Richert. Augusta, Maine.

Osborn, C.T., F. Llacuna, and M. Linsenbigler. 1995. *The Conservation Reserve Program: Enrollment Statistics for the Signup Periods 1–12 and Fiscal Years 1986–93.* U.S. Department of Agriculture, Economic Research Service Statistical Bulletin No. 925.

The Trust for Public Land and Land Trust Alliance. 2004. *Land Vote 2003. Americans Invest in Parks and Open Space.* Washington, District of Columbia: The Trust for Public Land.

U.S. Department of Agriculture, Economic Research Service. 2000. 'Farming's Role in the Rural Economy,' in *Agricultural Outlook* (June-July). Washington, District of Columbia.

U.S. Department of Commerce, Bureau of Economic Analysis. 2002. *Gross Domestic Product by Industry and the Components of Gross Domestic Product.* Prepared by the Industry Economics Division. Washington, District of Columbia.

U.S. Department of Commerce, Bureau of the Census. 2000. 'United States Census of Population and Housing.' Retrieved from:
http://www.census.gov/population/censusdata/urpop0090.txt.

U.S. Department of Transportation. 1999. *Highway Statistics 1998.* Prepared by the Federal Highway Administration. Washington, District of Columbia.

Van Kooten, G.C. 1993. *Land Resource Economics and Sustainable Development: Economic Policies and the Common Good.* Vancouver: University of British Columbia Press.

Vesterby, M., R.E. Heimlich, and K.S. Krupa. 1994. *Urbanization of Rural Land in the United States.* U.S. Department of Agriculture, Economic Research Service Agricultural Economic Report No. 673. Washington, District of Columbia.

Chapter 2

A Discussion of Recent Land-Use Trends

Mary Clare Ahearn and Ralph J. Alig

Introduction

The objective of this chapter is to provide a description of recent trends in rural land uses within the United States as the first step in developing an understanding of contemporary land-use issues. This discussion is placed in the context of recent policy discussions and hints at directions for future policy. Moreover, this description of recent trends provides a foundation for the subsequent assessments of the determinants and consequences of land-use change found in Chapters 6 through 12.

This chapter focuses on changes in land use within the United States from 1945 to 1997. The period immediately following World War II is often considered the beginning of the mechanical revolution in agriculture and forestry. Over time, public investments in infrastructure such as roads and highways have continued to significantly impact the path of development and land-use change.

We begin with an overview of measurement and data issues and a summary of the U.S. Department of Agriculture (USDA) data series, which serve as the basis of our historical assessment of rural land use. The discussion then turns to trends in land use, land ownership, and land quality.

Measurement of Land Uses

Before beginning our discussion of land-use trends, it is helpful to introduce terminology related to the measurement and description of land uses and land-use change. Terminology and data collection are important components of land-use research. A firm understanding of these concepts and measurement issues will improve interpretations of land-use data and policy recommendations.

Two common ways of classifying land are by its use and by its cover. Land use is defined as arrangements, activities, and inputs people undertake in a certain land cover to produce, change, or maintain it (di Gregorio and Jansen 1997). Land cover is the observed biophysical cover on the earth's surface. Use and cover classifications reference different aspects of lands and convey fundamentally different information. However, it is important to recognize that land cover can affect human uses of the land and that human uses can change land cover.

A second important consideration in reading this chapter relates to the land-use classification used by the federal government in the databases used/referenced here. Federal records may classify a single land area with a single land-use category, when in reality the land area has multiple uses. For example, some of the forestland managed by the U.S. Forest Service is also grazed, but this land is likely characterized as forestland in terms of use and cover. Multiple-use management of lands complicates the accounting of land uses.

Land-use data are collected by a variety of government agencies for a number of purposes, and no single land-use survey covers all land in the United States. In addition, some government agencies collect similar data, but with differing concepts and definitions, resulting in different statistical estimates. An important example of this are the different estimates of urban areas as measured by the U.S. Bureau of the Census and the USDA. Land-use surveys generally vary in terms of statistical data collection methods and temporal and spatial scope.

In order to provide a consistent and comprehensive understanding of land use, the USDA developed the Major Land Use Series. The Major Land Use Series is a data series of land use that is based on a variety of surveys and public administrative records of land use. In compiling the series, a significant amount of effort is devoted to reconciling the differences among the variety of data sources from which it draws, including the National Resources Inventory (NRI). In the discussion of changes in land use from 1945 to 1997, this chapter draws heavily on both the Major Land Use Series and the NRI. The land-use classifications and primary data resources of the Series and the NRI are described in the chapter appendix.

Recent Land-Use Trends in the United States

Data from the USDA's Major Land Use Series (Table 2.1) and the National Resources Inventory (NRI) data series (Table 2.2) serve as the basis of this discussion. Table 2.1 presents the number of acres by land-use classification for select years between 1945 and 1997. Table 2.2 is an NRI-based land use transition matrix for the 1982-1997 period: the columns and rows of the table represent acres in each land-use in 1982, and 1997, respectively. Entries on the matrix diagonal indicate acres that did not change use over the observed time period, while entries on the off-diagonal indicate a transition (for example, 11 million acres of land classified as cropland in 1982 were classified as rangeland in 1997). The data presented in Table 2.1 provide a comprehensive picture of the land-use allocation over time, while the transition matrix in Table 2.2 helps to provide insight into the direction of shifts in rural land uses.

The three major uses of land in the contiguous United States are grassland pasture and range, forestland, and cropland. In 1997, these three uses represented 84 per cent of all land in the 48 contiguous states. Their respective shares of the total land area have remained remarkably stable over more than five decades. The share of land in cropland was 24 per cent in 1945 and 1997, with minor variation in the intervening years. The shares of land in forestland and grassland were only slightly less in 1997 than in 1945, 29 compared to 32 per cent and 31 compared to 35 per cent, respectively.

These relatively small net changes at an aggregate level, however, mask the underlying dynamics of land-use change. The key point to note is where and when change occurs. With few exceptions (e.g., change to urban use), land-use shifts occur in both directions across land-use categories. For example, some land shifts from grassland to cropland during the same period that other cropland moves into grassland.

Table 2.1 Major land uses of the contiguous United States, 1945–1997 (million acres)[a, b]

Land Use	1945	1949	1954	1959	1964	1969	1974	1978	1982	1987	1992	1997
Cropland	451	478	465	458	444	472	465	471	470	464	460	455
Cropland Used for Crops	363	383	381	358	335	333	361	368	383	331	337	349
Cropland Idled	40	26	19	34	52	51	21	26	21	68	56	39
Cropland Used for Pasture	47	69	66	65	57	88	83	76	65	65	67	68
Grassland Pasture and Range	660	631	632	630	636	601	595	584	594	589	589	578
Forestland	602	606	615	611	612	603	599	583	567	558	559	553
Forestland Grazed	345	320	301	244	224	198	179	171	158	155	145	140
Forestland Not Grazed	257	286	314	367	388	405	420	412	410	404	414	412
Special Uses	100	105	110	124	145	143	148	167	177	191	194	207
Urban Land	15	18	19	27	29	31	35	44	50	56	58	64
Transportation	23	23	25	25	26	26	26	26	26	25	25	25
Recreation and Wildlife Areas	23	28	28	32	50	53	57	66	71	84	87	96
National Defense Areas	25	22	27	29	29	23	22	22	22	19	19	15
Misc. Farmland Uses	15	15	12	11	11	10	8	8	8	7	6	7
Miscellaneous Other Land	93	84	81	79	63	78	91	92	89	94	92	102
Total Land, 48 States	1,905	1,904	1,904	1,902	1,900	1,897	1,897	1,897	1,896	1,896	1,894	1,894

[a] Rounding may cause discrepancies between estimates of totals and summation of specific uses.
[b] Total land area differs over time due to re-measurement of the U.S. land area.

Sources: Major Land Use Series Data, Vesterby (2001).

Table 2.2 National Resources Inventory-based land use transition matrix, 1982–1997 (million acres) [a, b]

	Land use	Cropland	Rangeland	1982 Uses Forestland	Miscellaneous	Other	1997 Totals
	Cropland [c]	509	6	20	16	1	552
1997 Uses	Rangeland	11	395	3	5	3	416
	Forestland	6	2	380	12	2	403
	Miscellaneous [d]	3	1	3	116	—	123
	Other [e]	1	2	1	—	396	399
	1982 Totals [f]	529	406	407	149	402	1,893

[a] — equals less than 500,000 acres.
[b] Excludes Alaska. NRI data are not directly comparable with Major Land Use Series data in Table 2.1.   The NRI uses different data collection techniques and slightly different definitions of land use.
[c] Cropland includes all crops, idle cropland, summer fallow, and pasture.
[d] Miscellaneous includes other farmland, rural land, urban land, and roads.
[e] Other includes primarily federal land that is not inventoried.
[f] Sum of specific land uses may not add to estimated total due to rounding.

Source: Vesterby and Krupa (2001).

Urban Land and Other Special Land Uses

Although this category only accounts for 11 per cent of the total land in the 48 contiguous states in 1997, it accounted for the largest percentage increase in land area during the period from 1945 to 1997.   Acreage in the Special Land Uses classification increased by 107 per cent from 1945 to 1997.

Urban land, as defined in the Major Land Use series, more than quadrupled from 1945 to 1997 to 64 million acres. Based on the information provided in the transition matrix of Table 2.2, most of the increase in urban land (included in the Miscellaneous category) from 1982 to 1997 came from decreases in cropland and forest uses.   From 1982 to 1987, 1.3 million acres per year were converted from undeveloped to developed uses.   From 1987 to 1992, 1.5 million acres per year were converted.   And, for the most recent period, 1992 to 1997, 2.2 million acres per year were converted from undeveloped to developed uses (U.S. Department of Agriculture, Natural Resource Conservation Service 2001). The most common land cover that was developed between 1992 and 1997 was forestland (43 per cent).   Of the remaining new developed land in 1997, 25 per cent was converted from cropland, 17 per cent from pastureland, and 11 per cent from rangeland (*Ibid.*).   The increase in the annual rate of change in developed acres between 1992 and 1997 fueled an already keen national interest in better managing growth and conserving open lands.

While the rapid rate of conversion of undeveloped lands to developed land uses is of interest to policy-makers, the spatial distribution of population on these developed lands is also of preeminent importance. For example, the rate of increase in land classified as urban is significantly larger than the rate of increase in the population living in urban areas. From 1950 to 1990, the rate of increase of the urban population was less than 100 per cent, while the growth rate of land classified as urban was approximately 400 per cent over this period (U.S. Department of Commerce, Bureau of the Census 2002). The implication of this finding is that there is a significant increase in urban space per urban resident over this recent time period.

Natural Resources Inventory data from 1997 reveal a significant increase in developed and built-up areas outside of urban areas during the 1990s (U.S. Department of Agriculture, Natural Resource Conservation Service 2001). While the total land in rural areas decreased between 1980 and 1997 (by the amount of land that shifted to urban areas), the annual change in rural land converted to rural residences increased by 1.03 million acres over that same time period (Vesterby and Krupa 2001). In large part, this new use of previously undeveloped rural land is for rural residences, often times on the fringe of urban areas, and often times with large lot sizes. This is evidence of what is commonly called urban sprawl. A variety of definitions of urban sprawl exist, and there is limited consensus on a single definition. Most definitions, however, share a common emphasis on low-density development, geographic separation of essential places, and dependence on automobiles for travel (Heimlich and Anderson 2001).

Though not experiencing quite as high a rate of increase as acres in urban uses, land in recreation and wildlife uses increased substantially from 1945 to 1997. In 1997, 96 million acres were in recreation and wildlife areas, compared to 23 million acres in 1945. In 1997, about 23 million acres of land were used for roads and other transportation needs. The land area falling under this classification has changed very little over the past five decades. Land used for defense purposes declined by 40 per cent, to 15 million acres, from 1945 to 1997. Those changes support the notion of an urban population seeking recreation and preserved lands in rural areas. On the other hand, the road system appears to be largely in place with the major changes involving the upgrading of the quality of roads.

Grassland Pasture and Range

In 1945, at the beginning of the study period, there were 660 million acres of land in this land use category. Since that time, the number of acres in grassland pasture and range uses has declined. By 1997, there were 578 million acres of land in the 48 states that were classified as either grassland pasture or range. The 1982 to 1997 transition data shown in Table 2.2 for rangeland indicate that most of the recent movement of land out of and into this land use involved cropland uses. Approximately 11 million acres of rangeland moved into cropland uses during the 15-year period, but more than half of that number of cropland acres (six million) moved into rangeland.

Forestland

Forestlands account for the second largest use of land in the contiguous 48 states. From Table 2.1, the 553 million acres in forest uses in 1997 account for almost 29 per cent of the land in these states. Approximately 140 million acres of these forestlands were grazed in 1997, and 30 per cent of total forestland is federal land.

In 1945, there were 602 million acres in forest uses and this level was relatively stable until the 1970s. Since that time, there has been a slow but steady decline in the number of acres in this use, with about one quarter of the reduction in the South (U.S. Department of Agriculture, Forest Service 2000). There has also been a trend towards less grazing activity on forestlands. In 1945, the majority of forestland was grazed; the opposite holds true in 1997.

Table 2.2 indicates slightly more acres in forests in 1997 than in 1982. About three times as many acres moved from cropland to forest use as shifted from forest uses to cropland uses between 1982 and 1997. Approximately 12 million acres of forestland moved into a variety of miscellaneous uses between 1982 and 1997.

Cropland

In 1997, there were 455 million acres in cropland, which was very similar to the 451 million acres of cropland in 1945. However, there was movement below and especially above that net level throughout the study period. Aside from developed uses, cropland generally offers the highest economic return to landowners. Land owners and farm operators make cropland use decisions at key times of the year based on their assessments of the potential for return, which varies with supply and demand conditions and the government programs available to support growing crops or to set land aside from production. Hence, the variation in acres used for crops over the study period may be explained as a response to changing market conditions and government programs, such as the Conservation Reserve Program, which pays eligible farmers to idle their land in conserving uses.

Miscellaneous Other Land

The Miscellaneous Other Land classification, which includes land areas of little surface use, such as open swamps, rural commercial areas, such as golf courses, and lands not inventoried, accounted for approximately five per cent of the nation's land in 1997 (Table 2.1). Little change in acreage from 1945 to 1997 is observed for this land-use classification.

Recent Trends in Land Ownership

A discussion of recent trends in land use would be incomplete without consideration of trends in land ownership. The land area of the United States, including Hawaii and Alaska, is 2.3 billion acres. Twenty-eight per cent of this land (or 630 million acres) is owned by the federal government. Ownership type can affect the economic, social, and ecological roles of lands. Privately and publicly owned lands are sometimes viewed as distinct natural resources due to the differing land management strategies employed. As emphasized in Chapters 6 and 7 of this volume, a basic tenet of economics is that land resources are employed in their highest and best use. For private land, the highest use is typically equated with the greatest market return. Historically, public lands have generally had designated public good uses that are not necessarily related to their highest market return. Moreover, management philosophies for public lands are becoming increasingly complex as managers implement multiple-use management strategies, while considering tighter budget constraints and opportunities to generate revenue.

Federally Owned Lands

In recent times, the number of acres in federal ownership has changed slowly. For example, from 1982 to 1997, federally owned acres increased by about one per cent (U.S. Department of Agriculture, Natural Resource Conservation Service 2000). While the environmental movement in this country has likely contributed to interest in the use and expansion of federal lands, other movements rooted in the protection of private property rights may have opposed such increases (Opie 1987).

  In some regions of the United States, the spatial concentration of federal lands makes them critical factors in understanding ecological, economic, and social issues. The 630 million acres of land that were owned by the federal government, as of September 30, 1999, were not evenly distributed across the states (U.S. Department of Interior, Bureau of Land Management 2001). Federal lands, mostly forestlands and rangeland, are largely concentrated in the western United States. The federal government owns most of these lands, but a small share is simply under federal management. 42 per cent of forestland is publicly held (36 per cent, excluding Alaska). Most of that is owned by the federal government, but states own 19 per cent and local governments own three per cent of all forestlands (U.S. Department of Agriculture, Forest Service 2000). The ownership and distribution situation for land in pasture and rangeland uses is similar to that for forest uses. A significant share of these lands (26 per cent) is also owned by the federal government (U.S. Department of Agriculture, Forest Service 2000).

  Alaska has the greatest number of acres that are federally owned – 228 million acres, or nearly two-thirds of the state's total land area. As a proportion of the total acres of land in Nevada, the federal government owns 83 per cent. This ownership pattern is in contrast with the situation in five states where federal ownership is less than one per cent of the total land area: Connecticut, Delaware, Iowa, Maine, New York and Rhode Island. (U.S. Department of Interior, Bureau of Land Management 2001). The much greater federal ownership of land in the West is a function of many factors, not the least of which is the historic settlement of the country from the East. As new territories in the West were added to the original 13 eastern colonies of the United States, they first became the property of the U.S. government.

  Thus, while land in public ownership has remained relatively constant, this ownership, itself, and public expectations regarding the management of public lands have affected land use. A variety of federal agencies manage the federal lands for the public, including the Bureau of Land Management (264.3 million acres), the Forest Service (191 million acres), the Fish and Wildlife Service (91 million acres), the National Park Service (80.7 million acres), and several other agencies managing smaller areas (including the Bureau of Indian Affairs, Bureau of Reclamation, Department of Defense, and the Tennessee Valley Authority) (U.S. Department of Interior, Bureau of Land Management 2001). Federal management promotes the use of these lands for livestock grazing, production of forest products, wildlife refuges, watershed protection and water provision, and recreation. Furthermore, the philosophy behind the management of federal lands is evolving from one of single-type consumptive uses to one that recognizes multiple purposes. National forest lands were historically managed for optimal production of forest products, but with the evolving societal preferences for how public lands are managed, timber harvest volumes on national forests in 1997 were only about 30 per cent of levels in 1986 (Haynes et al. 2003). Today, timber harvests from national forests account for approximately six per cent of the timber harvested in the United States (U.S. Department of Agriculture, Forest Service 2000).

The biggest area of increasing use is recreation on federal lands (Cordell et al. 1999). National parks accounted for only 14 per cent of all recreational visits to federal lands. Recreational visits to forests managed by the Forest Service accounted for 45 per cent of the total visitor days to federal lands, with more than 200 million visits annually. Visits to Army Corps of Engineer sites accounted for 27 per cent of recreational visitor days, and the remaining visits were to areas managed by a variety of other agencies (*Ibid.*). Two drivers of changes in the use of federal lands are changing markets for natural resource products and changes in public preferences. Traditional timber industries have been affected by global competition, while the increasing urban population with increasing incomes view public lands as desirable recreation sites.

Privately Owned and Nonfederal Lands

The use of private land varies significantly across the 48 states. While most federal land is concentrated in the western states, the West also has large tracts of private rangeland and large areas of nonfederal land classified as barren. The coastal areas of the west have more cropland and developed land than other parts of the west, and they also have higher concentrations of population. The Great Plains are dominated by rangeland and cropland. The most dominant land use in the eastern U.S. is private forestland, and eastern states currently have some of the highest proportion of developed areas as well (U.S. Department of Agriculture, Natural Resource Conservation Service 2001).

Trends in uses of nonfederal land are of interest because they represent the major portion of our natural resource base, an even larger portion of our working lands, and are, for the most part, under the control of private individuals responding to market influences and government policies. In 1997, agricultural uses of nonfederal land accounted for about half of the land base (excluding Alaska). This included 406 million acres of rangeland, 377 million acres of cropland, 120 million acres of pastureland, and 33 million acres of agricultural land enrolled in the federal Conservation Reserve Program (CRP) (U.S. Department of Agriculture, Natural Resource Conservation Service 2000). The CRP is the major conservation program of the USDA under which land owners agree to place crop land in a conserving use over a long term (usually ten years) in exchange for annual rental payments. Forestland accounts for about 407 million acres of nonfederal land in the United States, including several million acres in the CRP.

Land Quality

The quality of agricultural and forestlands, not just quantity of acres, is an important element in the productive capacity of land. Economists and policy-makers are frequently interested in whether marginal or high quality lands are being converted to another use and to what extent these conversions reflect a migration towards higher or best uses. For example, policy-makers have consistently expressed an interest in the loss of high quality agricultural and forestlands.

Measuring land quality is recognizably problematic. Part of the reason for the difficulty in classifying land quality is because any classification of quality must be with respect to a particular use or goal. Since uses may be multiple, simple measures of quality can be misleading. Soil quality is often used as a proxy for suitability for agricultural use. The primary functions of soil are to serve as an input of agricultural production, to regulate water flow, and to act as an environmental filter. The traditional indicators of land quality, the Land Capability Class (LCC) and the prime farmland designation, are with respect to agricultural uses only.

The LCC is a reflection of the suitability of a portion of the land base for use in crop production. Overall, there are eight land classes, with subclasses that indicate erosion risk, wetness, shallowness, and climatic limitations. Higher classes indicate lesser suitability for crop production. In 1997, there were 31 million acres that were categorized as being the highest quality class, LCC I, and 285 million acres were in the next highest quality class, LCC II. Approximately 63 per cent of these acres were in cropland, 15 per cent were in forestland, nine per cent were in pastureland, and the remaining 13 per cent were in rangeland and other uses. In 1997, land capability classes IV and greater, which include lands designated as marginal for agricultural crops or having very severe limitations that restrict choice of crops to be grown, contained over 60 million acres of cropland, 270 million acres of forestland, 343 million acres of rangeland, and 52 million acres of pastureland (U.S. Department of Agriculture, Natural Resource Conservation Service 2001).

Table 2.3 Prime farmland by land use and year (million acres)

Year	Cropland	Conservation Reserve Program	Pastureland	Rangeland	Forestland	Other Rural Land	Total Prime Farmland
1982	230.9	0.0	37.7	20.2	46.8	6.3	341.9
1987	225.6	3.3	37.0	19.4	47.2	6.3	339.0
1992	216.0	9.7	36.8	18.9	47.6	6.3	335.5
1997	212.3	9.3	35.5	19.3	48.7	6.3	331.9

Source: USDA, Natural Resource Conservation Service (2000).

Prime farmland is land that has been designated as having the best combination of physical and chemical characteristics for producing food, feed, forage, fiber, and oilseed crops, and is also available for these uses. Table 2.3 displays the distribution of prime farmland across various land use categories from 1982 to 1997 (*Ibid.*). In 1997, 69 percent of prime farmland was in cropland or CRP, 11 percent was in pastureland, and five percent was in rangeland use. The remaining 14 percent of prime agricultural land was in forestland. In 1997, more than half of cropland was classified as prime farm land, compared to 30 percent for pasture, five percent for rangeland, 12 percent for forestland, and 13 percent for other rural land. Much of the prime farmland is concentrated in the eastern and central United States.

The decline in prime farmland for agricultural purposes from 1982 to 1997 represents a loss of ten million acres (Table 2.3). Most of the decline in prime farmland was due to urban and rural residential development during this period. From an agricultural production viewpoint, it is generally more desirable to convert less productive land to development than highly productive land. A higher proportion of rural land in metropolitan counties is classified as prime farmland than rural land in non-metropolitan counties. However, the data show that prime farmlands were no more likely to be developed than other rural land. About 24 per cent of all rural land was classified as prime farmland in both 1982 and 1997. However, because prime farmland and pressures for growth are not evenly distributed across states, concern about the loss of prime agricultural land varies across regions. From 1992 to 1997, the greatest increases in developed acreage took place along the coasts. Between 1992 and 1997, more than 800,000 acres were developed in Texas, Florida, and Georgia. Texas, notably, experienced the greatest absolute increase in the number of developed prime farmland acres.

It bears repeating that any single quality measure, such as acres of prime farmland, is a limited indicator. Many high value crops thrive in the non-prime farmland soils and climate of California and other states. Much of the value is located in metropolitan counties. Hence, the probability of future development of the agricultural land is greater than in non-metropolitan counties. Hoppe and Korb (2001) estimate that 34 percent of the value of agricultural production occurred in metropolitan areas in 1997, which shows a slight increase from 29 per cent in the previous decade (Ahearn and Banker 1990).

Conclusions

There is a relatively large quantity, and high quality, of land in the United States. The total land area, including Alaska, is approximately 2.3 billion acres. At the aggregate level, there is little concern that there will be a shortage of land for farm production and forestry needs. Net changes in the uses of land were relatively modest from 1945 through 1997. However, the net changes in land use mask a significant amount of change in and out of major land use categories. During the 1990s, a significant increase occurred in the acres of land used in developed purposes, such as in urban areas. While developed uses are still a small share of the total land base, land was converted to developed uses at the rate of 2.2 million acres per year from 1992 to 1997. As a result of this development and the generally irreversible nature of these conversions, urban sprawl and rural amenity preservation, including wildlife habitat, have emerged as high profile policy issues.

This chapter has painted a broad picture of land-use change in the United States; the remaining chapters of Part I address specific drivers of land use change in greater detail. This highlights the spatial concern for land use changes: because conversion is occurring close to residential areas, the land amenities people choose to live near are changing. In addition, the growing urban population has increasing demands for the use and management of rural lands, both in private and public ownership.

References

Ahearn, M. and D. Banker. 1988. 'Urban Farming Has Financial Advantages.' *Rural Development Perspectives* 5(1): 19–21.

Cordell, H.K., C.J. Betz, and J.M. Bowker, et al. 1999. *Outdoor Recreation in American Life: A National Assessment of Demand and Supply Trends*. Champaign, Illinois: Sagamore Publishing.

di Gregorio, A. and L.J.M. Jansen. 1997. 'A New Concept For A Land Cover Classification System,' in *Proceedings of the Earth Observation and Environment Information 1997 Conference*, Alexandria, Egypt, October 13–16.

Fuller, W.A. 1999. 'Estimation Procedures for the United States National Resources Inventory.' Presented at the Statistical Society of Canada Annual Meeting. Retrieved from http://www.nrcs.usda.gov/technical/nri/1997/stat_estimate.html.

Haynes, R., ed. 2003. '2000 RPA Timber Assessment.' U.S. Department of Agriculture, Forest Service General Technical Report PNW-GTR-560. Portland, Oregon: Pacific Northwest Research Station.

Heimlich, R.E., and W.D. Anderson. 2001. *Development at the Urban Fringe and Beyond: Impacts on Agriculture and Rural Land.* U.S. Department of Agriculture, Economic Research Service, Agricultural Economic Report No. 803. Washington, District of Columbia.

Hoppe, R.A. and P. Korb. 2001. *The Fate of Farm Operations Facing Development.* Draft manuscript. U.S. Department of Agriculture, Economic Research Service. Washington, District of Columbia.

Nusser, S. M., and J.J. Goebel. 1997. 'The National Resources Inventory: A Long-Term Multi-Resource Monitoring Programme.' *Environmental and Ecological Statistics* 4: 181–204.

Nusser, S.M., J.M. Kienzler, and W.A. Fuller. 1999. 'Geostatistical Estimation Data for the 1997 National Resources Inventory.' Retrieved from: http://www.nhq.nrcs.usda.gov/NRI/1997/stat_estimate.html.

Opie, J. 1987. *The Law of the Land: Two Hundred Years of American Farmland Policy.* Lincoln, Nebraska: University of Nebraska Press.

Smith, W.B., J.S. Vissage, D.R. Darr, R.M. Sheffield, et al. 2001. *Forest Resources of the United States.* U.S. Department of Agriculture, Forest Service General Technical Report NC-219. St. Paul, Minnesota: North Central Research Station.

U.S. Department of Agriculture, Economic Research Service. 2002. 'Agricultural and Environmental Indicators, 2000 and 1996–97.' Retrieved from: http://www.ers.usda.gov/publications/ah712/AH7121-1.PDF and http://www.ers.usda.gov/Emphases/Harmony/issues/arei2000/AREI1_1landuse.pdf.

U.S. Department of Agriculture, Forest Service. 2000. '1997 RPA Assessment: The United States Forest Resource Current Situation (final statistics).' Retrieved from: http://www.srsfia.usfs.mssstate.edu/wo/review.htm.

U.S. Department of Agriculture, Forest Service. 2001. *2000 RPA Assessment of Forest and Range Lands.* Washington, District of Columbia.

U.S. Department of Agriculture, Forest Service. 2002. 'Forest Inventory and Analysis.' Retrieved from http://fia.fs.fed.us/.

U.S. Department of Agriculture, National Agricultural Statistics Service. 2001. 'Census of Agriculture; 1997 Agricultural Atlas of the United States.' Retrieved from: http://www.nass.usda.gov/census/census97/atlas97/menu.htm.

U.S. Department of Agriculture, Natural Resources Conservation Service. 2000. *Summary Report 1997 National Resources Inventory* (revised December 2000). Ames, Iowa: Iowa State University Statistical Laboratory.

U.S. Department of Agriculture, Natural Resources Conservation Service. 2001. 'Natural Resources Inventory 2001.' Retrieved from: http://www.nhq.nrcs.usda.gov//technical/NRI/1997/summary_report/

U.S. Department of Commerce, Bureau of the Census. 1992. *1990 Census of Population and Housing. Summary Population and Housing Characteristics: United States, CPH-1-1.* Washington, District of Columbia.

U.S. Department of Commerce, Bureau of the Census. 2002. Retrieved from: http://www.census.gov/population/censusdata/urpop0090.

U.S. Department of Interior, Bureau of Land Management. 2001. 'Public Land Statistics 2000.' Retrieved from: http://www.blm.gov/nhp/browse.htm.

Vesterby, M. 2001. 'Land Use,' in *Agricultural, Resource, and Environmental Indicators*, Chapter 1.1, U. S. Department of Agriculture, Economic Research Service. Retrieved from: http://www.ers.usda.gov/Emphases/Harmony/issues/arei2000/.

Vesterby, M. and K. Krupa. 2001. 'Major Uses of Land in the United States, 1997.' U.S. Department of Agriculture, Economic Research Service Statistical Bulletin No. 973.

Appendix: The U.S. Department of Agriculture's Major Land Use Series

The USDA's Major Land Use Series is a unique resource because it enables national trends in land use, particularly in rural areas, to be assessed consistently over a lengthy period of time. This section describes the land-use classifications and primary data resources of the Major Land Use Series.

Land-Use Classifications

The land-use classifications include cropland, grassland pasture and range, forest land, special land uses, and miscellaneous land uses. The following descriptions of these classifications are based on Vesterby and Krupa (2001).

Cropland   Cropland includes land which is harvested, planted land with crop failure, and cultivated summary fallow. These data are developed from a variety of USDA sources, which are primarily provided by the National Agricultural Statistics Service on an annual basis. Cropland idled includes cropland on which no crops were planted and land in crops planted for cover and soil improvement purposes. Cropland that is idled under government programs is included in this category. Cropland used for pasture is land that is considered to be in long-term crop rotation.

Grassland pasture and range   Grassland pasture and range include open land used primarily for pasture and grazing. Pastureland is land managed primarily for livestock grazing. Management of pastureland usually includes fertilization and other cultural practices. Pastureland is more common in eastern states than in western states and primarily occurs on private land. Rangeland is land where the plant cover is suitable for livestock grazing but composed mainly of native grasses or introduced forage species that are managed like rangeland. Management of rangeland generally does not include the use of chemicals or fertilizers. Livestock in the West are more likely to be grazed on rangeland that is commonly owned and managed by federal agencies such as the U.S. Bureau of Land Management.

Forestland   Forestland includes land that is at least ten per cent stocked by trees of any size. However, forest lands in parks, wildlife areas, and other special purpose uses are excluded from this land-use classification. Forestland is further categorized into that used for grazing and that which is not. Forestland used for grazing includes forested areas of farms and forested areas not in farms.

Special land uses   Special land uses include urban land and land used for public infrastructure purposes. The Major Land Use Series employs the U.S. Census Bureau's definition of urban land, which is 'cities, towns, and Census designated places of 2,500 or more persons, including urbanized areas with populations of 50,000 or more' (U.S. Department of Commerce, Bureau of the Census 1992). Public infrastructure purposes include land in highways, roads, railroad rights-of-way and airports; federal and state parks, wildlife areas and wilderness areas; and national defense and industrial uses. Note that in some reports using the Major Land Use series, urban areas are classified as a miscellaneous land use (Vesterby and Krupa 2001).

Miscellaneous land uses This category includes other land uses such as industrial and commercial sites in rural areas, cemeteries, golf courses, mining areas, and quarry sites; areas with little surface use (e.g., marshes, swamps, sand dunes, bare rocks, deserts, tundra); and other unclassified land.

Primary Data Sources

The Major Land Use series is built from many survey and administrative data sources, two of which are described below. These sources – the National Resources Inventory (NRI) and the Forest Inventory and Analysis (FIA) – are the primary data sources of the Major Land Use Series and are data sources maintained by the USDA.

The National Resources Inventory The National Resources Inventory (NRI) conducted by the USDA is designed to assess land-use conditions on non-federal lands, and collects data on soil characteristics, land use, land cover, wind erosion, water erosion, and conservation practices (Nusser and Goebel 1997; Fuller 1999). Land-use data are collected on approximately 300,000 area segments and 800,000 points within those segments every five years. Geographic Information System (GIS) software is used to compile these data and organize estimates based on these sample points (Nusser et al. 1999). The first landmark national resources inventories were conducted in 1934 and 1945. However, the inventories did not have a common statistical design until 1982. The NRI is conducted by the USDA's Natural Resources Conservation Service in cooperation with the Iowa State University's Statistical Laboratory (U.S. Department of Agriculture, Natural Resources Conservation Service 2000, 2001). As a result of its statistical design, the NRI allows land-use transition matrices, such as that presented in Table 2.2 in the text, to be developed from 1982 onward. Transition matrices for other time periods are available at the USDA's Economic Research Service website (U.S. Department of Agriculture, Economic Research Service 2002).

A unique aspect of the NRI data is that they reflect the recent increase in development of rural land into rural residences. The NRI classifies developed land differently than the Major Land Use Series (discussed below). In the NRI, developed land consists of urban and built up areas (classified as large and small) and land devoted to rural transportation. The NRI classification of developed land covers more land area than the urban land classification adopted by the Major Land Use Series and the U.S. Bureau of the Census.

Forest Inventory and Analysis The Forest Inventory and Analysis (FIA), also conducted by USDA, is designed to provide objective and scientifically credible information on key forest attributes, such as forest stocks, growth, harvest, and mortality (U.S. Department of Agriculture, Forest Service 2002). Related data are collected by region, forest ownership category (e.g., forest industry versus non-industrial private forests), and cover type (e.g., oak-hickory). FIA inventories provide consistent forest inventory data for the nation back to 1952 (Smith et al. 2001). The FIA, in conjunction with the Resources Planning Act Assessments, now has four related databases in place: the Eastwide forest inventory database; the Westside forest inventory database; the national timber products output database; and a national summary database that draws upon these three and incorporates other federal data resources. Although sampling techniques for the NRI and FIA are similar, different sampling grids make the estimates from the two inventory systems statistically independent.

Chapter 3

Effects of Policy and Technological Change on Land Use

Ralph J. Alig and Mary Clare Ahearn

Introduction

Land use in the United States is dynamic, as discussed in Chapter 2, with millions of acres of land shifting uses each year. Many of these land-use changes are the result of market forces in an economy affected by modern technology and policy choices. Changes in land use are the result of choices made by individuals, corporations, nongovernmental organizations, and governments. This chapter considers forces that act at broad scales to affect land-use changes, operating via land markets, where they exist, and evidenced by the behavior of economic agents over a broad geography. The specific foci are the effects of policy and technology on land-use choices.

Land Markets

Land markets reflect the aggregation of individual decisions by sellers and buyers within the constraints imposed by land-use policies and regulations. The aggregation of these individual decisions determines the type and extent of land-use change. However, market failures exist (see Chapter 6), such that actions of individual buyers and sellers do not result in socially desirable outcomes. Policies designed to address such failures or to accomplish other public policy goals alter land supply and demand conditions. The political system has reacted to failures of land markets and interest in other public policy goals by the passage of legislation affecting land use, e.g., the 2002 Farm Security and Rural Investment Act ('2002 Farm Act').

Before introducing specific examples of land-use policies, we broadly characterize major drivers in land use among rural uses and then between urban and rural uses. In both cases, a number of factors influence land supply and demand conditions. Examples include changing consumer demand for goods and services produced on the land and for direct consumption of land, e.g., through housing developments. Other factors are increases in population size and personal income levels that lead to an increase in demand for agricultural and forest products (U.S. Department of Agriculture, Forest Service 1988, 1990). Changes in land supply or demand conditions can alter land rents, and landowners may react to such market signals by deciding to shift land use. The discussion of these drivers of land-use change will take a national perspective.

Competition Between Agriculture and Forestry Uses

As discussed in Chapter 2, more than 80 per cent of nonfederal land in the United States is in forests, crops, pasture, or range. Where climate and physiography permit, these rural uses can compete for the same land. More than 90 per cent of land-use changes on nonfederal lands in recent decades have been among uses of land for forestry and agriculture, and shifts between these two uses and other uses such as rural residential (U.S. Department of Agriculture, Natural Resources Conservation Service 2001).

Competition Between Urban Uses and Agriculture and Forestry Production.

Farm and forestry producers are sometimes adversely impacted by sprawling urban development. Areas of urban and other developed uses in the United States have expanded by more than one million acres annually since 1982 (see Chapter 2), as population and personal incomes have increased significantly (U.S. Department of Agriculture, Natural Resources Conservation Service 2001). A major contemporary focus of land-use policies is to manage the direction of this development or conversion of rural lands to other uses.

The basic factors of increasing population and real incomes are important drivers for the expansion of developed areas and have significant impacts on land- use change (Alig and Healy 1987; Heimlich and Anderson 2001). They lead to greater direct consumption of 'open' land for housing development. At the same time, greater incomes and population size can also lead to an increase in demand for agricultural and forestry products as well as for the environmental, recreational, and aesthetic services of the land (U.S. Department of Agriculture, Forest Service 1988, 1990).

Population and income pressures on land uses are not uniform across the nation. For example, shifts in population have occurred from the North to the South and the West in recent decades. The amount of land in urban and special uses increased more than 50 per cent since the 1960s in the South. From 1992 to 1997, six of the top ten states that lost cropland, forests, and other types of rural open space to urban development were in the South: Texas, Georgia, Florida, North Carolina, South Carolina, and Tennessee (U.S. Department of Agriculture, Natural Resources Conservation Service 2001).

The rural landscape in these regions has changed with rapid population growth as more land was needed for home sites, roads, airports, schools, commercial and industrial sites, parks, open space, and other uses to satisfy the demands of urbanizing areas. As urban areas expand into rural areas, competition for land in rural areas increases and the value of rural land rises (Reynolds 2001).

Consider that for the whole U.S., more than one-quarter of counties are currently classified as metropolitan. That compares with less than one-tenth 50 years ago. Even with constant tastes and preferences, a larger population base with higher income levels will add up to greater consumption and demands for developed space. For example, consumers may demand more shopping space, as demonstrated by the 27 per cent increase in U.S. shopping area, and the 24 per cent increase in the number of shopping centers, between 1990 and 2000 (U.S. Department of Commerce, Bureau of the Census 2001).

The amount of urban land added per additional person is higher for non-metropolitan than for metropolitan counties (Reynolds 2001; Zeimetz et al. 1976). Many Americans have a strong preference for the spreading out of development. They prefer to live in less-congested areas and will commute additional minutes or hours to realize their goals, a choice made possible by our excellent road system. Moreover, an increasing population of retirees has augmented out-migration from central cities and suburbs to rural areas that offer aesthetic amenities. Natural amenities may be a more important determinant of population growth than nearness to metropolitan centers or type of local economy (McGranahan 1999).

The market price of land can be decomposed into different sources of value, such as its current use in production and its expected use in alternative enterprises. In many areas adjacent to urban centers, the expectation of urban development has a greater influence on the value of land its current use in farm or forestry production (Alig and Healy 1987). For example, the market value of more than 15 per cent of farmland is significantly influenced by urban development. For those urban-influenced acres, urban development pressures account for two-thirds of their market value (Barnard 2000). Of course, many landowners welcome this urbanizing influence, as it greatly increases their net worth. This marked appreciation allows them to borrow more and perhaps expand their operations, or it allows them to sell their land and realize capital gains.

Although individual producers may be better off when they sell their land to developers, the checkerboard pattern of developed land and farm and forest production can have a variety of negative impacts on producers who choose to stay. Impacts include complaints by new residents about the noise and pollution associated with farm and forestry production, loss of local farm infrastructure, such as input suppliers, and difficulty in expanding for those producers who would like to purchase nearby parcels of land. For those who want to stay in agriculture or forest production, low profit margins do not allow producers to compete with developers for additional land as land prices are bid up by residential and other types of development encroachment. The checkerboard pattern of development can also have substantial ecological ramifications for wildlife species dependent on large blocks of forested or grassland habitat (Alig, Butler, and Swenson 2000).

Some producers have seen the urban sprawl trend as a business opportunity for staying in farm production. They have shifted their commodity mix to satisfy the nearby market demand for perishable fruits and vegetables, as well as other fresh commodities. Other producers have adjusted by catering to the demand by local residents for farm visits. In 2000, 28 per cent of sightseers surveyed indicated that a motivation for their trip was to visit a farm or agricultural setting (U.S. Department of Agriculture, Forest Service 2000–2002). These include visits to purchase farm products or visits to learn about farming and to enjoy the view on the farm. Pumpkin patches and you-pick operations are common in many urban areas. In addition, adjacent urban development has meant that farm operator household members have off-farm job opportunities. The average farm household earns more off-farm than on the farm (Ahearn, Perry, and El-Osta 1993). Off-farm opportunities in nearby urban areas have been key to the survival of many farms.

Technological Changes

Technological innovation is a major driver in land-use change. Technological change affects all sectors of the economy, including agricultural and forest production. At the same time, technological innovations in transportation, as discussed in Chapter 4, affect a broad set of economic activities and thereby influence land uses by reducing transportation time and costs.

Innovations in Agriculture and Forestry

Agriculture is a highly productive industry in the U.S. economy. Agricultural output grew at an annual average rate of nearly two per cent over the past 50 years. During this period, the use of land was relatively constant, while relative use of labor declined and use of intermediate inputs and capital increased (Figure 3.1). A major factor in this high level of productivity is the payoff from research in the form of new technologies. Studies have shown that the social rate of return on investment in public agricultural research ranges from 40 to 60 per cent. Rates of return on research investments in some forest products industries exceed 100 per cent annually, while others, such as in southern softwood growth and management research, do not begin to approach this range of results or those for the agricultural sector (Hyde, Newman, and Seldon 1992). Public and private research investments have led to the adoption of 'labor-saving' technologies. Other inputs, such as capital and farm chemicals, have been substituted for land and labor on the farm as part of this process (Ahearn et al. 1998).

Significant advances in agricultural technologies affect land use in a variety of ways. First, new technologies have allowed the relatively fixed agricultural land base to be farmed more intensively. New mechanical technologies have generally affected producers' cost structures and led to increasing economies of size. A constant feature of U.S. farm structure is a dwindling number of operations, and an increasing average farm size, although the number of small, primarily rural residence farms is stable. Although the total acres in agricultural uses has changed little since 1935, when the number of farms was greatest, the number of farms has fallen from 6.8 million to about two million in 1997 (U.S. Department of Agriculture, Economic Research Service 2002).

There are significantly more private landowners in forestry than in agriculture (about 10 million in total), with less than 10 per cent of forestland owners possessing three-quarters of all forestland (Birch 1994). Between 1978 and

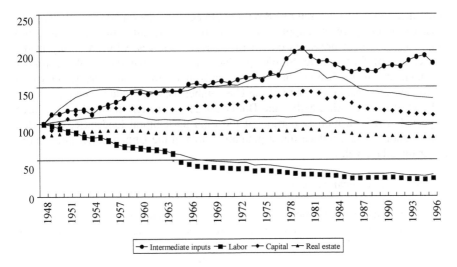

Figure 3.1 Index of farm input use in the United States (1948=100)

1994, there was a significant increase in forest ownership of plots smaller than 50 acres. With the continued pace of development into forestland documented in the 1997 National Resources Inventory, the average size of forest ownership is expected to decline (Sampson 2000). Part of the reason is that an increasing number of smaller forest properties (less than 25 acres) are used primarily for residential purposes; the number of larger-sized properties is more stable.

In spite of a relatively stable number of U.S. cropland acres, the innovations that have spurred production intensification have influenced land in two important ways. First, the scenic look of farmland has gradually changed over time. For example, confinement livestock operations have reduced the extent of livestock pasturing. Second, the production intensification permitted by some technologies has likely had a negative impact on soil quality (Batie 1993). However, other innovations, such as conservation tillage technologies or variable rate technologies, are believed to reduce the degradation of soil quality relative to conventional technologies.

One technological advance that may greatly affect both the agricultural and forest sectors is the use of genetically modified material. Yields per acre could be significantly increased under certain scenarios, and the use of environmentally degrading inputs could be reduced. While societal concerns may limit use of genetically modified organisms in some cases, adoption of these technologies in the land-intensive industries of agriculture and forestry could influence land exchanges between the two sectors if relative productivities shift.

One example of genetically modified material that affects the competition for land between agriculture and forestry involves the production of short-rotation woody crops (SRWCs), such as hybrid poplars. A national-scale analysis by Alig et al. (2000) showed that growing demand for wood fiber and tightening supply could mean that introduction of SRWCs could act to temper market price rises and bolster reliable aggregate supplies of woody fiber. Expanded fiber farming could reduce management pressures on existing forest resources, while resulting in the conversion of farmland to SRWC production. Even without SRWCs, timber management intensification on private lands over the years has generated a significant increase in the share of the U.S. timber harvest produced on plantations (Alig et al. 1999b; Alig, Mills, and Butler 2002). Although the total SRWC area projected will be a modest portion of the total agricultural land base, expanded SWRC supply could reduce forest plantation area in the United States and lead to lower forestland values.

Innovations in Communication

Innovations in communication have been a driver behind changing land rents and uses because they have reduced the transactions costs of locating outside of central cities for some businesses and households. Before the current suite of telecommunication innovations existed, most businesses were required to operate in urban areas. The impact of the dispersion of businesses into less developed regions of the country is multiplied by the relocation of downstream industries and associated housing developments. For example, telecommunication-dependent firms, such as catalog retail operations, can successfully function in rural communities.

In addition, though not large in numbers, some individuals are able to successfully conduct private consulting and other business pursuits from any location through telecommunication. Major communication innovations affecting population dispersion are personal computers and the internet. Although non-metropolitan use of computers on the job has lagged that for metropolitan areas, 40 per cent of non-metropolitan job holders used computers on the job in 1997, as compare to 18 per cent in 1964. In addition, there is a wage premium of ten per cent associated with using computers on the job (Kusming 2002).

Policies

The U.S. has a long and varied history of influencing private land use through policies at the national, state, and local levels. These land-use policies include land-use taxes or subsidies, transfer of development rights, easements, and regulations, such as zoning and growth control. In addition, many other policies that are not primarily targeted to land-use management sometimes impact land use. These include agriculture and forest production policies, public policies governing investment in public infrastructure, tax policies (e.g., property taxes for school funding), and trade policies.

Land-use policies guide how land will be used, usually to achieve some stated or implicit objective. Early land-use policies in the United States extend back to the 'Broad Arrow Policy.' In 1691, this was when a shortage of ship masts in Europe led England to blaze pine trees 24 inches or more in diameter within three miles of water in the northeastern U.S. with the mark of a broad arrow; these trees were to be reserved for use by the Royal Navy. Later milestones include the disposal and retention of public lands. Contemporary land-use policies as a whole are multi-objective in nature. This is evident in a 1983 policy directive of the U.S. Department of Agriculture (USDA):

> It is the USDA's policy to promote land use objectives that are responsive to current and long-term economic, social, and environmental needs. This policy recognizes the rights and responsibilities of State and local governments for regulating the uses of land under their jurisdiction. It also reflects the USDA's responsibility to (a) assure that the United States retains a farm, range, and forest land base sufficient to produce adequate supplies, at reasonable production costs, of high quality food, fiber, wood, and other agricultural products that may be needed; (b) assist individual landholders and State and local governments in defining and meeting needs for growth and development in such ways that the most productive farm, range, and forest lands are protected from unwarranted conversion to other uses; and (c) assure appropriate levels of environmental quality (U.S. Department of Agriculture, 1983).

A major contemporary focus of land-use policies is to manage the direction of development; 'urban sprawl' has been cited as one of the leading concerns of Americans (Pew Center 2000). According to the Pew report, approximately 1,000 measures were introduced in state legislatures in the late 1990s, attempting to change planning laws and to make U.S. development more orderly and conserving.

State and local governments use a variety of tools to protect farm and forestlands as production resource bases. These tools include agricultural zoning, differential farm tax assessments, right to farm laws, agricultural districts, purchase and transfer of development rights, comprehensive land-use planning, and urban growth boundaries. In addition, the USDA complements the purchase of development rights programs of state and local governments with the Farmland Protection Program for agricultural lands and the Forest Legacy Program for forestlands. The purchase of development rights provides government agencies with the option of conserving open space for future use in farm or forest production without necessitating government acquisition. The land will not necessarily be required to stay in a current farm or forestry use, but under a program that purchases development rights, a land owner will not be allowed to develop the parcel. Because the cost of cultivating undeveloped land is considerably less than the expense associated with reversing development, purchasing development rights is viewed as an investment in food and forestry security for future generations. Conservation easements and other partial interests in land have also been increasingly used to accomplish particular natural resource protection goals such as maintaining open space that provides scenic beauty and wildlife habitat (e.g., Wiebe et al. 1996).

Agriculture and Forestry Policies

The role of government in the agriculture sector is pervasive. Various types of farm support have been in place since 1933 (after the Great Depression), and are aimed at ensuring farm viability by guaranteeing a minimum income level for farmers producing certain crops. Such programs have taken different forms over the years including production limits, acreage reduction programs, deficiency payments, farm credit, and non-recourse loans.

Funding for farm programs has also varied widely over time, depending on agricultural markets and on the programs in effect at any one time. Direct government subsidies to farmers and farmland owners are the most obvious example of government intervention in agriculture. Figure 3.2 presents the trend in direct subsidies from 1996 to 2000. In 2000, direct government payments amounted to $23 billion, only $1.6 billion of which was for conservation programs. This compares to a total net farm income in 2000 of $46 billion. Moreover, direct government payments represent only a portion of total subsidies. Kennedy estimated that 33 per cent of total policy transfers were in the form of direct payments, with other transfers (including subsidization by consumers through higher prices resulting from import quotas or other policies) accounting for the remaining share (Kennedy 1990).

This extensive transfer of wealth to the farm sector has significant impacts on land use and land tenancy. Producers that receive direct government payments are more likely to rent-in land from landlords, than are producers who do not receive payments. 50 per cent of the acreage on farms that receive payments was rented-in in 1999 (U.S. Department of Agriculture 2001). A major channel for the impacts of government payments on land use is through the capitalization of subsidies into the value of farmland. Barnard et al. (1997) found that the rate of capitalization varied considerably over regions, from less than ten per cent to 69 per cent of land values. Only about one-third of farming operations receive direct payments. Hence, the acres in these operations have benefited from the capitalization of payments, while other acres in the sector have received less benefit. In part, this is because eligibility for payments is tied to the historical production 'base' of specific farmland. Subsidies help to keep land in agricultural uses, relative to other uses. Payments lead to higher land prices and higher land prices tend to reduce the migration of land out of agriculture (Barkley 1990). The 2002 Farm Act calls for a large increase in direct payments to farmers, with a projected total cost of $190 billion over the next decade.

In contrast to spending on agriculture, in 1986, federal funding for forestry programs for private tree planting, forest stand management, and technical assistance totaled about $57 million. This was less than half of one per cent of direct agricultural payments to farmers (Lee and Alig 1991). This suggests that agricultural policies may be more likely to have affected rural land uses than forest policies. From a land-use perspective, policies that increase the land rent of agriculture, without affecting forest rents, are expected to increase the land in agriculture use (all other things held constant). Alig, Adams, and McCarl (1998b) showed this empirically in a national analysis, where agriculture area increased and forest area decreased relative to a baseline, with restoration of farm programs after their proposed near elimination in the 1996 Farm Act. Lubowski (2002) found that government crop subsidies contributed to decreased forest area in the United States

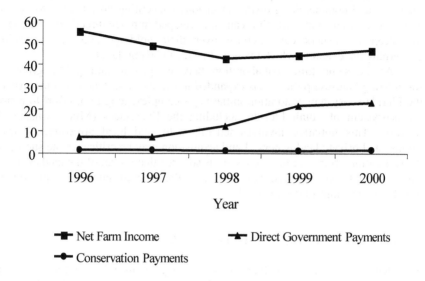

Figure 3.2 Farm income and government payments in the United States, 1996–2000 ($ billion)

between 1982 and 1997, relative to the level that would have resulted without such government farm payments. Lubowski also reported that the government is directly competing with itself in providing incentives for landowners to retire environmentally sensitive crop lands. This involves government crop payments reducing the incentive for farmers to enroll acreage in the Conservation Reserve Program.

Environmental Policies

Federal programs, such as the Endangered Species Act, can also be used to promote conservation on private lands. Among the many competing interests in land-use policies, there is perhaps none more fundamental than the potential conflict between the presumed rights of private property owners and the received rights of the general public. Recent years have seen a substantial debate over how to balance these interests. This debate has included the emergence of a property rights movement in response to the increasing emphasis on protecting environmentally sensitive land.

From a planning perspective, Schiffman (1996) sees the property rights question as the central legal (and political) issue in the making of planning and environmental policy. This issue is of particular importance, and the subject of increasing controversy, in the rural and urbanizing communities of America. Planning officials wrestle with the challenge of how they can address the process of land development so as to protect the environmental, cultural, aesthetic, and fiscal character of the locality, while meeting the need for new housing, industrial facilities, and commercial growth. Decisions concerning how land is to be used and the conditions under which it can be developed impinge directly on the control that property owners can exercise over their holdings and raise questions concerning the extent to which the use of land can be regulated.

At the same time, collaboration between private and public groups in formulating land-use policies has expanded in some cases. One example involves the Florida ecosystem restoration initiative, a complex, long-term effort to restore the ecosystem of South Florida, including the Everglades (Milon, Chapter 10 herein). This initiative involves federal, state, and local governments, tribal groups, and private landowners. Land acquisition may be critical to the success of the restoration effort, but the ecosystem is so large that not all of the lands within it can be bought and preserved, which requires the different interest groups to work together to accomplish desired goals.

The Future and Challenges for Land-Use Policymakers

Knowledge of the drivers behind land-use change is useful for informing policy discussions. Policymakers must anticipate future conditions and estimate the effects that proposed policies are likely to produce. Value in charting the future includes providing ideas to policymakers of the potential future demands on rural land, and, given that some land reallocation will occur, how the future outcome may differ with and without changes in land-use policies. Given the drivers discussed above, the importance of U.S. agricultural and forest lands in providing improved water quality, food, fiber, timber, fish and wildlife habitat, recreational opportunities, erosion control, and other environmental services is likely to increase in the future.

This 'multifunctionality' of rural lands has been recognized by many countries, and is a major issue in continuing international debates about trade and production subsidization (OECD 1998). World growth in human populations and income has resulted in social, economic, and technological changes that profoundly affect the global management and use of rural lands. The world population will continue to grow, possibly from six billion now to nine billion by 2050. The U.S. population will also continue to grow, particularly in the southern and western regions, with a projected increase of more than 120 million people by 2050 (U.S. Department of Commerce, Bureau of the Census 2001). Such a population increase and changes in economic activity could lead to an increase of more than 30 million acres in urban and developed area in the U.S. (Alig et al. 1999a). A key question involves how society can make positive progress towards sustainability in the face of needing more developed land to serve more people in the future.

Interconnections among land use, policies, technological changes, and market forces involve two-way relationships, with changes as society evolves. In addition to the role of markets and prices in deciding whether alternative technologies will be used in production and thereby affect land use, public choice discussions may increasingly affect the application of technology, as in the case of genetic modifications. Policy debates affect public land-use and management decisions, as in the case of public forest policy in the U.S., and are also increasingly affecting private land use and the associated use of technology.

A confluence of economic, environmental, and social forces has influenced how the nation's fixed land base is used. As drivers of land-use change within a market-based economy, policy and technology are influenced by other exogenous factors, such as world political events, and by potential changes in related global conditions such as climate change (Sohngen and Alig 2000). It may not be sufficient to simply extrapolate from experience to look at the future implications of major economic and technological forces. As with all future gazing, one's understanding of future technology becomes murkier the further into the future one attempts to look. The interplay between the policy environment and technological change can be important. An example of such interplay in a global climate change context is Edmonds et al.'s (2000) finding that technological innovation can be 'induced' by policies to stimulate research and development expenditures, energy prices, taxes, and subsidies. While we understand some parts of the innovation process, the science of understanding the full process of induced technological change is in its infancy.

References

Adams, D.M., R.J. Alig, J.M. Callaway, B.A. McCarl, and S.M. Winnett. 1996a. 'The Forest and Agriculture Sector Optimization Model (FASOM): Model Structure and Policy Applications.' U.S. Department of Agriculture, Forest Service General Technical Report PNW-RP-495. Portland, Oregon: Pacific Northwest Research Center.

Adams, D.M., R.J. Alig, J.M. Callaway, B.A. McCarl, and S.M. Winnett. 1996b. 'An Analysis of the Impacts of Public Timber Harvest Policies on Private Forest Management in the United States.' *Forest Science* 42(3): 343–58.

Ahearn, M., J. Yee, E. Ball, and R. Nehring. 1998. 'Agricultural Productivity in the United States.' U.S. Department of Agriculture, Economic Research Service Agricultural Information Bulletin No. 740. Washington, District of Columbia.

Ahearn, M., J. Perry, and H. El-Osta. 1993. 'The Economic Well-being of Farm Operator Households.' U.S. Department of Agriculture, Economic Research Service Agricultural Economic Report No. 666. Washington, District of Columbia.

Alig, R., T. Mills, and R. Shackelford. 1980. 'Most Soil Bank Plantings in the South Have Been Retained: Some Need Follow-up Treatments.' *Scientific Journal of Applied Forestry* 4(1): 60–64.

Alig, R. 1986. 'Econometric Analysis of Forest Acreage Trends in the Southeast.' *Forest Science* 32(1): 119–134.

Alig, R., and R. Healy. 1987. 'Urban and Built-up Land Area Changes in the United States: An Empirical Investigation of Determinants.' *Land Economics* 63(3): 215–236.

Alig, R., D. Adams, B. McCarl, J. Callaway, and S. Winnett. 1997. 'Assessing Effects of Strategies for Mitigating Global Climate Change With an Intertemporal Model of the U.S. Forest and Agriculture Sectors.' *Environmental and Resource Economics* 9: 259–274.

Alig, R., D. Adams, and B. McCarl. 1998a. 'Ecological and Economic Impacts of Forest Policies: Interactions Across Forestry and Agriculture.' *Ecological Economics* 27: 63–78.

Alig, R., D. Adams, and B. McCarl. 1998b. 'Impacts of Incorporating Land Exchanges Between Forestry and Agriculture in Sector Models.' *Journal of Agricultural and Applied Economics* 30(2): 389–401.

Alig, R., F. Benford, R. Moulton, and L. Lee. 1999a. 'Long Term Projections of Urban and Developed Land Area in the United States,' in the Keep America Growing Conference Proceedings, June 6–9.

Alig, R., D. Adams, J. Chmelik, and P. Bettinger. 1999b. 'Private Forest Investment and Long Run Sustainable Harvest Volumes.' *New Forests* 17: 307–327.

Alig, R., D. Adams, B. McCarl, and P. Ince. 2000. 'Economic Potential of Short-Rotation Woody Crops on Agricultural Land for Pulp Fiber Production in the United States.' *Forest Products Journal* 50(5): 67–74.

Alig, R., B. Butler, and J. Swenson. 2000. 'Fragmentation and National Trends in Private Forestland: Preliminary Findings from the 2000 RPA Assessment,' in *Proceedings, Forest Fragmentation 2000*, eds., N. Sampson and L. DeCoster. September 17–20, 2000, Annapolis, Maryland. Washington, District of Columbia: American Forests.

Alig, R. 2001. 'Finite Land, Infinite Futures? Sustainable Options on a Fixed Land Base.' U.S. Department of Agriculture, Forest Service *Science Findings* 31. Portland, Oregon: Pacific Northwest Research Station

Alig, R. and R. Haynes. 2002. 'Sustainable Forest Management and Land Use Changes,' in proceedings of the National Convention of the Society of American Foresters. Denver, Colorado. September 2001.

Alig, R., J. Mills, and B. Butler. 2002. 'Private Timberlands: Growing Demands, Shrinking Land Base.' *Journal of Forestry* 100(2): 32–37.

Barkley, A. 1990. 'The Determinants of the Migration of Labor Out of Agriculture in the United States, 1940–85.' *American Journal of Agricultural Economics* 72(3): 567–73.

Barnard, C., G. Whittaker, D. Westenbarger, and M. Ahearn. 1997. 'Evidence of Capitalization of Direct Government Payments into U.S. Cropland Values.' *American Journal of Agricultural Economics* 79(5): 1642–50.

Barnard, C. 2000. 'Urbanization Affects a Large Share of Farmland.' U.S. Department of Agriculture, Economic Research Service, Rural Conditions and Trends. Washington, District of Columbia.

Batie, S. 1993. *Soil and Water Quality: An Agenda for the Future*. Washington, District of Columbia: National Academy Press.

Birch, T. 1994. 'Private Forest-Land Owners of the United States, 1994.' U.S. Department of Agriculture, Forest Service Resource Bulletin NE-134. Radnor, Pennsylvania: Northeastern Forest Experiment Station.

Cordell, K. 1999. *Outdoor Recreation in American Life: A National Assessment of Demand and Supply Trends*. Champaign, Illinois: Sagamore Publishing.

Edmonds, J., J. Roop, and M. Scott. 2000. 'Technology and the Economics of Climate Change Policy.' Pew Center Report. Washington, District of Columbia.

Haynes, R.W., J.A. Stevens, and R.J. Barbour. 2000. 'Criteria and Indicators for Sustainable Forest Management at the U.S.A. National and Regional Level,' in *Forests and Society: The Role of Research Sub-Plenary Sessions Volume 1*, eds., B. Krishnapillay, E. Soepadmo, N.L. Arshad, H.H. Wong, S. Appanah, S. Wan Chick, N. Manokaran, L.T. Hong, and K.C. Khoo: 238-26.

Haynes, R., ed. 2003. '2000 RPA Timber Assessment.' U.S. Department of Agriculture, Forest Service General Technical Report PNW-GTR-560. Portland, Oregon: Pacific Northwest Research Station.

Heimlich, R. and W. Anderson. 2001. 'Development at the Urban Fringe and Beyond: Impacts on Agriculture and Rural Land.' U.S. Department of Agriculture, Economic Research Service Agricultural Economic Report No. 803. Washington, District of Columbia.

Hyde, W., D. Newman, and B. Seldon. 1992. *The Economic Benefits of Forestry Research.* Ames, Iowa: Iowa State University Press.

Kennedy, R. 1990. 'Exports and the Farm Sector.' In *The U.S. Farm Sector Entering the 1990s: The 12th Annual Report on the Status of Family Farms*, eds., T. Carlin and S. Mazie. U.S. Department of Agriculture, Economic Research Service Agricultural Information Bulletin No. 587. Washington, District of Columbia.

Kline, J. and D. Wichelns. 1996. 'Public Preferences Regarding the Goals of Farmland Preservation Programs.' *Land Economics* 72(4): 538–549.

Kline, J. and R. Alig. 1999. 'Does Land Use Planning Slow the Conversion of Forest and Farm Land?' *Growth and Change* 30(1): 3–22.

Kusming, L. 2002. 'Wage Premiums for On-the-Job Computer Use: A Metro and Nonmetro Analysis.' U.S. Department of Agriculture, Economic Research Service Rural Development Research Report No. RDRR95. Washington, District of Columbia.

Lee, K. and R. Alig. 1991. 'Public Policies and the Southern Forest Landscape,' in proceedings of the 1991 Southern Economics Workshop. Washington, District of Columbia.

Lubowski, R. 2002. 'Determinants of Land-Use Transitions in the United States: Econometric Analysis of Changes Among the Major Land Use Categories.' Ph.D. dissertation, Harvard University.

Mauldin, T., A. Plantinga and R. Alig. 1999. 'Land Use in Maine: Determinants of Land Use in Maine With Projections to 2050.' *Northern Journal of Applied Forestry* 16(2): 82–88.

McGranahan, David. 1999. 'Natural Amenities Drive Rural Population Change.' U.S. Department of Agriculture, Economic Research Service Agricultural Economic Report No. 781.

Milon, W. 2003. 'Land Use Change and Ecosystems: The Consequences of Private and Public Decisions in South Florida,' in *The Economics of Land Use Change*, eds., K. Bell, K. Boyle, A. Plantinga, and J. Rubin. Aldershot, England: Ashgate Press.

Moulton, Robert J. 1999. 'Tree Planting in the United States. 1997.' *Tree Planter's Notes.* 49(1): 5–15.

Organisation for Economic Co-operation and Development. 1998. 'Multifunctionality: A Framework for Policy Analysis.' *AGR/CA* (98)9, December.

Opie, J. 1987. *The Law of the Land: Two Hundred Years of American Farmland Policy.* Lincoln, Nebraska: University of Nebraska Press.

Pew Center. 2000. 'Sprawl Now Joins Crime as Top Concern.' Retrieved from http://www.pewcenter.org/about/pr_ST2000.html.

Plantinga, A., R. Alig, and H. Cheng. 2001. 'The Supply of Land for Conservation Uses: Evidence from the Conservation Reserve Program.' *Resources, Conservation, and Recycling* 31: 199–215.

Reynolds, J. 2001. 'Land Use Change and Competition in the South.' *Journal of Agricultural and Applied Economics* 33(2): 271–281.

Samspon, N. 2000. 'People, Forests, and Forestry: New Dimensions in the 21st Century.' In Proceedings, *Forest Fragmentation 2000*, September 17–20, 2000, Annapolis

Maryland, eds., N. Sampson and L. DeCoster. Washington, District of Columbia: American Forests.

Schiffman, I. 1996. 'The Property Rights Challenge: What's a Planner to Do?' *Planning Commissioners Journal* 21(Winter): 11–12.

Sohngen, B., R. Mendelsohn, and R. Sedjo. 1999. 'Forest Management, Conservation, and Global Timber Markets.' *American Journal of Agricultural Economics* 81: 1–13.

Sohngen, B. and R. Alig. 2000. 'Mitigation, Adaptation, and Climate Change: Results From Recent Research on U.S. Timber Markets.' *Environmental Science and Policy* 3: 235–248.

Stavins, R. and A. Jaffe. 1990. 'Unintended Impacts of Public Investments on Private Decisions: The Depletion of Forested Wetlands.' *American Economic Review* 80(3): 337–352.

U.S. Department of Agriculture. 1983. *Land Use Policy.* Environmental Compliance Land Use Policy Departmental Regulation, 9500–3, March 22, 1983.

U.S. Department of Agriculture, Economic Research Service. 2002. 'Farm Structure Briefing Room.' Retrieved from http://www.ers.usda.gov/Briefing/FarmStructure/

U.S. Department of Agriculture, Forest Service. 1988. 'The South's Fourth Forest: Alternatives for the Future.' Resource Report No. 24. Washington, District of Columbia.

U.S. Department of Agriculture, Forest Service. 1990. *An Analysis of the Timber Situation in the United States: 1989–2040.* General Technical Report RM-199. Ft. Collins, CO: Rocky Mountain Forest and Range Experiment Station.

U.S. Department of Agriculture, Forest Service. 2000–2002. *National Survey on Recreation and the Environment (NSRE): 2000–2002.* The Interagency National Survey Consortium, Coordinated by the Recreation, Wilderness, and Demographics Trends Research Group, Athens, Georgia and the Human Dimensions Research Laboratory, University of Tennessee, Knoxville, Tennessee.

U.S. Department of Agriculture, National Agricultural Statistics Service. 2001. *1997 Census of Agriculture. Agricultural Economics and Land Ownership Survey (1999).* Vol. 3, Part IV, Ac97–4.

U.S. Department of Agriculture, Natural Resources Conservation Service. 2001. '1997 National Resource Inventory.' Retrieved from www.usda.gov.

U.S. Department of Commerce, Bureau of the Census. 2001. 'Statistical Abstract of the United States.' Retrieved from http://www.census.gov/prod/www/statistical–abstract–us.html.

Wiebe, K., A. Tegene, and B. Kuhn. 1996. 'Partial Interests in Land: Policy Tools for Resource Use and Conservation.' U.S. Department of Agriculture, Economic Research Service Report No. 744. Washington, District of Columbia.

Wu, H. 2003. 'Land Use Changes and Regulations in the U.S. West Coast,' in *The Economics of Land Use Change*, eds. K. Bell, K. Boyle, A. Plantinga, and J. Rubin. Aldershot, England: Ashgate Press

Zeimetz, K.A., E. Dillion, E.E. Hardy, and R.C. Otte. 1976. 'Dynamics of Land Use in Fast Growth Areas.' U.S. Department of Agriculture, Economic Research Service Agricultural Economic Report No. 325. Washington, District of Columbia.

Chapter 4

Transportation and Land-Use Change

Jonathan Rubin

Introduction

Any discussion of rural land-use change in the United States since World War II must recognize the ascendance of privately owned cars, trucks, and more recently, minivans and sport utility vehicles (collectively know as light-duty vehicles). In fact, much of the current concern and discussion about changes in rural land use cannot be thought about separately from the use of private, light-duty vehicles.

The great expansion in private, light-duty vehicle use (described below) has taken place in the context of large technological advances in vehicle safety, performance, and value. North Americans have also become wealthier and can afford to purchase more private, personalized transportation services.

Early economic theory on the economics of land use employed monocentric models to recognize the tradeoff between location, travel costs (monetary and commuting time to a central business district) and land rent gradients (Alonso 1964; Muth 1969). These theories predict decentralization in response to lower transportation costs.

In their 1995 book, *At Road's End*, Carlson et al. argue that the federal highway program, more dramatically than any other single public policy, has changed the sense of place in urban, suburban and rural communities. They argue that new roads open land to development, alter the environment, create congestion and degrade the quality of life that the new roads were meant to improve.

Giuliano (1996) maintains that our current state of decentralization was not an accident, but the result of a confluence of government support for the federal interstate highway system, policies that have kept car and fuel prices low, federal tax and mortgage policies that favor suburban development, and policies that have enabled suburban residents to avoid the social and fiscal problems of the inner city. In an even stronger statement, Hansen (1992) argues that our current transportation system, based on and designed largely for the automobile, has been systematically subsidized in a way that produces a more dispersed settlement pattern than would have otherwise evolved.

Regardless of the direction of causality – whether (underpriced) private vehicle use spurs low density development, or whether the demand for low density development (the result of attitudes, lifestyles and wealth) encourages people to drive – the relationship between land-use change and private vehicles continues to be interwoven. Economic modeling of rural land-use change must take into account these complex relationships.

This chapter examines the economic interactions of light-duty vehicle transportation and land-use patterns.[1] These interactions are complex, not one-directional. Recognition of these interactions is essential for understanding the limitations and ability of public policy to shape rural land-use change via transportation regulation. It warrants emphasis to note that there are important differences between the potential for public policy to influence rural, as opposed to urban, land-use change. In urban areas, transportation systems are highly developed and new transportation projects and policies are likely to have more limited impacts.[2]

Vehicle Population and Use

Aggregate Vehicle Use

The availability of affordable, private light-duty vehicle transportation and a growing interstate highway system were important historical factors affecting land-use change in the United States. In 1950, the U.S. population of 152 million people used 43 million cars and trucks to drive 458 million miles. By 1999, the U.S. population had grown to 272 million, driving 2.7 billion miles in 209 million vehicles (Davis 2001, Table 11.1). This represents an increase in per-capita driving from roughly 3,029 to 9,713 miles per year (see Figure 4.1). While the population increased by 78 per cent, the number of miles driven increased by 468 per cent, and the number of vehicles in use grew by 377 per cent. This vehicular traffic was made possible by extensive road construction that has grown to constitute 3.9 million miles (U.S. Department of Transportation 2000) and a vehicle ownership rate that almost tripled from 0.28 to 0.77 vehicles per capita (Davis 2001, Table 11.2).

Trip Decomposition

Contrary to popular belief, this tremendous increase in driving is not due solely to increases in the daily commute to work in single-occupancy vehicles; the journey to or from work represented only about 27 per cent of all household vehicle-miles in 1995 (Davis 2001, Table 11.9). Nonetheless, in the daily commute, the use of alternatives to single-occupancy private vehicles used has fallen. U.S. census data shows that the percentage of workers who carpooled dropped from 19.7 per cent to 11.2 per cent, and the percentage of workers using public transit declined from 6.4 per cent to 5.2 per cent between 1980 and 2000 (Davis 1999, Table 11.13; Davis 2001, Table 11.14). The remainder of household vehicle travel is for family and personal business, shopping, recreation, and vacations (see Figure 4.2).

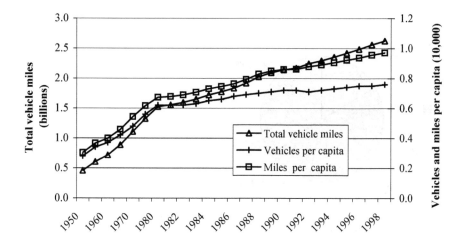

Figure 4.1 Vehicle population and use

Source: Adapted from Davis (2001), Table 11.1.

Low-Density Development

A second important factor affecting rural land-use change has been the increased demand for lower-density residential development. Within U.S. metropolitan areas, which themselves contain 80 per cent of the total U.S. population, the suburban proportion increased from 54 per cent to 63 per cent between 1970 and 1996. Unlike the historical rural to urban migration, much of the current suburban growth is from the movement of the population from central cities to the suburban areas (Littman 1998).

Competing Theses of Transportation

The literature on linkages between transportation and land use contains many nuances. Emphasizing two important lines of argument is helpful: one views sprawl as the result of underpriced transportation services, the other views dispersion as the natural, and perhaps inevitable, result of increases in wealth combined with attitudinal and lifestyle choices. As stressed above, both discussions take place with the backdrop of rapidly improving technology for light-duty vehicles.

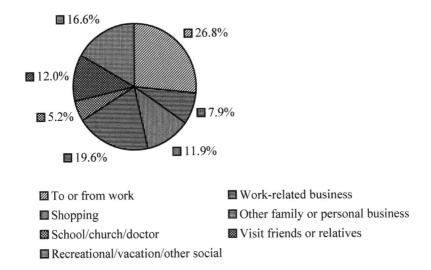

To or from work 26.8%
Work-related business 7.9%
Shopping 11.9%
Other family or personal business 19.6%
School/church/doctor 5.2%
Visit friends or relatives 12.0%
Recreational/vacation/other social 16.6%

🡕 To or from work   ▤ Work-related business
▥ Shopping   ▤ Other family or personal business
▨ School/church/doctor   ▨ Visit friends or relatives
▦ Recreational/vacation/other social

Figure 4.2 Vehicle miles by trip purpose

Source: Adapted from Davis (1999), Table 11.8.

Sprawl Thesis

An important theme in the transportation-land-use relationship is the classic economic question: are transportation services from private vehicles priced correctly? Are private light-duty vehicles systematically subsidized in a way that encourages a more dispersed settlement pattern than would have otherwise been the case (Hansen 1992; Litman 1997; MacKenzie et al. 1992)?

As Cervero and Landis (1996) clearly state, investments in transportation systems strongly affect urban conditions including land-use patterns, urban densities, and housing prices. 'Given today's distorted transportation marketplace, we are not surprised that the coordination of transportation and land use programs has to date yielded suboptimal outcomes. However, this is an indictment of pricing policies, not land use planning,' (Cervero and Landis 1996, p. 11). They continue, '[p]roper pricing, such as congestion fees and mandatory parking charges, would likely eliminate the need for efforts to balance jobs and housing or build transit-oriented communities.'

Are Private Vehicles Subsidized?

Important to the sprawl thesis is the notion that the level of private vehicle use is too great because the direct (marginal) price of private vehicles is too low. Several researchers have attempted to estimate the magnitude by which private marginal or average vehicle costs differ from social marginal or average vehicle costs. These include the work of MacKenzie et al. (1992), Hansen (1992), Litman (1996), and Delucchi (1998). The most comprehensive analysis is by Delucchi who, in a monumental twenty volume series, attempts to estimate all annualized social costs of motor-vehicle use in the U.S., from vehicle ownership to human health effects to crop losses attributable to vehicle emissions. Fortunately, Delucchi is aware of the difficulties in undertaking such an enormous task and offers his estimates for what they are – his best appraisal using a combination of secondary data and original analysis. These estimates provide a useful starting point to address the question as to whether or not motor vehicles are underpriced.

Delucchi breaks down vehicle costs into personal, private sector, public-sector, and external costs. These categories are broken down further to recognize both monetary and non-monetary components. Important personal non-monetary costs include: travel time, accidental injuries and death, and personal time spent buying, selling, refueling and repairing vehicles. Public sector costs include public highways not paid for out of the federal or state gasoline excise taxes, highway patrols, regulating air pollution, energy and vehicle research and development, some portion of military expenditures in the Persian Gulf, and stocking and maintenance of the strategic petroleum reserve.

External costs of vehicle use receive the most attention from researchers and the public. Table 4.1 shows Delucchi's estimates of the monetary externality cost of motor vehicles ranges from $43 to $104 billion per year.

Delucchi also estimates the non-monetary costs of vehicles. These range from $68 billion to $730 billion, and are dominated by the value of accidental pain suffering and death, human morbidity from air pollution, and travel delay that displaces unpaid activities. As is shown in Table 4.2, Delucchi estimates monetary and nonmonetary externalities to be between seven per cent and 25 per cent of the total costs of motor vehicle use.[3] As Delucchi points out (p. 33), the aggregated totals are shown in order to provide a sense of magnitudes, not because such aggregated totals are themselves useful. Bearing this caution in mind, it is instructive to note that motor vehicle services produced and priced in the private sector roughly represent only 30 per cent to 50 per cent of the total costs of vehicle services. To the extent that these estimates are remotely correct, this lends significant economic justification to the notion that vehicles are used more than they otherwise would be if all costs were borne directly by the user. To the extent that vehicle use is related to low-density development, this evidence does provide support for the sprawl thesis. The magnitude of its importance, however, is difficult to gauge. Moreover, as Delucchi (2000) also argues, the lack of marginal cost pricing of light-duty vehicle transportation services undermines otherwise well-intentioned efforts to internalize external costs.

Table 4.1 Monetary externalities of motor-vehicle use (billion 1991$)

Cost item	Low	High	Q*
Monetary costs of travel delay imposed by others: foregone paid work	9.1	30.5	A2
Monetary costs of travel delay imposed by others: extra consumption of fuel	2.3	5.7	A2
Accident costs not accounted for by economically responsible party: property damage, medical, productivity, legal and administrative costs	26.0	28.0	A2/B
Expected loss of GNP due to sudden changes in the price of oil	1.8	31.5	C
Price effect of using petroleum fuels for motor vehicles: increased payments to foreign countries for oil used in other sectors	3.8	8.0	A3
Monetary, non-public-sector costs of net crimes related to using or having motor-vehicle goods, services, or infrastructure	0.1	0.4	A3
Monetary costs of injuries and deaths caused by fires related to motor-vehicle use	0.0	0.1	A3
Total	43.1	104.2	

*Quality of the estimate, roughly A=high, D=low, see Table 1.3 in the source for additional detail.

Source: Adapted from Delucchi (1998), Table 1–8. Reproduced with permission from the author.

Wealth and Attitude Thesis

Increasing wealth may encourage private vehicle use both directly and indirectly. Increasing wealth directly encourages increased use of light-duty private vehicles if individuals view them as normal goods. As Dunn points out in his book, *Driving Forces*, critics of the U.S. car and truck culture are deeply averse to acknowledging the material and psychological value of the auto to millions of individuals. That is, if we accept that individuals desire private, personalized transportation, as opposed to public transportation, then increases in wealth, *ceteris paribus*, encourage or enable its use.

Table 4.2 Summary of the costs of motor-vehicle use

	Total cost (billion 1991$)		Percentage of total	
	Low	High	Low	High
(1) Personal non-monetary costs of motor-vehicle use	527	968	32	29
(2) Motor-vehicle goods and services produced and priced in the private sector (estimated net of producer surplus, taxes, fees)	827	980	49	30
(3) Motor-vehicle goods and services bundled in the private sector	76	279	5	8
(4) Motor-vehicle infrastructure and services provided by the public sector	131	247	8	7
(5) Monetary externalities of motor-vehicle use	43	104	3	3
(6) Non-monetary externalities of motor-vehicle use	68	730	4	22
Grand total: social cost of highway transportation	1,673	3,308	100	100
Subtotal: monetary cost only (2+3+4+5)	1,077	1,610	64	49

Source: Adapted from Delucchi (1998), Table 1–10. Reproduced with permission from the author.

This point is supported by Giuliano (1999), who, after reviewing the relationships between international car ownership rates and incomes, argues that car ownership is significantly related to per capita income. In particular, she argues that higher incomes imply a higher value of time, making travel time relatively more important in the travel choice decision. Shown in Table 4.3 are data from the 1983, 1990 and 1995 National Personal Travel Surveys showing Journey-to-Work Statistics (Davis 2001, Table 11.13). The journey-to-work using public transportation takes about twice as long as private transportation, though there is only a slight difference in travel distance.

Rising per capita income also increases the demand for consumer goods, including housing. Reviewing the evidence, Giuliano (1999) argues that there is increasing demand, even internationally, for single-family housing. Thus, she argues that rising incomes, changing demographics, and economic structures have all played a key role in the land-use and travel patterns that we observe today. Giuliano argues that continued geographic decentralization and increased use of private vehicles is likely to occur.

In a different approach to these issues, Kitamura et al. (1997, p. 126) ask: 'Is the observed association between travel and land use real, or is it an artifact of the association between land use and the multitude of demographic, socioeconomic, and transportation supply characteristics which also are associated with travel?' Rather than asking whether personal vehicle use causes low-density development, Kitamura et al. are concerned with whether properly formulated land-use polices can help control travel demand. Their approach is to perform statistical tests of association on a unique data set consisting of land-use characteristics, roadway networks, public transit information, and the socioeconomic, travel behavior, and attitudinal characteristics of residents from several neighborhoods in the San Francisco Bay area. Kitamura et al. find that attitudes toward the environment, lifestyles, and mobility are at least as strongly, and perhaps directly, associated with travel as are land-use characteristics. They conclude that land-use policies that promote higher densities may not materially alter travel demand without also changing individuals' attitudes. Although not the focus of this research, it suggests that economists interested in modeling land-use change may need to incorporate explicit attitudinal characteristics into their behavior models.

Sperling argues in *Future Drive* (1995) that it is important to respect individuals' preferred mode of travel, the private car. He argues that measures such as the greater use of public transit, walking, biking and telecommuting are useful, but they are limited in their effectiveness to reduce private vehicle use because they fail to give sufficient weight to the attachment people have to cars. This attachment derives from the unprecedented freedom, privacy, convenience, and security that cars provide. Moreover, these trip reduction measures do not lead to clean and efficient vehicles. The question then becomes, what technologies are on the horizon that could reduce the external costs of private, light-duty vehicles?

Sperling convincingly makes the case that the key to a more benign future lies with electric propulsion, either powered by batteries or fuel cells. After surveying the literature, Sperling concludes that the cost reductions resulting from improved technology and mass production will not bring the cost of battery-powered electric vehicles down to that of gasoline vehicles if they attempt to have the same range and performance as gasoline vehicles. But, as Sperling sees it, electric vehicles do not have to be completely comparable. Households could own a short-range city car, a long-range minivan, and perhaps a third specialty vehicle such as a sport-utility vehicle or a small neighborhood car. The key is that, within a household vehicle choice framework, every vehicle need not do everything. Sperling compares the introduction of electric vehicles to the introduction of microwave ovens. Both are appliances with a new set of functional features that

Table 4.3 U.S. journey-to-work statistics (1983, 1990, and 1995 National Personal Transportation Surveys)

Year	Private transportation	Public transportation
Average travel time (minutes)		
1983	17.6	39.8
1990	19.1	41.1
1995	20.1	42.0
Average trip length (miles)		
1983	8.9	11.8
1990	11.0	12.8
1995	11.8	12.9
Average speed (miles per hour)		
1983	30.2	17.8
1990	34.7	18.2
1995	35.4	19.3

Source: Adapted from Davis (2000), Table 11.12.

complement, but need not replace, their conventional counterparts. In the longer term, neighborhoods could be redesigned to accommodate 'neighborhood electric vehicles,' small lightweight vehicles built specially for short trips, not for highway travel.

Similar considerations also apply to fuel cell vehicles, which, although expected to be much cleaner and more quiet than conventional internal combustion vehicles, are also not likely to be cost competitive without substantial public subsidies. For public policy purposes, and for economic modeling of rural land-use change, the challenge is how to effectively allow for and utilize the coming diversity of vehicle technologies and attributes. These changes may have little impact on the current trend in land-use patterns while yielding substantial improvements in air quality.

Changes in the Cost of Vehicle Purchase and Use

Regardless of the merits of these competing theses, land-use changes from vehicle use, as distinct from (nonmarket) regulatory and attitudinal changes, clearly depend on the price of vehicle services over time as well as changes in income and the cost of substitute or complementary services. The total costs of operating an automobile are the sum of the fixed costs, including depreciation, insurance, finance, and license fees, and the variable costs which depend on the amount of travel.

Capital Costs

The American Automobile Manufacturers Association (AAMA) has compiled a data series that estimates the cost over time of purchasing a new car and a 1967 'comparable car' (AAMA 1998). The AAMA data show that the purchase price of an average car has increased from $3,212 in 1967 to $20,447 in 1997 in nominal dollars.   Simply converting these prices to constant dollars would give a misleading indication of the relative change in cost of a car over time because of the changes in household income and the fact that cars themselves are not the same. Cars today have many more safety, emissions, and consumer convenience features than those produced in 1967.

The AAMA estimate for a 1967 comparable car shows that, without additional consumer features and emissions and safety equipment, cars have roughly tripled in price in three decades. Added emission and safety equipment has added about $4000 to the price of a 1967 comparable car and upgrades have added another $7000 beyond that.

Cars are not the only thing that has changed, so has household income. The cost of a car in terms of the number of weeks of median family income is perhaps an economically more relevant measure of the relative cost of a car. In terms of weeks of median income, the AAMA data show that the average new car, including all safety, emissions equipment, and model upgrades, was slightly more expensive in 1997, costing an average of 23.5 weeks of median household income as compared to 21.1 weeks in 1967. Using this definition, the AAMA data indicate that, relative to income, a 1967 new car today would cost 15.3 weeks in 1997 compared to 20.9 weeks in 1967. If consumers fully value safety and emissions equipment, a 1967 comparable car today would cost only 10.7 weeks of median family income.

These data clearly show that, relative to income, an average new car today is more expensive than one purchased in 1967, but only because households choose to purchase vehicles with more amenities. Even allowing that emissions and safety equipment may not be completely valued by households, a comparable 1967 vehicle is 25 to 50 per cent less expensive today, taking purchasing power into account.

Variable Vehicle Costs

Clearly, vehicle use, as opposed to ownership, depends importantly on variable operating costs. As can be seen from Figure 4.3, maintenance and tire costs have essentially remained constant over the 1975–1999 time period, while gasoline and oil costs have declined. The net effect is that (monetary) variable costs (equal to the sum of gas, oil, tires, and maintenance costs) of motor vehicle use have declined at an average annual rate of 4.9 per cent for the period 1975–1984 and 1.1 per cent per year since 1985. They currently comprise only about 19 per cent of total vehicle costs (fixed plus variable), based on 10,000 miles per year of driving (Davis 2000, Table 5.12).

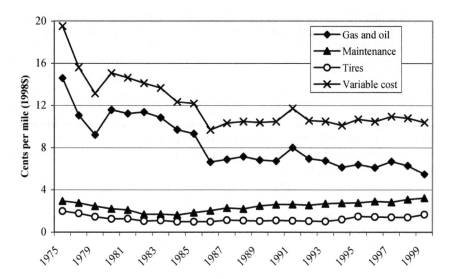

Figure 4.3 Real variable vehicle costs

Source: Adapted from Davis (2000), Table 5.12.

Variable Price Sensitivity

Especially important from a policy perspective is not just the long-term trend in variable vehicle costs, but also the sensitivity of consumers to changes in variable costs. Concentrating on the fuel portion of variable costs, the quantity of gasoline used per household in a given year (Q_t) is a function of both the vehicle miles traveled (VMT) and the fuel efficiency (miles per gallon [MPG]) of the household vehicles: $Q_t = \dfrac{VMT_t}{MPG_t}$. Following Dahl (1986), the price elasticity of demand for fuel use can be decomposed into the difference between the elasticities of VMT and fuel efficiency with respect to fuel price as follows: $\varepsilon_{Q,P} = \varepsilon_{VMT,P} - \varepsilon_{MPG,P}$. Given the changing fuel efficiency of vehicles over time, the most relevant elasticity for considering the interactions of light-duty transportation and land use is the fuel price elasticity of VMT, $\varepsilon_{VMT,P}$, since this tells us how sensitive households are in their demands for driving with respect to fuel prices.

In her 1986 survey, Dahl concluded that the empirical literature provided average estimates of long-run fuel price elasticities of -0.55 for VMT and 0.57 for MPG, summing to an overall long-run price elasticity of -1.12.[4] In their 1990 survey, Dahl and Sterner find an average long-run price elasticity of gasoline demand of -0.80. Also, importantly, Dahl and Sterner observe that there is fairly strong evidence that the average long-run income elasticity of demand for gasoline is greater than one.

In a more recent look at the literature, Greene (1998) finds the elasticity of VMT with respect to fuel cost per mile to be about -0.2 in the long-run. He explains that this new lower estimate is the result of greater variation in fuel price and fuel economy, taking into account the oil price shock of 1979–1982, the oil price collapse of 1986, the oil price rise of 1991, and the increase in light-duty fuel economy during the 1980–1995 period. Greene, who is concerned with how fuel economy affects fuel use and the efficacy of corporate average fuel efficiency (CAFE) regulations, concludes that the observed 80 per cent increase in light-duty vehicle travel from 1975 to 1995 has only resulted in an increase in fuel use of 20 per cent, with the difference attributable to a 50 per cent increase in on-road fuel economy over the same period.

What does this mean for rural land-use change? Simply, that if you accept Greene's recent findings, straightforward advocacy of higher fuel prices is not likely to reduce the trend towards increased driving, per capita and in total. Even using the older, higher elasticity estimates, arguments that we can use taxes – in any politically feasible range – as an effective policy instrument to reduce driving are likely to be wrong. One may want to increase fuel taxes for reasons such as internalizing external effects or for revenue recycling, but this increase in taxes is not likely to have much effect on the amount of driving or rural land-use change.

This discussion also highlights the importance of explicitly taking into account changes in vehicle fuel efficiency for medium and long-term modeling of transportation costs in land-use models. Vehicle fuel efficiency is, of course, partly endogenously determined by individual choice, and partly the result, on a fleet-wide basis, of CAFE established by the US Energy Policy and Conservation Act.

Observations

Changes in rural land use have historically been, and remain, intimately connected with changes in light-duty vehicle use, technology, and policy. The evidence presented by Delucchi (1998, 2000) supports the notion that private vehicle use is significantly underpriced, especially in terms of marginal expenses per trip. At the same time, getting the prices right is not likely to be the panacea for undesirable land uses, as is hoped for by full cost advocates. Nonetheless, there is no justification for ignoring known external costs or for not considering the land-use implications of bundling vehicle costs into housing or shopping developments. Correct pricing of light-duty vehicle transportation ought to be pursued.

Growing wealth and preferences for private vehicle transportation and detached housing also account for our growing geographic decentralization. These trends are likely to lead to increasing decentralization and to additional development of rural lands.

Regardless of the direction of causality – underpriced (and non-marginal priced) private vehicle use spurring low-density development or demand for low-density development encouraging people to drive – the relationship between land-use change and private vehicle use continues to be interwoven. Economic modeling of land-use change must take into account this relationship.

Notes

1   There is a vast literature on land use and transportation, most of it from an urban
     planning perspective. The Victoria Transport Policy Institute (http://www.vtpi.org/)
     maintains an Excel database with more than 2,000 publications related to
     transportation economics, transportation policy, planning and modeling, transportation
     benefit and cost analysis, and existing transportation cost studies.
2   For urban transportation economics, see Small (1997).
3   Despite the comprehensive nature of Delucchi's reports, some costs such as air and
     water pollution damages to natural ecosystems, vibration damages, esthetic damages
     of highways, and others, are not estimated.
4   It is important to emphasize that for land-use change, one should focus on the long-
     run price elasticities which can vary by a factor of three as compared to short-run
     elasticities.

References

Alonso, W. 1964. *Location and Land Use: Toward a General Theory of Land Rent.*
     Cambridge, Massachusetts: Harvard University Press.
American Automobile Manufacturers Association (AAMA). 1998. *Motor Vehicle Facts
     and Figures 1998, Table 'New Car Expenditures,'* p. 64.
Carlson, D., L. Wormser, and C. Ulberg. 1995. *At Road's End: Transportation and Land
     Use Choices for Communities.* Washington, District of Columbia: Island Press.
Cervero, R. and J. Landis. 1996. 'Why the Transportation-Land Use Connection is Still
     Important.' *TR News* 187: 9–11. National Research Council, Transportation
     Research Board.
Dahl, C. 1986. 'Gasoline Demand Survey.' *The Energy Journal* 7(1): 67–82.
Dahl, C. and T. Sterner. 1991. 'Analysing Gasoline Demand Elasticities: A Survey.'
     Energy Economics 13(3): 203–210.
Dunn, J.A. Jr. 1998. *Driving Forces: The Automobile, Its Enemies, and Politics of
     Mobility.* Washington, District of Columbia: Brooking Institution Press.
Davis, S.C. 1999. *Transportation Energy Data Book, Edition 19.* Prepared for the Oak
     Ridge National Laboratory, Center for Transportation Analysis. Oakridge, Tennessee.
Davis, S.C. 2000. *Transportation Energy Data Book, Edition 20.* Prepared for the Oak
     Ridge National Laboratory, Center for Transportation Analysis. Oakridge, Tennessee.
Davis, S.C. 2001. *Transportation Energy Data Book, Edition 21.* Prepared for the Oak
     Ridge National Laboratory, Center for Transportation Analysis. Oakridge, Tennessee.
Delucchi, M. 1998. 'The Annualized Social Cost of Motor-Vehicle Use in the U.S., 1990–
     1991: Summary of Theory, Data, Methods, and Results.' University of California,
     Davis, Institute of Transportation Studies Report No. 1, UCD-ITS-RR-96-3 (1).
Delucchi, M. 2000. 'Should We Try and Get the Prices Right?' *Access* 16: 10–14.
Giuliano, G. 1995. 'The Weakening Transportation-Land Use Connection.' *Access* 6: 3–11.
Giuliano, G. 1996. 'Transportation, Land Use, and Public Policy.' *TR News* 187: 12–13.
Giuliano, G. 1999. 'Land Use Policy and Transportation: Why We Won't Get There From
     Here.' *Transportation Research Circular* 492, National Research Council,
     Transportation Research Board.
Greene, D.L. 1998. 'Why CAFE Worked.' *Energy Policy* 26(8): 595–613.
Hansen, M.E. 1992. 'Automobile Subsidies and Land Use: Estimates and Policy
     Responses.' *Journal of the American Planning Association* 58(1): 60–71.

Kitamura, R., P.L. Mokhtarian, and L. Laidet. 1997. 'A Micro-Analysis of Land Use and Travel in Five Neighborhoods in the San Francisco Bay Area.' *Transportation* 24: 125–158.

Kleit, A.N. 1990. 'The Effect of Annual Changes in Automobile Fuel Economy Standards.' *Journal of Regulatory Economics* 2: 151–172.

Litman, T. 1996. *Transportation Cost Analysis: Techniques, Estimates and Implications.* Victoria, Canada: Victoria Transport Policy Institute.

Litman, T. 1997. 'Policy Implications of Full Social Costing.' *Annals of the American Academy of Political and Social Sciences* (553): 143–156.

Littman, M.S. 1998. *A Statistical Portrait of the United States: Social Conditions and Trends.* Lanham, Maryland: Bernan Press.

MacKenzie, J.J., R.C. Dower, and D. Chen. 1992. *The Going Rate: What It Really Costs to Drive.* Washington, District of Columbia: World Resources Institute.

McCarthy, P.S. 1996. 'Market Price and Income Elasticities of New Vehicle Demands.' *The Review of Economics and Statistics* LXXVII(3): 543–547.

Muth, R. 1969. *Cities and Housing.* Chicago, Illinois: University of Chicago Press.

Small, K.A. 1997. 'Economics and Urban Transportation Policy in the United States.' *Regional Science and Urban Economics* 27: 671–691.

Sperling, D. 1995. *Future Drive: Electric Vehicles and Sustainable Transportation*, with contributions from Mark A. Delucchi, Patricia M. Davis, and A.F. Burke. Washington, District of Columbia: Island Press.

U.S. Department of Transportation, Federal Highway Administration. 2000. *Highway Statistics 2000, Table HM-10*. Retrieved from: http://www.fhwa.dot.gov/ohim/hs00/index.htm.

Chapter 5

Patterns and Processes in the Demographics of Land-Use Change in the United States

Deirdre M. Mageean and John G. Bartlett

Introduction

The 2000 decennial census records the population of the United States as 281,421,906 – a figure that represents a growth of 13.1 per cent over the 1990–2000 period (U.S. Department of Commerce, Bureau of the Census 2001a). The 1996 population of 265 million was approximately twice as many people as were residents in 1940. The growth in population during the last half-century, however, has been uneven. From 1930 to 1940, the country's population increased by only 7.2 per cent. During the 1950s (the baby boom era), growth rebounded and population increased by 18.5 per cent from 1950 to 1960. Thereafter, growth rates declined, and during the 1980s the population increased by less than ten per cent (Murdock 1995).

The addition of some 32.7 million new Americans since 1990 represents the largest numerical increase in population ever recorded in a decade by the census and the largest percentage gain since the 1960s (Kent et al. 2001). The growth in population during the last decade is remarkable not only in absolute numbers but also for its high rate relative to all other industrial democratic countries. Unique among industrial countries, the United States simultaneously experiences three strong population trends, namely international migration, natural increase, and residential mobility. Together these forces result in widespread growth and redistribution of the population, which, in turn, has a considerable impact on rural land uses such as agriculture and forests. While the United States has a population density of 77 people per square mile – low in comparison to most European and Asian countries – both the pace and pattern of population growth, particularly at the regional and local level, are affecting the conversion of land throughout the U.S. Current projections are that the U.S. population will reach 346.0 million in 2025 and 413.5 by 2050 (Kent et al. 2001). Where and how these people will settle will have enormous implications for the environment. Hence, it is important to understand the dynamics of the interaction between population and land. In this chapter we will examine the broad patterns of population and land-use change in recent decades. In particular, we will look at regional shifts in population, urbanization and the growth of edge cities, those low-density, sprawling suburban centers that have become the new 'hot spots' of residential growth in the 1990s. As we will see, the patterns of change, and the constraints on them, are distinctly different from one part of the country to another.

During the decade 1990–2000, the U.S. population grew by just over three million people per year. Although growth was widespread – almost every state recorded population gain – growth in certain cities and states has been dramatic. Overall, the western and southern states grew the fastest while the midwestern and northeastern states grew the slowest. The flow of population to the West over the last few decades is one of the most significant population shifts to occur in the U.S. Growth in some of the Rocky Mountain States has been particularly dramatic. Arizona (40 per cent), Colorado (30.6 per cent), Idaho (28.5 per cent), Nevada (66.3 per cent) and Utah (29.6 per cent) were the five fastest growing states in the country. Nevada, which has been the fastest growing state in the country for the past 15 years, increased its population from 1.2 to almost two million people, while Arizona grew from 3.6 to 5.1 million people.

In the Pacific West, Oregon and Washington grew by 20.4 and 21.1 per cent respectively. Because of its sheer size, any growth in California is significant. While its growth rate of 13.6 per cent was less than the previous decade's 26 per cent, it managed to record the single greatest numerical increase – 4.1 million people – of any state. Between April 2000 and July 2002, the state grew by 630,000 people, which accounts for almost one-fifth of the country's entire growth.

Because of its consistently high rates of growth, the West will soon become the second most populous region of the U.S. As of July 2001, its total population reached 64.5 million people, just 0.2 million shy of the Midwest's population, and 11 million more than the Northeast which it overtook after 1990.

In the South, the country's most populous region with 101.8 million people, the states of Georgia (26.4 per cent), Florida (23.5 per cent), Texas (22.8 per cent) and North Carolina (21.4 per cent) were the fastest growing. Like California, Florida's growth, although slower than that experienced in the previous decade, was significant in sheer numbers, with an additional three million people, making it the third largest numerical increase in the country.

Metropolitan Growth and Conversion of Land to Urban Use

The particularly rapid rates of growth highlighted above – faster than many developing countries – are in large measure due to population flows and are reflective of both new centers of economic growth and amenity-driven migration. Dramatic though some of the state's growth rates are, sub-state areas, such as metropolitan counties, have experienced even more dramatic growth. Metropolitan counties include: central and fringe counties of one million people or more; counties in metropolitan areas of 250,000 to one million people and counties in metropolitan areas of fewer than 250,000 people (U.S. Department of Agriculture, Economic Research Service 2002). In 1990, 39 areas achieved major metropolitan

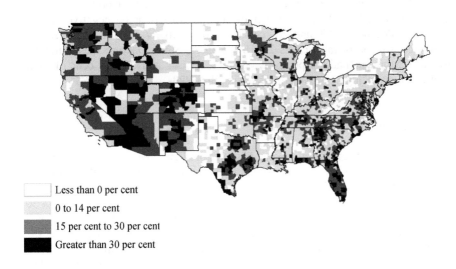

Less than 0 per cent

0 to 14 per cent

15 per cent to 30 per cent

Greater than 30 per cent

Figure 5.1 Percentage change in county population, 1990–2000

status (those with populations greater than one million) and, for the first time in U.S. history, a majority of the population lived in these major metros (Frey 1995). The growth in metropolitan counties during the last decade, a period of population growth in most of the country's metropolitan areas, is clearly seen in Fig. 5.1.

In 2000, 80 per cent of the U.S. population lived in metropolitan areas. The continuing concentration of the nation's population in large urban centers is one of the most notable and enduring trends in the demography of the United States (Frey 1995). Other than during a period in the 1970s, when many non-metropolitan areas grew faster than metropolitan areas, this trend toward population concentration was strong throughout the twentieth century. In the 1990s, the majority of U.S. metropolitan areas experienced population growth. While growth in these areas was widespread, it was particularly fast, an average of 19 per cent, in metropolitan areas with populations between one million and five million (Kent et al. 2001). In Figure 5.1 we can clearly see the very rapid growth (30 per cent and above) in the counties around large cities, such as Atlanta and Augusta, Georgia., Charlotte and Raleigh-Durham, North Carolina, Orlando and Naples, Florida, Phoenix, Arizona, Las Vegas and Reno, Nevada, Boise, Idaho, Provo and Salt Lake City, Utah, Bolder, Denver and Fort Collins, Colorado, and San Bernardino county, east of Los Angeles, California.

Reflecting overall growth in the last decade, the metropolitan areas in the South and West grew the most rapidly – 20 per cent on average compared to less than ten per cent in metropolitan areas in the Midwest and Northeast. The desert cities of Las Vegas and Phoenix continued their spectacular growth at 83.3 and 45.3 per cent respectively, while retirement meccas in Florida, such as Naples, registered growth of 65.3 per cent. Population declines during the same period were widespread but concentrated primarily in the Midwest. North Dakota and Nebraska recorded the largest number of counties experiencing negative growth during the decade at 89 and 57 per cent, respectively (U.S. Department of Commerce, Bureau of the Census 2001b). Kansas, South Dakota, West Virginia, Iowa and Montana had, respectively, 54, 48, 47, 44 and 39 per cent of their counties experiencing negative growth during the 1990s.

The Shaping of Metropolitan Growth

The forces behind these rapidly expanding metropolitan areas vary from region to region, as do the patterns of metropolitan growth. A major force in the growth of the United States, and, in particular, metropolitan areas, has been international migration. Of the total U.S. population increase between 1990 and 1998, about 30 per cent was contributed by immigration (Martin and Midgley 1999). International immigration has proceeded at the rate of just over one million per year during the last two decades, but the selected flow of immigrants has contributed substantially to the growth of these metropolitan areas (Chiswick and Sullivan 1995). For instance, all of the 1985–1990 migration gains for Los Angeles, New York, and San Francisco were due to international migration. In the early 1990s, international migration continued as a more significant force than rural to urban migration for these large metropolitan areas.

In contrast to these cities, the majority of migration gains for Atlanta, Seattle, and Phoenix came from internal migrants from other parts of the U.S. (Frey 1995) It has been the flow of domestic migrants which has shaped the broader pattern of urbanization. Some cities, such as Charlotte and Raleigh-Durham, have grown as people have moved away from older, more congested areas in the Northeast and Midwest. These cities have developed with the new economy of the South and offer a lifestyle more akin to traditional suburbs than the urban areas in the Frost Belt. Similarly, cities in the Mountain West, such as Boise, Idaho, have attracted Californians disenchanted with dense, congested, and hectic urban centers in their home state (Kent et al. 2001).

Shorter distance migration has given rise to a notable phenomenon of the last two decades, namely the growth of edge cities: those residential, rural or mixed-use areas on the perimeters of large cities, which were initially the locus of homes and malls for those who worked in the central cities and, eventually, became the areas where new jobs were created and emerged as cities in their own right. Garreau (1991, 1994) identified 203 edge cities inside 36 large metropolitan areas. Examples include the Interstate-95 loop encircling Boston, Massachusetts, interstate highways 287 and 78 in New Jersey, and the 'bedroom community' of Irvine, California, south of Los Angeles.

Kent et al. (2001) have recognized that the growth of metropolitan areas varies substantially across the country, but the patterns of growth fall into three broad categories:

(1) Slow-growing metropolitan areas where the central city grew slowly or not at all, while outlying counties grew rapidly, such as the Kansas City, Missouri, and Minneapolis-Saint Paul, Minnesota metropolitan areas;
(2) Rapidly growing metropolitan areas, mainly in the South, such as Atlanta, Georgia, that exemplify a typical sprawl pattern of fast growth with rapid development occurring on the edges of the area, following major highways;
(3) Rapidly growing metropolitan areas in the West where population becomes more concentrated due to constraints of land availability, including physical features such as mountain ranges, desert and coastlines, and the federal ownership of large blocks of land.

Such large-scale urbanization patterns are reflected in the concomitant pattern of land-use conversion seen in Figure 5.2. Even at this coarse scale, one can detect (1) the radial pattern of rural agricultural land conversion around Kansas City, (2) the irregular patchiness of forest conversion in the greater Atlanta region and, (3) the relatively constrained land conversion in the western cities.

Population Growth in Rural America

About one in four Americans still live in rural areas (defined as living outside places that have a population of 2,500 or more), but of these, a mere seven per cent live on farms (Littman 1998). With the reorganization of agriculture and a decline in the need for labor in that and other extractive industries, rural America has been experiencing a steady decline in population. The one notable exception to this was a period in the seventies when population growth in non-metropolitan areas outstripped that in metropolitan areas. This period, known as the 'rural renaissance' was hailed as an expression of Americans' desire to live in small communities, a desire that could be facilitated by advances in technology and communication. However, the renaissance proved to be short-lived and was due more to economic forces than environmental preferences. The 1980s pattern reverted to one of population growth slow-down and decline in rural areas, a trend that continued into the 1990s.

Trends in county-level population growth between 1990 and 2000 in non-metropolitan areas followed state-level trends in many respects. Negative growth in non-metropolitan counties was concentrated in the Midwest and Central Atlantic states and in New England (U.S. Department of Agriculture, Economic Research Service 2002). Some states had positive growth in 100 per cent of their non-metropolitan counties, including Arizona, Florida, Massachusetts, Tennessee, Oregon, Washington, and Wisconsin. Five mid-western states had greater than 50 per cent of their non-metropolitan counties experiencing negative growth in the 1990s, namely North Dakota, Nebraska, Kansas, South Dakota, and Iowa. States outside the Midwest that experienced negative growth in greater than 25 per cent of their non-metropolitan counties included New York, Arkansas, Louisiana, and Pennsylvania. Areas considered completely rural (population less than 2,500)

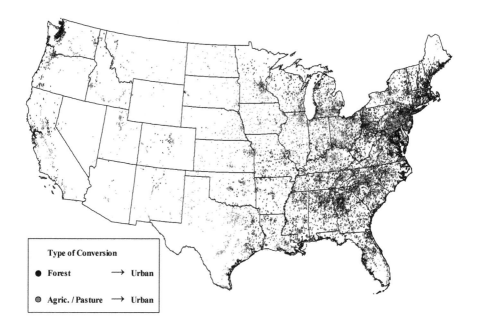

Type of Conversion

● Forest   ⟶ Urban

◉ Agric. / Pasture ⟶ Urban

Figure 5.2 Urbanization in the United States, 1992–1997

Source: U.S. Department of Agriculture, Natural Resource Conservation Service (2001).

followed the same national patterns as non-metropolitan counties (*Ibid.*). Small pockets of growth in rural counties were recorded in many states and were often associated with recreational amenities and pristine natural resources such as national parks and forests. These areas include the Upper Peninsula of Michigan, the Southern Appalachian Mountains of northern Georgia, South Carolina and western North Carolina, the Ozarks of Arkansas, the Pocono Mountains of Pennsylvania and the San Juan Mountains of Colorado.

The 1990 census reveals that between 1980 and 1990, nine states became more rural, i.e. experienced an increase in the percentage of their population living in rural areas (U.S. Department of Commerce, Bureau of the Census 1995). For six of these nine states (New York, Pennsylvania, West Virginia, Mississippi, Louisiana and Montana), however, the difference in percentage points was less than one. The most significant change, both relatively and in percentage points, occurred in four states in New England – Maine, New Hampshire, Vermont and Rhode Island. Maine, the third most rural state in the country, saw its rural population increase from 52.5 per cent in 1980 to 55.4 per cent in 1990, a relative change of 5.52 per cent, or 2.9 percentage points. However, this apparent increase in the rural population was not due to any great revival of Maine's rural communities but to that state's peculiar experience of sprawl. Much of the growth can be attributed to movement out of the state's service centers to the suburbs. In the case of Maine, a state with a small population distributed over many small communities, those suburbs were mainly areas with populations of 2,500 or below. New Hampshire and Vermont, the country's most rural states, experienced relative changes of 2.5 and 2.3 per cent and witnessed the same phenomenon. Although Rhode Island has a relatively small rural population, the state experienced a relative change of 7.69 per cent, with an increase in the rural population from 13 to 14 per cent. The experience of Maine, Vermont, and New Hampshire is largely an artifact of its population distribution across small towns resulting in its experience of sub-urbanization to register as a growth in rural population.

Examination of those non-metropolitan areas in the United States that continued to grow through the otherwise declines of the 1980s and 1990s reveals some interesting patterns. In the 1980s, two kinds of rural areas sustained growth. The first was that of exurban counties, those adjacent to metropolitan areas, which were strongly connected by commuting. The second was non-metropolitan counties that were retirement destinations, which attracted populations of elderly people with discretionary incomes. As Frey (1995) notes, both type of areas were populated by people who could enjoy the benefits and amenities of rural life without being dependent on their economies for employment.

The reasons for current non-metropolitan rural population growth are complex and varied. Nowhere can this be better seen than in the New West. Non-metropolitan areas of the western United States have experienced considerable population fluctuations over the last 30 years, best characterized as boom-bust cycles (Beyers and Nelson 2000). The Mountain West – the area around the Rocky Mountains – has experienced very rapid growth (25.4 per cent) during the 1990s (Hansen et al. 2002). While much of this has occurred in the urban centers of Denver and Salt Lake City, a number of rural counties have experienced similarly strong growth.

Some of this growth is a result of redistribution of people within the region from the High Plains, an area of continued population loss, to the mountains of the West. Some is due to in-migration from other areas of population loss, such as the Midwest, and large metropolitan areas on the East Coast (Hansen et al. 2002). The forces behind this growth appear to lie in a combination of economic and non-economic factors, namely the new economy (high technology and service industries), niche marketing of traditional resource based industries, and a high level of amenities (Beyers and Nelson 2000).

We do not yet have a complete understanding of the role of recreation and natural amenities as a pull factor in migration. However, the land and associated amenities can be considered a factor in attracting and retaining people and businesses, and analysis of economic development needs to recognize the role of natural amenities in population growth (Rasker and Hansen 2000). As such, it brings a new perspective on land as a resource in the West. A resource that was once extracted or used through logging, mining, and agriculture now provides scenic beauty, amenities, and recreation, which attract in-migrants. While this new economic base does not impact the land in the same manner as extractive industries, there is concern that these areas can be degraded by rural growth and sprawl and by high-impact recreational activities.

Forest Loss in the Southeast

Although the South, with 102 million people (in July 2001), is the most populous region in the country, it is the least urbanized – 68.6 per cent in 1990. However, the combined forces of economic and population growth in the New South are already registering effects in land transition, particularly in some metropolitan areas and in Florida.

Four out of the top five sprawling major metropolitan areas are in the Southeast, namely Nashville, Tennessee, Charlotte and Greensboro, North Carolina, and Atlanta, Georgia. With few natural barriers to impede or constrain growth, and with major highways creating natural corridors for development, metropolitan growth in this region typifies Kent's second pattern of metropolitan growth. Indeed, sprawl along Interstates 85 and 20 is creating what has been referred to as a 'string city' that stretches 600 miles between Raleigh-Durham, North Carolina and Birmingham, Alabama (USA Today 2001).

With the decline in returns to agriculture relative to forestry, the South has become the dominant timber-producing region in the country. Indeed, the South is now the largest agricultural-style timber-producing region in the world (*Ibid.*). One of the key findings of the report is that the South is forecast to lose 12 million forest acres (eight per cent) to developed uses between 1992 and 2020. An additional 19 million acres are forecast for development between 2020 and 2040 with most losses concentrated in the eastern South. Figure 5.3 shows the trends in land cover for the nation and 13 southern states over the period 1982 to 1997. Note that, as with the national picture, the only upward trend in land cover is in the urban class. This is particularly important because forest-to-urban conversion is a one-way process: only one in every 21,000 inventory points were converted from urban to non-urban uses between 1982 and 1997, according to the National Resources Inventory (NRI) (U.S. Department of Agriculture, Natural Resource Conservation Service 2001).

Point data from the NRI provide a detailed picture of recent land-use change in the region. Figure 5.4 shows land-use conversion for three five-year periods and reveals that most of the increase in urban land use was concentrated in states along the Atlantic coast. Loss of forestland was mainly concentrated in areas of rapid population growth and urbanization. These coastal states have experienced strong population gains, with North Carolina, Georgia, and Florida registering increases in excess of 20 per cent over the last decade. The map also reveals substantial forest loss in rapidly growing areas around Atlanta, Georgia, Richmond, Virginia, Raleigh-Durham and Charlotte, North Carolina, Nashville, Tennessee, Charleston, South Carolina, and the cities of northern Florida. The pattern in Florida is particularly spectacular. While the state is significantly more urban than most

Southern states (85 per cent in 1990), a number of cities continue to experience substantial population growth. Growth has tapered off since the dramatic rates seen in the eighties, but northern Florida areas such as Melbourne, Ocala, and Orlando registered growth between 20 and 35 per cent in the last decade. Further, according to population projections for 2000 to 2020, seven of the 20 fastest growing counties will be in Florida (Woods and Poole 1997).

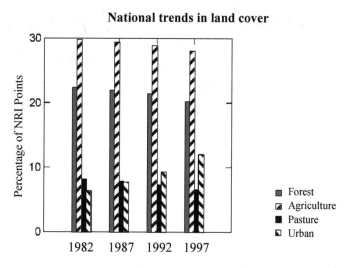

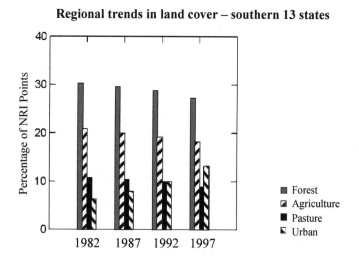

Figure 5.3 National and regional trends in land cover

Source: U.S. Department of Agriculture, Natural Resource Conservation Service (2001).

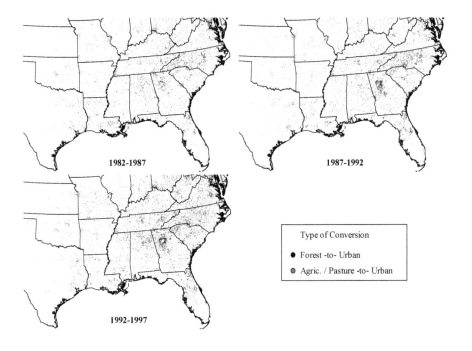

Figure 5.4 Urbanization in the southern United States

Land-Ownership Constraints in the Desert Southwest

As noted above, and in a recent computation of a sprawl index (USA Today 2001), geography is a factor limiting or allowing sprawl. Oceans, mountains and other physical features can force a metropolitan area to grow compactly. Flat land, on the other hand, can permit development of any kind. USA Today (2001) cites the example of Los Angeles as a once sprawling city whose growth is constrained by the ocean and mountains encircling it, forcing the city to turn inwards to grow.

An underappreciated constraint on the pattern of spatial development of metropolitan areas is the prevailing land ownership. In the West, large swaths of land are in federal ownership and, thus, are not available for development. In Figure 5.5 we present a blow-up of the rural land conversion in Nevada with federal ownership and the highway system superimposed. As stated earlier, Nevada has been the fastest growing state in the nation for the last 15 years. A desert state, whose economy is based largely on tourism, recreation and government employment, it has become a destination for retirees and migrants seeking jobs, the climate, and the lifestyle. Its population has grown from 800,000 in 1970 to two million today. The extraordinary population growth rates of 50 and 66 per cent in the last two decades have occurred mainly in cities. By 1990, 88 per cent of Nevada was urban, as people poured into cities such as Las Vegas and Reno, as well as smaller cities such as Henderson City, the fastest growing city in the country with a growth rate of 169 per cent in the last decade.

As Figure 5.5 shows, the vast majority of land is federally owned, and consists of a mixture of national forests, defense ranges, wildlife ranges, and Indian Reservations. A notable exception is a tract of land along the Humbolt River, which was given over to ranching early in the state's history and through which now winds Interstate 80. The map shows how urban development is concentrated into pockets of non-federal land, most notably the Reno and Carson City cluster in the northwest, along the border with California, and the Las Vegas, Henderson and Bolder City cluster to the southwest, along the border with Arizona. Both clusters depend on, but are additionally constrained by, large water borders, i.e. Lake Tahoe and Lake Mead.

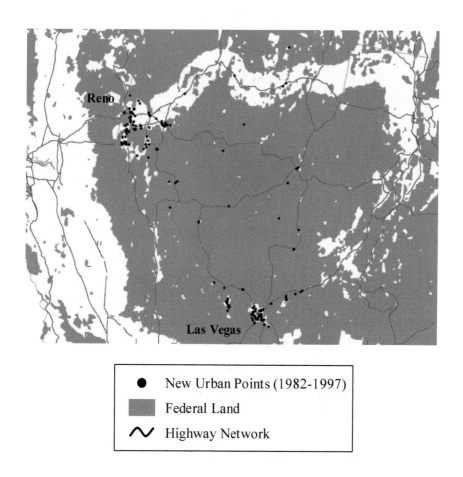

●	New Urban Points (1982-1997)
▮	Federal Land
∿	Highway Network

Figure 5.5 Urban development in Nevada, 1982–1997

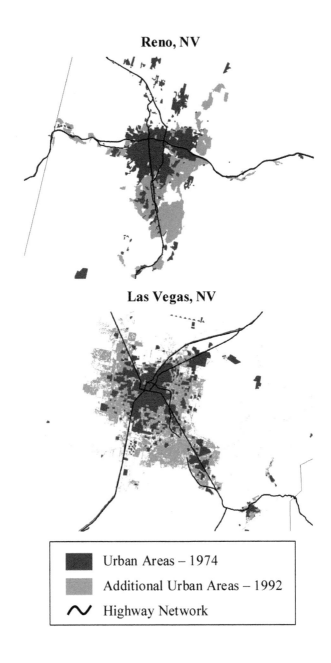

Figure 5.6 Urban expansion in Nevada, 1974–1992

A more detailed look at how urban development has followed highways is afforded by Figure 5.6, which shows how the city of Reno has developed over the last 25 years. While the nucleus of the city was formed around the intersection of a number of highways, new urban development has followed the fingers of highways radiating out from the center.

The prevalence of federal land ownership around Las Vegas, in southern Nevada, and concomitant development pressure in the relatively pristine Lake Tahoe Basin in western Nevada, prompted Congress to pass the Santini-Burton Act in 1980. The act authorized the U.S. Forest Service to sell surplus federal land in the Las Vegas area and to earmark the proceeds for purchase of environmentally sensitive lands in the Lake Tahoe Basin (U.S. Department of Agriculture, Natural Resource Conservation Service 2001). The act helped to alleviate a mosaic pattern of public-private ownership that was crippling the systematic development of Las Vegas and Henderson City.

Some of the same problems are becoming evident in the eastward expansion of the greater Los Angeles Metropolitan area into the Mojave Desert (Hunter 2001). Portions of the desert landscape have already been negatively impacted by population growth and related development patterns. In the area examined by Hunter, the population of the incorporated cities grew by over 350 per cent, increasing from 70,000 in 1970 to over 300,000 in 1990. If the current trend continues, population is projected to increase by nearly 900,000 people during the period 1990–2020, representing a 200 per cent increase (*Ibid.*). The expansion of urbanization, which has already swept out along Highway 15 to reach Victorville, is projected to expand significantly towards Barstow which itself will become a major center of urbanization (*Ibid.*). While federal land, mainly defense bases, offer some buffer to further land use, only high density development offers some measure of protection against further land-use change and habitat loss in the Mojave region.

Coastal Development

The high rates of population growth in the southern coastal states typify a major demographic pattern in the United States, namely the increase in population residing in coastal counties. Growth rates in coastal areas of the U.S. are triple the national average (Clark 1996). In 1998, population density in coastal areas was, at 341 people per square mile, more than four times the national average. This concentration is expected to increase such that nearly 75 per cent of all Americans will live in coastal areas by 2025 (Hinrichsen 1998).

Recent work by Bartlett et al. (2001), which examined the relationship between demographic patterns and a range of environmental variables, revealed a particular continental form of settlement that was characterized by population growth and building construction that was differentially located away from settlement. As such, this pattern contrasts with the traditional patterns discussed above, where urban expansion encroaches onto prime farmland (or forestland).

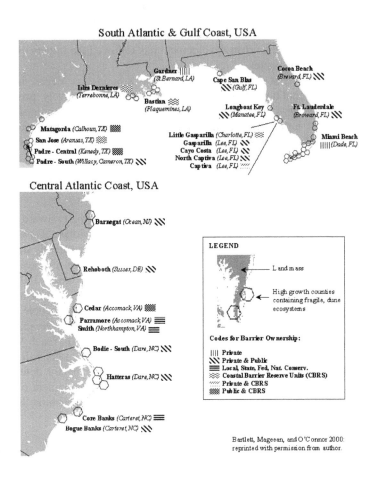

Figure 5.7 Coastal barriers with high rural population growth

This form of settlement was particularly concentrated into areas with fragile dune systems, particularly along the coasts and barrier islands of the Carolinas and points south and round into the Gulf of Mexico. Figure 5.7 shows the location of these large (greater than two km^2) coastal dune ecosystems. With few exceptions, each county associated with these coastal ecosystems had disproportionately higher population densities along their coastal margins. Accompanying these areas of high population growth were larger counts of building permits (single-unit, multi-unit and hotels alike) than elsewhere. However, areas under federal, state, or non-governmental organization ownership were not consistent with this pattern. Other forms of protection, such as the Coastal Barrier Reserve System (CBRS), can also discourage development. CBRS classification prohibits federal subsidies for infrastructure development and flood insurance (U.S. Department of the Interior 1987). The shortage of coastal and barrier land has created considerable pressure for reclassification of CBRS lands to allow other forms of development. These proposals have major implications for conservation, since these lands make up 29 per cent (183,700 hectares) of all Atlantic and Gulf Coast barrier beach acreage (Mageean 2001).

Road Development as a Driver of Rural Land Conversion

We made reference above to the conversion of rural forestland to urban use, but did not consider whether the spatial configuration of the forest was at all associated with such development. In the East, approximately 35 per cent of forestland is in patches of contiguous forest greater than 17 acres in size, while 8.5 per cent of forestland is in contiguous patches of greater than 163 acres in size, and less than 0.5 per cent of forestland is in contiguous patches greater than 1,458 acres in size (Bartlett, unpublished). The remaining forests comprise a variety of types of what may loosely be termed fragmentation. At one extreme, such fragmentation consists of patterns of perforation in which small pockets of non-forestland punctuate otherwise continuous forest, in much the same way as islands of non-federal lands perforate the federal lands of central Nevada in Figure 5.5. At the opposite extreme is the inverse pattern of small islands of forest persisting in a matrix of otherwise non-forested lands, either in isolation or as islands joined by wooded corridors, and in between are various forms of edges where forest abuts non-forestland.

Analysis of the relative size of forest patches prior to urbanization between 1992 and 1997 in the East, using National Resource Inventory (NRI) data and a forest fragmentation map (Riitters et al. 2000), shows nine categories of forest fragmentation in Figure 5.8 (ranked from intact forest on the left to residual mosaics on the right). NRI points not experiencing a land-use conversion were disproportionately concentrated in patchy forests (Figure 5.8a), while points that were converted to roads between 1992–1997 were relatively rare (n=1,340) and distributed relatively evenly across the nine fragmentation categories (Figure 5.8b). Forested NRI points experiencing a small urban conversion (Figure 5.8c) were most common in patchy forest fragments, and those points experiencing a large urban conversion (greater than ten acres of development, Figure 5.8d) were the most common urbanization type on the landscape (n= 7,599), occurring mostly in fragmented forests.

The first conclusion to reach is that rural land conversion is not independent of the spatial configuration of the forest (a uniform distribution of the bars in Figure 5.8 would have resulted were this the case). The second conclusion is that road construction and small and large urban build-up are more common in fragmented forests than in intact forests (Figure 5.8). The third conclusion is that road development is more likely to occur in intact forests than in small and large urban build-up (Figure 5.9a, b), and small urban build-up is more likely to occur in forest interior areas than in large urban build-up (Figure 5.9c). This has a significant message for forest planning: that intact forests are less prone to rural land conversion than are mosaic arrangements of forestlands. It is also significant with respect to urban development along highways through desert landscapes (Figure 5.6) and to the hop-scotch urban growth patterns for large metropolitan areas, such as Atlanta, that expanded along major highway corridors (Kent et al. 2001).

Roads have historically tended to follow the easier paths, along river valleys and along the contours of mountains rather than directly over them, for example, so one explanation of these urbanization-highway associations is that of use of the most accessible land. The results in Figure 5.8 and 5.9, however, suggest, at least to the extent that intact forests are not confined to difficult terrain, that dispersion of forest stands across the landscape predisposes that landscape to an initial road development that is subsequently the seed for later urbanization. This piecemeal development is in contrast to the planned growth of new cities in Europe where zoning laws impose Green Belts and other controlled zones around existing urban

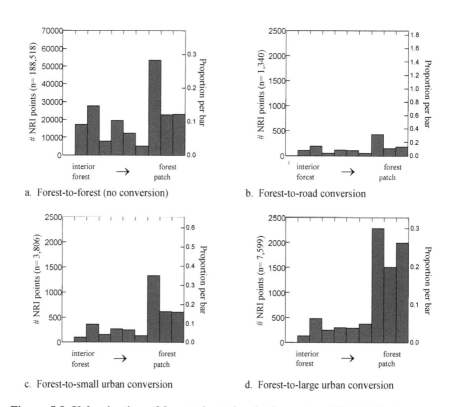

a. Forest-to-forest (no conversion)   b. Forest-to-road conversion

c. Forest-to-small urban conversion   d. Forest-to-large urban conversion

Figure 5.8 Urbanization of forested patches in the eastern United States (66 hectare scale)

centers, restricting further urbanization to in-filling of existing urban areas and the occasional planned construction of entirely new cities.

Further evidence as to the significance of roads in shaping small-scale development comes from a study by Mageean et al. (2001) of the scaling of population processes. They built a statistical model of population density across the conterminous United States, in terms of climate and continental land cover variables, and showed several continent-wide and regional factors correlated with density. However, when they considered the residuals about the models, they found the higher residuals to be clumped around highways and towns, i.e. it was the social (including travel) infrastructure provided by roads and towns that promoted densities above those predicted by the biophysical model.

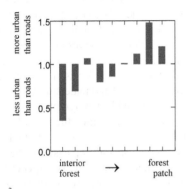

a. Roads vs. small urban build-up

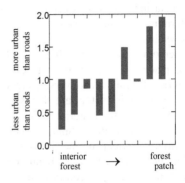

b. Roads vs. large urban build-up

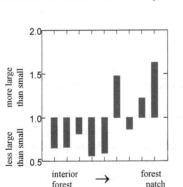

c. Small urban vs. large urban

Figure 5.9 Conversion-type ratios across forest fragmentation classes (66 hectare scale)

Discussion

Urbanization and rural land conversion are at times assumed to be a single or unitary phenomenon, typically reflecting the outwards expansion of existing centers. Bartlett et al's. (2000) analysis of U.S. Census data shows that demographic patterns in the contiguous 48 United States are more consistently interpreted as reflecting two independent patterns of urban development. The first, which they termed alpha settlement, reflects the conventional urban peripheral expansion. The second, termed beta settlement, describes a pattern of green field development in areas far from urban centers. Bartlett et al. show that such settlement was particularly high in Atlantic coastal areas (e.g., barrier islands and seashores) from the Carolinas to Florida, along the Gulf of Mexico from Florida to Texas, and in desert areas in the Southwest. The beta index thus captures two of the major thrusts of urbanization described here. Nevertheless, a later version of the beta index in which economic data were used instead of demographic data (to determine the role of sectoral economic activities in urban and rural development) shows that the spread of urbanization across the United States is the result not merely of demographic changes, but also of the economic milieu in which those changes take place. Hence an understanding of the underlying economies is necessary if patterns of rural land conversion are to be correctly interpreted and understood.

Economic factors are themselves often correlated with demographic forces. It is clear from the material reviewed here that migration is changing the face of the metropolitan United States. While international migration has had major quantitative effects on the size of the U.S. population, its spatial impacts have been relatively limited to a small number of states and metropolitan areas, especially ports of entry. In contrast, internal migration has been the major driver of populating growth in the West and in the Southeast, typically attracted by the combination of favorable climate and economic opportunity. Our earlier work (Mageean et al. 2001a, 2001b), in particular, shows that while climate accounts for regional redistribution of population, the details of local population concentration are contingent on local factors. However, the surrogate local predictors considered – towns and roads – reflect a social and economic organizational influence most likely based in associated economics, be they related to size of markets or access thereto.

A related issue emerging in several of the topics discussed above is the effect of topographic and ownership constraints in shaping development. Development along highways is readily understood in terms of access, while the proliferation of subdivision along lakeshores and ecological edges likely reflects the value of natural amenities. In addition to shaping the spread of subdivisions illustrated in detail here for Nevada, federal ownership also serves to limit development along the barrier islands and beaches identified as vulnerable to subdivision by Bartlett et al. (2000).

The final broad issue to emerge here was the role of landscape (especially forest) configuration in promoting or hindering subdivision. Housing encroachment is the major cause of loss of agricultural land in the U.S. and the finding here that the extent of road distribution and of subdivision are a function of the pattern of fragmentation has important policy implications. In particular, the results suggest that land maintained as intact forest is more resistant to encroachment than is forestland already fragmented. The clear message is that land-use change in forested areas is best consolidated into a few large patches and not allowed to spread piecemeal across the landscape. The economics for and against in-holdings, road development, and so on therefore need to be assessed against a landscape of fragmentation, and forecasts of future land value need to be based on an understanding of such changes by those charged with its long-term management.

References

Bartlett, J. Unpublished data. Department of Wildlife Ecology, University of Maine.

Bartlett, J., D. Mageean, and R.J. O'Connor. 2000. 'Residential Expansion as a Continental Threat to U.S. Coastal Ecosystems.' *Population and Environment* 21(5): 429–468.

Beyers, W.B. and P.B. Nelson. 2000. 'Contemporary Development Forces in the Nonmetropolitan West: New Insights from Rapidly Growing Communities.' *Journal of Rural Studies* 16: 459–474.

Chiswick, B.R. and T. Sullivan. 1995. 'The New Immigrants,' in *State of the Union: America in the 1990s, Vol. 2: Social Trends*, ed. R. Farley. New York, New York: Russell Sage Foundation.

Clark, J. 1996. *Coastal Zone Management Handbook*. New York, New York: Lewis Publishers.

Cordell, K. and C. Overdevest. 2001. *Footprints on the Land: An Assessment of Demographic Trends and Future of National Resources in the United States.* Champaigne, Illinois: Sagamore Publishing.

Farley, R. 1996. *The New Reality: Who We Are, How We Got Here, Where We Are Going.* New York, New York: Russell Sage Foundation.

Frey, W.H. 1995. 'The New Geography of Population Shifts,' in *State of the Union: America in the 1990s, Vol. 2: Social Trends*, ed., R. Farley. New York, New York: Russell Sage Foundation.

Garreau, J. 1991. 'Edge City: Life on the New Frontier.' *American Demographics* 139: 24–31.

Garreau, J. 1994. 'Edge Cities in Profile.' *American Demographics*, 162: 24–33.

Hansen, A.J., R. Rasker, B. Maxwell, J.J. Rotella, J.D. Johnson, A.W. Parmenter, U. Langner, W.B. Cohen, R.L. Lawrence, M.P.V. Kraska. 2002. 'Ecological Causes and Consequences of Demographic Change in the New West.' *BioScience* 52(2): 151–168.

Hinrichsen, D. 1998. *Coastal Waters of the World: Trends, Threats, and Strategies.* Washington, District of Columbia: Island Press.

Hunter, L. 2001. 'Land Use Futures for the California Mojave Desert: Integrating Social, Economic and Biophysical Dimensions.' Paper delivered to the 2001 Annual Meeting of the Population Association of America, Washington, District of Columbia.

Kent, M.M., K.M. Pollard, J. Haaga, and M. Mather. 2001. 'First Glimpses From the 2000 U.S. Census.' *Population Bulletin* 562(2). Washington, District of Columbia: Population Reference Bureau.

Littman, M.S. 1998. *A Statistical Portrait of the United States: Social Conditions & Trends*. Lanham, Maryland: Bernan Press.

Mageean, D.M. 2001. 'Human Dimensions of Coastal Management.' White Paper Prepared for the United States National Oceanographic and Atmospheric Administration Sciences Division.

Mageean, D.M., J.G. Bartlett, and R.J. O'Connor. 2001. 'Environmental and Legacy Constraints to Population Growth in the Desert South-West.' Paper presented at the Population Association of America Annual Conference, Washington, District of Columbia.

Mageean, D.M., J.G. Bartlett, and R.J. O'Connor. 2001. 'Scale Identification in Spatially Explicit Population-Environment Modeling.' Proceedings of the 2001 Open Meeting of the Human Dimensions of Global Environmental Change Research Community, Rio de Janeiro, Brazil. Available at http://sedac.ciesin.org/openmeeting/

Martin, P. and E. Midgley. 1999. 'Immigration to the United States.' *Population Bulletin* 54(2): 3–40. Washington, District of Columbia: Population Reference Bureau.

Murdock, S.H. 1995. *An America Challenged: Population Change and the Future of the United States*. Boulder, Colorado: Westview Press.

Nusser, S.M. and J.J. Goebel. 1997. 'The National Resources Inventory: A Long-Term Multi-Resource Monitoring Programme.' *Environmental and Ecological Statistics* 43: 181–204.

Rasker, R. and A. Hansen. 2000. 'Natural Amenities and Population Growth in the Greater Yellowstone Region.' *Human Ecology Review* 72(2): 30–40.

Riitters, K.H., J.D. Wickham, J.E. Vogelmann, and K.B. Jone. 2000. 'National Land-Cover Pattern Data.' *Ecology* 812: 604.

U.S. Department of Agriculture, Economic Research Service. 2002. 'Rural America.' Retrieved from: http://www.ers.usda.gov/.

U.S. Department of Agriculture, Forest Service. 'The Southern Forest Resource Assessment Report Draft Summary Report.' Retrieved from: http://www.srs.fs.fed.us/sustain.

U.S. Department of Agriculture, Natural Resource and Conservation Service. 2000a. '1997 National Resources Inventory: Highlights.' Retrieved from: http://www.nrcs.usda.gov/technical/land/pubs/97highlights.html.

U.S. Department of Agriculture, Natural Resource and Conservation Service. 2000b. '1997 National Resources Inventory Summary Report.' Retrieved from http://www.nrcs.usda.gov/technical/NRI/1997/summary_report/index.html.

U.S. Department of Agriculture, Natural Resources Conservation Service. 2001. *The National Resources Inventory, 1982–1997*.

U.S. Department of Commerce, Bureau of the Census. 1995. 'Urban and Rural Population: 1900 to 1990.' Retrieved from: http://www.census.gov/population/censusdata/urpop0090.txt.

U.S. Department of Commerce, Bureau of the Census. 1999. *1990 Census of Population and Housing, Population and Housing Unit Counts; State Population Estimates: Annual Time Series*.

U.S. Department of Commerce, Bureau of the Census. 2000a. '1990 Census of Population and Housing, Supplementary Reports, Metropolitan Areas as Defined by the Office of Management and Budget, June 30, 1993.

U.S. Department of Commerce, Bureau of the Census. 2000b. *1990 Census of Population and Housing, Population and Housing Unit Counts; Population Estimates for Cities with Populations of 10,000 and Greater*.

U.S. Department of Commerce, Bureau of the Census. 2001. *Statistical Abstract of the United States*. Washington, District of Columbia: Government Printing Office.

U.S. Department of the Interior. 1987. 'Coastal Barrier Resources System: Executive Summary.' Draft Report Prepared for Congress. Washington, District of Columbia: Coastal Barrier Study Group.

USA Today. 2001. 'The U.S.A. Sprawl Index.' *USA Today*, February 22, 2001.

Waggoner, P.E., J.H. Augubel, and I.K. Wernick. 1996. 'Lightening the Tread of Population on the Land: American Examples.' *Population and Development Review* 223: 531–545.

Wear, D. 2002. 'Socio-1: Land Use,' in *Southern Forest Resource Assessment – Technical Report*, eds. D. Wear and J.G. Greis. US Department of Agriculture, Forest Service General Technical Report SRS-53. Asheville, North Carolina: Southern Research Station.

Wear, D. and J.G. Greis. 2002. *Southern Forest Resource Assessment – Summary Report*. US Department of Agriculture, Forest Service General Technical Report SRS-054. Asheville, North Carolina: Southern Research Station.

Woods and Poole Economics Incorporated. 1997. *Socio-Economic Forecast Data*.

PART II
DETERMINANTS OF
LAND-USE CHANGE

Chapter 6

Theoretical Background

Kathleen Segerson, Andrew J. Plantinga, and Elena G. Irwin

Introduction

At the heart of most discussions or debates about land use are two basic
questions: (1) how are land-use decisions made, and (2) how should land be
used? The first question concerns the study of the factors that determine the
choice among alternative uses and how changes in those factors are likely to
affect land-use decisions. This lies within the realm of what economists
generally term 'positive' analysis. The second question involves 'normative'
analysis, or a comparison and judgment regarding alternative decisions or
outcomes. It requires the designation of some criteria for determining which
land-use decisions or patterns are somehow more desirable. From an economic
perspective, the criterion that is most often used is economic efficiency. Under
this criterion, the second question asks what configuration of land uses ensures
that land is used in a way that maximizes the aggregate social net benefits that
are reaped from the land resource.

In the absence of market failures, private land-use decisions are expected to
be socially efficient, i.e., to maximize the net social return from use of the land.
However, in reality many land-use decisions involve market failure. In
particular, they can generate external costs or benefits, i.e., costs or benefits that
are not borne by the private parties making the land-use decisions. For example,
use of land for agricultural production can generate external costs from the use of
fertilizers and pesticides (e.g. causing water pollution) or from the odors
associated with certain production activities (e.g., hog farms). On the other
hand, agricultural use of land also generates open space amenity benefits for
surrounding communities. In such cases, the private net return from a given land
use differs from the social net return, and private land allocation decisions will
not necessarily be socially efficient.

There is an extensive body of theoretical and empirical literature on both
the positive and normative aspects of land-use decisions. Our intention in this
chapter is not to provide a comprehensive review of that literature. For this, we
refer the reader to a bibliography compiled by Plantinga (1999). Rather, our
purpose is to provide an overview of the economic analysis of land-use
decisions. Using a very simple model of the private land allocation decision, we
illustrate some basic principles that underlie nearly all economic models of land

use (both positive and normative).[1] We then use the basic principles embodied in this simple model to discuss more complex scenarios in which optimal private allocation decisions are affected by a number of factors. In particular, we consider (1) the role of land characteristics such as land quality, (2) intertemporal or dynamic influences stemming from the existence of stock effects or changes in returns over time, (3) the impact of uncertainty about returns stemming, for example, from uncertainty about future demand for certain goods or services, and (4) the importance of the location of land, such as its proximity to markets or cities or to other related land uses. Each of these extensions introduces an additional consideration in the optimal private allocation decisions (which often complicates the theoretical modeling), but the qualitative nature of that decision remains unchanged. We emphasize this common underlying structure throughout the chapter. This common structure, as will be explained at the end of the chapter, serves as the conceptual basis of economic analyses of land-use change, and policies that preclude or stimulate such changes.

We also emphasize the applicability of this common structure to a wide range of land-use contexts. It applies to any land allocation context, whether it be an allocation between agricultural and non-agricultural land (e.g., forestland), developed and undeveloped land, residential and urban or agricultural land, cropland and pastureland, or even land in corn and land in soybeans. In addition, this basic model applies equally to land-use decisions in production (e.g., allocating land as an input to multiple agricultural outputs) and consumption (e.g., allocating land to residential uses based on preferences). In all of these cases, the underlying principles are the same. To highlight this, we illustrate the basic principles using a variety of contexts that offer specific examples of decisions regarding different types of land uses in both production and consumption cases.

Lastly, this structure is extended to consider socially optimal land allocation decisions. In particular, we consider how externalities result in disparities between private and social returns from land and how such disparities, in turn, distinguish optimal private land allocation decisions from socially optimal land allocation decisions. This extension provides the foundation for out discussion of public policy instruments such as taxes, subsidies, zoning regulations, and conservation easements. The modeling structure is further adapted to highlight the potential of these public policy instruments to align private and social returns.

The chapter is organized as follows. We begin with an overview of the positive analysis of land-use decisions. As noted above, we first present the simplest model of a private land allocation decision and then extend the model to incorporate additional considerations. We then turn to the normative issues that arise from land-use externalities. Again drawing on the simplest land allocation model, we briefly review the nature of the resulting inefficiency. We then discuss policies that can be used to correct the associated allocation distortions.

Private Land-Use Decisions

The Simplest Land Allocation Problem

We consider here the simplest form of the land allocation decision in which a landowner has a fixed amount of land, A, to allocate between two alternative uses. Let a_i denote the amount of land allocated to use i, where $i=1,2$ and $a_1+a_2=A$. As noted above, the specific uses of interest will vary with the application. For example, $i=1$ could denote agricultural land and $i=2$ non-agricultural land (e.g., forestry), or $i=1$ could denote undeveloped land and $i=2$ developed land. In a crop choice model (where land is allocated across crops), i indexes crops. The general structure of the basic allocation problem is the same in all cases.[2] Each use generates a private net return, which we denote R_i. These returns will depend upon a number of factors that will vary with the application. For example, in crop choice models, the returns will depend on the output prices of the crops, the prices of non-land inputs used to produce the crops, and the production technologies.[3]

The basic land allocation problem is to maximize the total return from the land, subject to the constraint that the sum of land in the two uses must equal the total amount of land available. This problem can be written as:[4]

(1)   Maximize $R=R_1 + R_2$,
      a_1,a_2

       subject to $a_1+a_2=A$
                      $0 \leq a_1 \leq A$
                      $0 \leq a_2 \leq A$.

We consider first the case where the net returns are linear in the amount of land allocated to the two uses, i.e., $R_i=r_ia_i$, where the return from an additional acre of land in use i, r_i, does not depend on a_i. This assumption is generally appropriate at the level of the individual landowner who uses the land to produce a product or service that is sold in a competitive market. For example, for an individual farmer, the return from an acre of land used to produce corn will generally be independent of the number of acres of corn the farmer has. However, maintaining this assumption ignores any economies of scale that might be associated with the existence of fixed costs at the farm level.

With linear returns, the solution to this problem is to set $a_1=A$ and $a_2=0$ if $r_1>r_2$, and set $a_1=0$ and $a_2=A$ otherwise. In other words, all of the land should be put into the use with the higher per acre return. The result is a 'corner solution' in which only one land use is chosen. Note that if $r_1=r_2$, then the landowner should be indifferent between putting the acre into use one or use two.

The extension to multiple alternative uses is straightforward. In this case, $i=1,2,...,n$, where n is the number of possible uses. The optimal allocation rule then becomes the following. Assuming that net returns are linear in acres, a given acre of land should be put into use k if for that acre the following condition holds:[5]

(2) $r_k > r_j$ for all $j \neq k$.

The assumption that returns are linear in acreage generates the corner solution for the problem given in (1). In some contexts, linearity is not a realistic assumption. For example, at a more aggregate level, the returns from putting an additional acre of land into agriculture rather than forestry will generally depend upon the amount of acreage already devoted to the two land uses. Under diminishing returns, the marginal return from any given land use would decrease with an increase in the acreage devoted to that use. In this case, $R_i = R_i(a_i)$, where $R_i' > 0$ and $R_i'' < 0$.

Under diminishing marginal returns, the solution to (1) must satisfy:[6]

(3) $R_1'(a_1) = R_2'(a_2)$.

Thus, in this case, the optimal allocation rule is to allocate the land between the two uses such that, at that allocation, the marginal returns from the two uses are equal. If the marginal return was higher in one use than the other, the total returns could be increased by reallocating some of the land from the low-return to the high-return use. When the two marginal returns are equal, it is not possible to reallocate land to increase the total return. The resulting allocation (a_1^*, a_2^*) is depicted graphically in Figure 6.1.

The basic allocation rule in (3), or the analogous rule for the case of *n* land uses, forms the basis for nearly all economic models of optimal land allocation. However, the simple model that generated these rules can be made more realistic by recognizing that, in reality, the marginal returns from a given land use can depend on a number of factors (in addition to simply the amount of acreage devoted to each use). For example, as noted above, marginal returns could also be a function of land quality, time, other variables that might be uncertain at the time of the allocation decision, and/or location. By generalizing the returns functions to incorporate these factors, their role in determining land allocation decisions can be explored in more detail. For ease of exposition, we examine each of these factors separately, although in some contexts it might be important to consider multiple factors simultaneously.[7]

The Role of Land Quality

For many land uses, particularly agricultural uses and forestry, the return from that use depends on the physical characteristics of the land, such as soil type, slope, and water-holding capacity. A number of authors have extended the basic model presented above to include land characteristics (e.g., Lichtenberg 1989; Stavins and Jaffee 1990; Parks and Murray 1994; Wu and Segerson 1995; Plantinga 1996; Hardie and Parks 1997; Miller and Plantinga 1999).

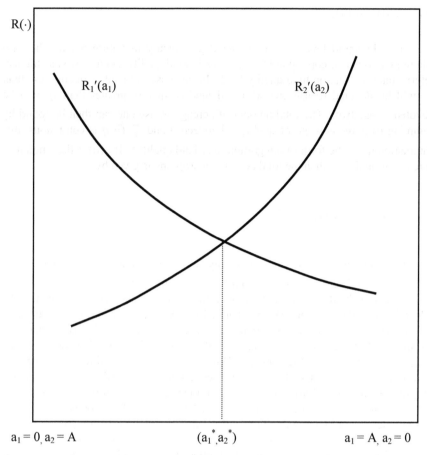

$a_1 = 0, a_2 = A$ (a_1^*, a_2^*) $a_1 = A, a_2 = 0$

Figure 6.1 Optimal allocation of land to uses a_1 and a_2 under diminishing marginal returns

Assume for simplicity that the vector of land characteristics can be summarized by an index of land quality, denoted q, where the index is defined so that $0 \leq q \leq 1$ (e.g., Lichtenberg 1989).[8] If marginal returns are independent of the amount of acreage allocated to each use, then the marginal return functions can simply be written as $r_i(q)$. The decision rule for the linear model (the analogue of (2)) is then to allocate an acre of quality q to land use k if

(4) $r_k(q) > r_j(q)$ for all $j \neq k$.

If q varies continuously between 0 and 1, then in the case of two alternative uses we can define a cut-off or threshold value of q, $\bar{q}$, by:[9]

(5) $r_1(\overline{q}) = r_2(\overline{q})$.

The threshold level of q is depicted graphically in Figure 6.2 for the case where increases in q correspond to increases in land quality and use two has higher returns than use one on high quality land. In this case, all land of quality less than $\overline{q}$ will be devoted to use one while all land of quality greater than $\overline{q}$ will be devoted to use two. The total amount of acreage in use one can then be found by summing over the acreage of quality q between 0 and $\overline{q}$ (if q is continuous, this summation takes the form of integration over land quality). If $\sigma(q)$ is the amount of acreage of quality q, then the total acreage in crop one is given by:

$$a_1 = \int_0^{\overline{q}} \sigma(q)dq = \Sigma(\overline{q}),$$

where $\Sigma(\overline{q})$ is the total acreage of quality less than or equal to $\overline{q}$ (Lichtenberg 1989). The total acreage allocated to use two is then $a_2 = A - a_1$.

The threshold or switching points for specific land uses, and hence the allocation of total acreage, can be changed by exogenous changes in factors that affect the profitability of different land uses on land of differing qualities. Examples of exogenous shifters that can affect land allocations include improved irrigation technology (Lichtenberg 1989), increases in public infrastructure investments (Stavins and Jaffe 1990), reductions in agricultural price support programs (Plantinga 1996), and incentives for carbon sequestration (Plantinga et al. 1999; Stavins 1999). Exogenous changes such as these will shift one or both of the return functions in Figure 6.2, which will in turn change the land-use pattern.

In the above models, the individual land-use decisions are based on a deterministic allocation model, which implies that all land of a given quality is allocated to a single use, a property that carries through to the aggregate shares. For empirical work, this is an overly restrictive formulation since it is commonly observed that land of a given quality is put to more than one use. The allocation of land of a given quality across alternative uses can be explained by introducing uncertainty over returns (e.g., Plantinga 1996). Following the random utility formulation of McFadden (1974), equation (4) is rewritten:

(6) $r_k(q) + \varepsilon_k(q) > r_j(q) + \varepsilon_j(q)$ for all $k \neq j$

where $r_k(q)$ and $\varepsilon_k(q)$ are, respectively, deterministic and random components of returns to use k on quality q land. Whether (6) holds or not depends, of course, on the realization of the random variables, which are unknown to the analyst. However, the condition in (6) can be used to derive the probability that land is allocated to use k, as a function of the deterministic (observable) components of returns to all uses. Under this formulation, land of quality q is allocated across alternative uses (rather than a single use k) according to these probabilities, which provide a theoretical justification for the observed land-use shares.

Another explanation for the allocation of land to alternative uses is the existence of diminishing returns. The discussion of land quality above assumes that returns are linear in acreage, which implies that land of a given quality will be devoted entirely to a single use. While this assumption is reasonable at the individual plot level, at a more aggregate level the total returns functions will not necessarily be linear in acreage. In this case, the optimal allocation rule will take the form of (3), where the marginal return functions, and hence the optimal amount of acreage in each use, are functions of q. Graphically, the positions of the marginal return functions in Figure 6.1 will vary with land quality. The intersection point will determine the optimal allocation for a given q. The total amount of land devoted to use one can then be found by summing over different land qualities:

$$a_1 = \int_0^1 a_1^*(q)dq,$$

where $a_1^*(q)$ is the optimal amount of land of quality q devoted to use one. This model also yields a system of land-use share equations, where the shares depend on the distribution of land quality (see Lichtenberg 1989; Wu and Segerson 1995).

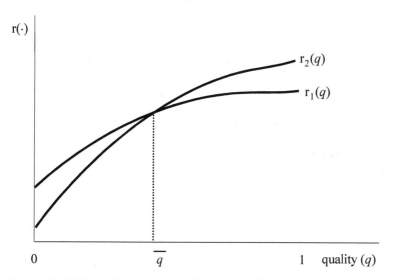

Figure 6.2 Optimal land use with heterogeneous land quality

Land Allocation Over Time

In addition to varying with land quality, net returns from alternative land uses can also vary over time. Temporal variation in returns can stem from exogenous changes in factors that affect returns, such as exogenous changes in input or output prices over time. However, the presence of this type of temporal variation does not necessarily imply the need for intertemporal land-use decisions. If prices vary over time but current land-use decisions do not affect future returns, then those decisions can still be made period-by-period, responding in each period to the prices for that period. The optimal allocation rule would be to allocate a given acre to use k in period t if $r_k(t) > r_j(t)$ for all $j \neq k$, where $r_i(t)$ is the net return to use i ($i = k, j$) in period t.[10]

However, period-by-period decisions are not optimal when land-use decisions affect returns not only in the period in which they are made but also in subsequent periods. The link between present decisions and future returns usually stems from one of two possible sources: (1) the total or partial irreversibility of some land-use decisions, such as the decision to convert land from a natural state to a developed use or to convert it from forest to agriculture,[11] or (2) the presence of stock effects, where current land-use decisions affect the stock of a variable (e.g., soil quality or the stock of a pollutant) that in turn affects future land-use returns. When there is some irreversibility or some stock effect resulting from current land-use decisions, then the optimal land-use decision is based on the solution to a dynamic or intertemporal land allocation problem.

Optimal time of conversion One of the simplest intertemporal land-use models considers the case of the optimal timing of the conversion of a piece of land from one use to another when that conversion is totally irreversible (for example, the subdivision of a large parcel into residential lots that are then developed). The returns from the alternative uses are implicitly assumed to be linear in acreage, so that the conversion occurs all at once rather than over time. This is analogous to the linear models discussed above where decisions can be made on an acre-by-acre basis and each acre (of a given quality) is devoted to only one land use. In this case, there is a single decision to be made, namely, the time of conversion. The potential desirability of eventual conversion is usually assumed to stem from an exogenous increase over time in the returns from the land in the converted use (e.g., the demand for developed land in Capozza and Helsley 1989).

In its simplest form, the irreversible conversion problem with exogenous intertemporal variation in returns takes the following form. Let $r_1(t)$ be the net return from a given acre in use one in period t, where we assume that use one is the pre-conversion use. It is possible, of course, that $r_1(t)$ *equals zero*, as might be the case, for example, when the pre-conversion use is simply idle land. Let $r_2(t, D)$ be the net per-acre return from the post-conversion use, use two, in period t. We allow the returns from the conversion to depend on the period in which the conversion occurs, denoted D, in order to reflect the influence of time-varying conversion costs incurred at time D and amortized over the life of the investment. The optimal time for development, i.e., the optimal intertemporal allocation of the land between the two uses, maximizes the present value of the stream of returns from the land over time. This has two components: (1) the present value of the stream of returns from the land in the pre-conversion use from the initial period to the time of conversion, D, and (2) the present value of the stream of returns when the land is in the converted use from time D onward. Thus, the optimal choice of D solves:

(7) $\text{Max } R(D) = \int_0^D r_1(t)e^{-\delta t}\,dt + \int_D^\infty r_2(t,D)e^{-\delta t}\,dt,$

where δ is the discount rate, the integral sums the returns over time and the term $e^{-\delta t}$ converts the return at time t to its present value. Assuming the second order conditions are met, the value of D that maximizes total returns $R(D)$ is given by the first-order condition:

(8) $r_1(D) - r_2(t,D) + \int_0^\infty \partial r_2(t,D)/\partial D \cdot e^{-\delta(t-D)}\,dt = 0.$

Note that, if the returns from conversion are a function of time but not directly a function of the time of conversion, i.e., if $\partial r_2/\partial D=0$, then this condition simply states that the land should be converted when the net return to the land in the converted use equals the net return in the original use, i.e., at the time D when $r_1(D)=r_2(D)$. This is analogous to equation (3) in the simple static allocation model. Figure 6.3 illustrates the optimal conversion time, D', for this case. The third term in (8) equals the discounted value of future changes in the net returns to use two. This term will be negative if conversion costs are increasing over time. In this case, the optimal conversion time occurs later than D', at D'' in Figure 6.3, in order to defer the higher costs of conversion.

The condition in (8) can be written in a number of different ways that provide different interpretations for the optimal conversion time. For example, it can be written as:

(9) $H'(D)/H(D) = \delta - r_1(D)/H(D),$

where

$H(D) = \int_0^\infty r_2(t,D) \cdot e^{-\delta(t-D)}\,dt$

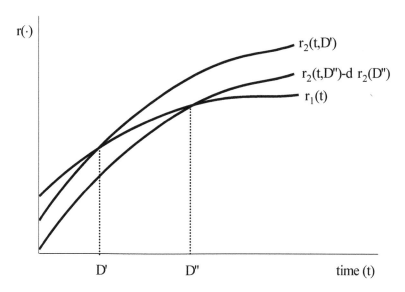

Figure 6.3 The optimal time of land conversion

is the sum of the stream of returns from the converted use, discounted to the time of conversion, or, equivalently, the value of the property in the converted use at the time of conversion.   In this form, the optimal decision rule states that the land should be converted when the rate of increase in the value of the land in the converted use is equal to the discount rate less the opportunity cost of conversion, expressed as a rate (Anderson 1993a).   Alternatively, (9) can be written as

(10) $(H'(D)+r_1(D))/H(D) = \delta,$

which states that the land should be developed at the time when the growth rate in the value of the land, including the value of development and the instantaneous return from use one, equals the discount rate.   In the absence of returns from the current use, (10) gives the standard investment rule that an asset be exploited when its value is rising at the discount rate.[12]   This basic model can be easily extended to incorporate other factors that affect the optimal timing of conversion, such as property taxes (Anderson 1993a) and externalities (Anderson 1993b).

Gradual conversion   The above problem assumes that conversion occurs all at once.   In some cases, complete conversion at one point in time may not be feasible or desirable, and it may instead be necessary or desirable to convert the land from one use to another gradually over time.   For example, Parks (1995) and Parks and

Kramer (1995) consider the optimal conversion of agricultural land to forests and wetlands (a wetlands reserve), respectively, where, in both cases, there is assumed to be a maximum rate at which conversion can occur due to short-run labor and capital constraints. The irreversibility of the conversion makes the optimal conversion problem analogous to the problem of optimal depletion of an exhaustible resource over time (see Conrad and Clark 1987).

Consider, for example, the conversion of agricultural land (use one) to forestry (use two) (Parks 1995). In this case, the optimal conversion rate $(c(t))$ solves:

$$(11) \quad R(c(t)) = \int_0^\infty \{R_1(a_1(t),t) + R_2(a_2(t),t)\} e^{-\delta t} \, dt \, ,$$

subject to
$$\dot{a}_1 = -c(t)$$
$$a_2 = c(t)$$
$$0 \le c(t) \le c_{\max}$$
$$0 \le a_1(t) \le A$$
$$0 \le a_2(t) \le A \, ,$$

where $a_1(0)+a_2(0)=A$, c_{max} is the maximum conversion rate, and a dot over a variable denotes a change over time.[13] The first constraint states that the amount of land in use one (agriculture) is reduced each period by the amount of land converted from use one to use two during that period, $c(t)$. The second constraint states that the amount of land in use two (forestry) is correspondingly increased by the amount of land converted. The third constraint limits the amount of conversion that can occur during any given period. The final two constraints simply state that the amount of land in any given use at any given time cannot exceed the amount of land available.

Because this problem is linear in the conversion rate, $c(t)$, the solution is a 'most rapid approach path (MRAP)' or 'bang-bang' solution, which is analogous to a corner solution in the static models discussed above.[14] In the agriculture versus forestry example considered by Parks (1995), it implies that land should be converted to forest as rapidly as possible (that is, at the rate c_{max}) whenever the net value of an additional acre in forest exceeds the marginal opportunity cost of land in agriculture. That is, whenever

$$(12) \quad \lambda_2(t) > \lambda_1(t),$$

where $\lambda_2(t)$ and $\lambda_1(t)$ are the shadow values of having an additional acre in forest and agricultural land at time t, respectively. This condition is analogous to the static decision rule in (2) for the case where returns are linear in acreage. However, here the shadow value or overall return from putting an additional acre into either land use includes both the instantaneous returns and the 'capital gains' or changes in the value of the land in that use. More specifically, at the optimal allocation,

(13a) $\lambda_1(t) = \partial R_1 / \partial a_1 + \dot{\lambda}_1(t)$

(13b) $\lambda_2(t) = \partial R_2 / \partial a_2 + \dot{\lambda}_2(t)$,

where the first term is the instantaneous return in period t and the second term is the change in the value of the land in that use. Thus, the optimal conversion decision depends not only on annual returns from the alternative land uses but also on how those returns are expected to change over time. Making conversion decisions on a period-by-period basis, i.e., without consideration of future changes in returns, will generally lead to suboptimal conversion rates.

Stock effects   In the above problem, the amount of unconverted land is viewed as a stock that can be 'depleted' over time, and land-use (here, conversion) decisions determine the rate at which it is depleted. Land-use decisions can also affect the stocks of other variables, such as the soil stock (quality or quantity) (e.g., Orazem and Miranowski 1994; Goetz 1997) or the stock of a pollutant in the air or water (Goetz and Zilberman 1999).

   Consider the allocation of land between two uses, both of which affect soil quality or quantity, or, following Orazem and Miranowski (1994), what we will term 'soil capital'. Let $s(t)$ be the stock of soil capital at time t. Changes in soil capital over time depend on the amount of acreage in each land use and the current capital stock, i.e.,

(14) $\dot{s}(t) = f(a_1(t), a_2(t), s(t))$.

In addition, the amount of soil capital is assumed to affect the returns from the alternative land uses. Thus, the return functions become $R_i(a_i(t), s(t), t)$. For example, if the soil quality (or quantity) has been depleted so that quality at a given time is low, then productivity and hence net returns from the land in a given use will be low. Conversely, higher quality will imply higher productivity and hence higher returns.

   When soil capital affects returns, the optimal time paths for $a_1(t)$ and $a_2(t)$ will maximize the present value of the stream of returns from the two land uses over time, given by:[15]

(15) $\displaystyle \text{Max} \int_0^{\infty} \{R_1(a_1(t), s(t), t) + R_2(a_2(t), s(t), t)\} \cdot e^{-\delta t} dt$,

subject to (14) and the constraints that $a_1(t) + a_2(t) = A$ and $0 \le a_i(t) \le A$ for all t. If both net returns and the change in soil capital are linear in acreage, i.e., if the marginal contribution of an additional acre in each land use does not depend on the acreage in that use (as in Goetz 1997), then the above problem is linear in the choice variables, a_1 and a_2, and hence again the solution is a MRAP. In particular, if changes in soil quality or quantity result from erosion, the solution is to put all of the land into use one (e.g., crop one) if the return minus the cost of erosion for use one exceeds that for use two, i.e., if

$$(16) \quad r_1(s(t),t) - \lambda e_1(s(t),t) > r_2(s(t),t) - \lambda e_2(s(t),t),$$

where λ is now the shadow value of an additional unit of soil capital and $e_i(s(t),t)$ is the per-acre reduction in soil capital from erosion when the land is put into use i (and $e_i<0$ if use i enhances soil capital). When the stock of soil capital reaches a level at which (16) holds as an equality, then the land allocation is set to maintain equality of the net marginal returns (the returns net of erosion costs). Again, (16) is analogous to (2) in the basic land allocation model, where here the optimal land allocation depends on both the instantaneous returns and the associated effects on soil capital.

The Effect of Uncertainty

The above discussion of intertemporal land allocation assumes that future returns from the alternative land uses are known with certainty. In reality, future returns are uncertain, due, for example, to uncertainty about future demand for the goods and services produced by the land in alternative uses. The existence of uncertainty can affect the optimal allocation of land in a number of ways.

Risk aversion For example, if future returns from a given land use are uncertain and landowners are risk averse, the rule for optimal land allocation must be modified to reflect the extent of risk aversion. Parks (1995) considers the optimal timing of conversion (from agricultural to forest use in his example) when there is uncertainty about future returns from both uses and landowners are risk averse. More specifically, the return from having $a_i(t)$ acres in land use i in period t is assumed to take the form

$$(17) \quad R_i(a_i(t),t) = \mu_i(a_i(t),t) + a_i(t)\varepsilon_i(t),$$

for some function μ_i, where $\varepsilon_i(t)$ is a random variable with a mean of zero and a variance of σ_i^2. The optimal conversion problem is then essentially the same as (11) except that the landowner is assumed to maximize the present discounted value of the expected utility of total returns, $EU(R_1(a_1(t),t)+R_2(a_2(t),t))$, rather than simply the present discounted value of total returns, where U is a von-Neumann-Morgenstern utility function with U'>0 and U''<0. If the post-conversion use is riskier, the result is that conversion is delayed since the net benefits from conversion are reduced by a 'risk premium' that reflects both the extent of the landowner's risk aversion and the relative riskiness of the two land uses (as well as the covariance of the two risks). If landowners are risk neutral, this risk premium vanishes and the conversion decision is identical to the corresponding decision under certainty with the certain returns replaced by their means.

Learning   However, even with risk neutrality, uncertainty about future returns can affect land allocation decisions if those decisions are (at least partially) irreversible and information about future demand will be (exogenously) revealed between now and the future, i.e., if passive learning is possible. The importance of learning about future demand has been well-recognized in the literature on land preservation versus development (e.g., Arrow and Fisher 1974; Fisher and Hanemann 1987; Hanemann 1989; Albers 1996). In particular, when development is irreversible, the possibility of having better information in the future reduces the desirability of development in the current period by increasing the benefits associated with preservation.[16] Preserving the land in the current period preserves the flexibility to respond to new information when it becomes available. This generates a 'quasi-option value' from preservation, which equals the expected value of the information, conditional on the land being preserved at the current time (Conrad 2000).

The possibility of learning can be incorporated into an intertemporal optimal land allocation model in the following way (see Arrow and Fisher 1974; Fisher and Hanemann 1987; Hanemann 1989). For simplicity, consider a simple two-period version of the optimal land conversion model given in (11), where use one is preservation and use two is development. The linearity of the model implies that, if development is desirable in a given period, all of the land will be developed, i.e., there is a corner solution. If we introduce uncertainty into this model, but do not allow for the possibility of learning, we would simply maximize the present discounted value of the sum of expected returns, subject to the constraints. Let r_{it} be the return from use i in period t. The model is solved recursively. Given the expected second period returns from the two land uses, we first determine the optimal land-use decision (i.e., develop or preserve) in the second period, assuming the land was not developed in the first period. In particular, it is optimal to develop in the second period if and only if

(18) $E(r_{22}) > E(r_{12})$.

The maximum expected return achievable in the second period, given preservation in the first period, is then simply the higher of the two expected second period returns, i.e., $max\{E(r_{22}), E(r_{12})\}$. If the land is developed in the first period, then, given the irreversibility of development, the maximum expected return achievable in the second period is simply the expected return from development, $E(r_{22})$. Given these expected second period returns from the two uses, it is optimal to preserve the land in the first period if the total expected return from preservation over the two periods exceeds the total expected return from development over those two periods, i.e., if

(19) $E(r_{11}) + max\{E(r_{22}), E(r_{12})\} > E(r_{21}) + E(r_{22})$.

Suppose now that information about the future returns to the two uses will become available before the period two land-use decision must be made. In this case, if the land is preserved in the current period, the period two land-use decision can be based on actual rather than expected returns. Thus, the land will be developed in period two if and only if

(20) $r_{22} > r_{12}$.

The expected maximum return in the second period, given preservation in the first period, is then the expected value of the higher of these two returns, i.e., $E(max\{r_{22}, r_{12}\})$. Given this, it is now optimal to preserve in the first period if

(21) $E(r_{11}) + E(max\{r_{22}, r_{12}\}) > E(r_{21}) + E(r_{22})$.

Since $E(max\{r_{22}, r_{12}\}) \geq max\{E(r_{22}), E(r_{12})\}$, the possibility of learning increases the expected return from preservation in the first period (Fisher and Hanemann 1987).[17] Thus, the presence of uncertainty and the possibility that information about future demand will be revealed over time affects the optimal land-use decision, making preservation in the current period more desirable than it would be in the absence of demand uncertainty. More specifically, since preservation maintains the flexibility to respond to new information about future demand for preserved vs. developed land, it is more likely that preserving the land now is optimal.

The above model considers the impact of uncertainty in a simple two-period model. In an infinite-horizon framework, Capozza and Helsley (1990) consider the impact of uncertainty about future land rents (resulting from uncertainty about future household incomes) on the optimal timing of conversion from agricultural to urban use. Again, information about the future returns from alternative land uses is exogenously revealed over time and the landowner must decide whether to take an irreversible action (development) now or wait until better information is available. Under specific assumptions about the nature of the uncertainty, Capozza and Helsley show that the effect of uncertainty is to delay the time of conversion.[18] This conclusion is consistent with the conclusion of the two-period model discussed above.

The Effect of Location

In the above models, the optimal land allocation decisions were independent of the actual location of the land since net returns from different uses did not depend on location. In some cases, location is a key determinant of net returns. The effect of location generally stems either from (1) the existence of transportation costs or (2) the existence of spatial externalities, i.e., external benefits or costs that one land use creates for neighboring land uses. When location matters, it is necessary to modify the simple land allocation model so that the net return from at least one of the land uses (e.g., residential use) depends on the location of the land.

Transportation Costs

Consider first the situation where people or products are transported to a specific location where business is transacted. Examples include residents who reside in suburbs and commute to a central business district (CBD) for work, and products that are produced in one location but shipped to a central market for sale. If transportation costs are significant, then the net return from a given land use decreases with the distance from the center. If the costs of commuting to a central business district are an important component of a household's budget, then a household's net income decreases with increasing distance from the CBD and the rent the household is willing to pay will be lower at a location that is far from the CBD than at a location nearer to the center. This generates the classic 'bid rent gradient' that is a key component of models of urban land use (Alonso, 1964; Muth, 1969) that were inspired by von Thünen's original model of agricultural land use.

The implications of location can be seen from a simple model of the allocation of land between residential use and agricultural use, where it is assumed that households commute to a CBD (Fujita, 1989). Each household is assumed to derive utility from the consumption of a quantity of residential land or housing (h) and other goods (x). The household has a given income (y) to spend on housing, other goods, and transportation. Let transportation costs be denoted by $T(z)$, where z is the distance to the CBD and $T'(z) > 0$. The budget constraint is given by:

$$(22) \quad y - T(z) = x + \phi(z)h,$$

where $\phi(z)$ is the rent paid for residential use of a unit of land (h). The household then chooses its consumption of housing and other goods as well as its location to maximize its utility subject to this budget constraint.

The household's optimal location decision is determined by a trade-off between transportation costs and land expenditures. To see this, consider the maximum rent that the household is willing to pay per unit of land at location z while maintaining some constant utility level, denoted $\Phi(z)$.[19] This defines the household's 'bid rent' function given by:

$$(23) \quad \Phi(z) = \frac{y - T(z) - x^*(z)}{h^*(z)},$$

where $x^*(z)$ and $h^*(z)$ are the optimal consumption levels for x and h, given a location z. By applying the envelope theorem, we can show that the household's willingness to pay decreases with distance, i.e., the bid rent gradient is negative:

(24) $\Phi'(z) = \dfrac{-T'(z)}{h*(z)} < 0.$

The equilibrium location of the household is then determined by the distance, z^*, at which the household's marginal bid-rent is just equal to the marginal cost of land at z^*, i.e. $\Phi'(z^*) = \pi'(z^*)$, where $\pi(z)$ is the market land rent curve. Replacing $\Phi'(z^*)$ with $\pi'(z^*)$ in (24) shows that the household's equilibrium location is characterized by the point at which the marginal transportation costs, $T'(z)$, are just equal to the marginal land cost savings, $-\pi'(z)h^*(z)$. Figure 6.4 illustrates this optimal choice as a function of z.

The shape of the land rent curve is determined by the number of bidders in the residential land market, as well as their preferences and incomes. In the simplest case in which all bidders have identical incomes and preferences and total population is exogenously fixed, households have identical bid rent functions and the land rent curve is equal to the common bid rent function. In the case in which households are differentiated by income and/or preferences, the land rent curve will be determined by the highest bid rent curve at each location. Thus the land rent

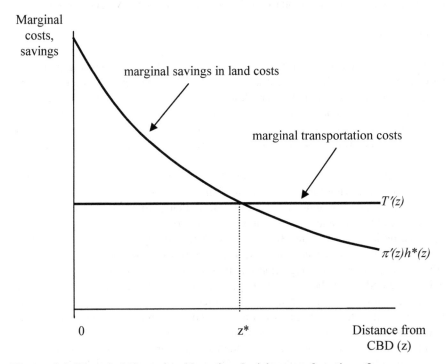

Figure 6.4 Household's optimal location decision as a function of transportation and land costs

curve gives the returns to residential land use at location z. If we view residential land use as land use one, then in terms of our previous notation $r_1(z)=\pi(z)$, where the return to land in residential use depends on its location. The returns to agricultural use of the land (use two) are assumed to be independent of location, i.e., r_2 is not a function of z.[20]

Based on (2), the optimal land allocation rule states that the land at location z should be allocated to residential use if and only if:

(25) $r_1(z) = \pi(z) > r_2$.

The value of z for which (25) holds as an equality defines the urban fringe boundary, $\bar{z}$. The resulting equilibrium land-use pattern is such that all land located at $z \leq \bar{z}$ is in residential use and all land located at $z > \bar{z}$ is in agricultural use. Using comparative statics, the land-use pattern can be further characterized to show that the urban fringe boundary will expand with an increase in either population or household income and will retract with an increase in either agricultural returns or transportation costs (e.g., see Fujita 1989). Given a decrease in marginal transportation costs and an increase in income, the model predicts a flattening of the land rent and population density gradients. This result is often used to explain suburbanization trends in the U.S. and other developed countries.

Spatial Externalities

In the above model, location plays an important role because transportation costs vary with distance from a central location. Alternatively, location may be important because of spatial externalities or spillovers among neighboring land uses. In this case, one landowner's allocation decision is influenced by another landowner's allocation decision, implying an interdependence among neighboring agents that is determined by their location relative to each other. Spatial spillovers can occur across a variety of different land uses. For example, external economies among firms, in the form of informational and technological spillovers, are often cited as the underlying force of city formation (Ogawa and Fujita 1980). Pollution externalities caused by industrial land use located close to residential, commercial, or other industrial land use can lower the returns to development located at neighboring locations (Li and Brown 1980). Alternatively, positive amenities from neighboring open space can increase the returns to residential land use (Irwin 2002). When there are congestion externalities from traffic, transportation costs will be dependent on the level of congestion at any particular location, which in turn is determined by residential location choices (Vickery 1965). Contiguous land in agricultural or forest use can lower average costs of production due to increasing returns to scale, whereas the net returns to agricultural land fragmented by development may be lower due to higher transportation costs and potential congestion effects from development. The value of a preserved land area may increase quickly once a minimum critical size is reached to support wildlife and biodiversity (Albers 1996).

The existence of spatial externalities can affect private land-use decisions and hence the nature of the equilibrium in the land market. To see this, consider a simple model of air pollution in which industrial air pollution negatively affects households who make residential location decisions. Following the basic structure of the location model described above, suppose the polluting industrial plants are located in the city center and that the amount of pollution remaining in the air decays (and hence air quality increases) with distance from the city center (Henderson 1985). This effect is represented by $m(z)$, where $m(z)$ is the air quality at location or distance z, and $m'(z)>0$. Air quality enters positively into the household's utility function, given by $U(x,h,m)$, where $U_x > 0$, $U_h > 0$, and $U_m > 0$.

Solving the household's constrained utility maximization problem for the optimal levels of x and h, which will depend on income (net of transportation costs), $y-T(z)$, land rent, $\Phi(z)$, and air quality, $m(z)$, and substituting the optimal quantities of x^* and h^* back into the utility function yields the indirect utility function: $V^*(y-T(z),\ \Phi(z),\ m(z)) = U\{x^*(y-T(z),\ \Phi(z),\ m(z)),\ h^*(y-T(z),\ \Phi(z),\ m(z))\}$. Totally differentiating the indirect utility function and solving for the bid rent gradient, $d\Phi/dz$, yields the following expression:

$$(26)\quad \frac{d\Phi}{dz} = \left[\frac{dV^*}{d\Phi}\right]^{-1}\left[\frac{dV^*}{d(y-T(z))}\frac{dT}{dz} - \frac{dV^*}{dm}\frac{dm}{dz}\right]$$

Since $dV^*/d\Phi$ is negative, the sign of $d\Phi/dz$ will be opposite the sign of the second bracketed term in (26). Because transportation costs increase with distance, the first part of this term is positive. The second part, $\dfrac{-dV^*}{dm}\dfrac{dm}{dz}$, will be negative since locations that are further from the CBD have higher air quality. If the improvement in air quality from moving outward is sufficiently high, then the externality effect may offset the transportation effect and a positive land rent gradient would result.

This model provides an example of a static externality, in which the activities of one party affect the wellbeing of another party at the time that they occur. However, external effects can be dynamic as well. For example, the spatial allocation of land use in period t, which is influenced by spatial externalities that exist during that period, can generate spatial externalities that influence households' and firms' location decisions in future periods. This leads to endogenous externalities that influence the dynamic path of land-use allocations over time. In the presence of such endogenous externalities, the evolution of land-use change is path-dependent and multiple equilibria are possible, some of which will be more efficient than others. The actual development pattern is determined by the particular sequence – in time and space – of land use conversion.[21]

Socially Optimal Land Allocation

The discussion thus far has focused on the factors that influence land allocation decisions made by private landowners and/or allocations that result from land markets. In the absence of any market failures, these private allocations will coincide with the socially efficient allocation of land, i.e., the allocation that maximizes not only the private but also the social returns from the land. However, as noted above, many land uses generate externalities – benefits or costs associated with a particular land use that are not directly captured or borne by the landowner – that create market failures. For example, agricultural use of the land can cause negative externalities, such as surface water or groundwater contamination from the runoff of fertilizers and pesticides. Agricultural use can also create positive externalities, since it provides open space and other amenity values for the local community. Likewise, land in forestry provides ecological and wildlife benefits that are not reaped by the owner of the land, but timber harvesting can cause negative externalities from erosion. When land uses generate external costs or benefits, private land-use decisions will not generally be socially efficient. In this case, there is a role for public policy to improve societal welfare.

Why Do Externalities Create Inefficiencies?

When externalities exist, private costs and benefits differ from social costs and benefits (the total costs and benefits for society as a whole). Since private land-use decisions are based on private costs and benefits, they do not reflect any external costs and/or benefits associated with the private land use. As a result, in the presence of external costs associated with a given land use, the private allocation of land to that use will exceed the amount that would be socially efficient. Conversely, when a land use generates a positive externality, the private allocation will be less than the amount that would be socially efficient.[22]

The existence of external costs or benefits associated with a particular land use (say, use one) can be easily reflected in a model of the socially optimal allocation of land. Let $R_i(a_i)$ continue to denote the private returns from a_i acres of land in use i. Let $G(a_1)$ denote the external costs or benefits associated with having a_1 acres in use one. If $G'>0$, then use one generates a positive externality (implying that the social return from putting more land into use one exceeds the private return), while $G'<0$ implies a negative externality (i.e., a social return that is less than the private return). For simplicity, we assume that G is linear in acreage, i.e., $G(a_1)=ga_1$, where g is the per-acre external cost or benefit.

While the private land allocation is still given by (1), the objective function for the socially efficient allocation problem becomes:

(27) $R_1(a_1) + ga_1 + R_2(a_2).$

In the presence of the externality, the optimal allocation will satisfy:

(28) $R_1'(a_1) + g = R_2'(a_2)$.

With the externality, the social marginal return differs from the private marginal return, and hence the socially optimal allocation of land is different from the allocation that is privately optimal. This effect is depicted graphically in Figure 6.5 for the case where $g<0$ (a negative externality). In this case, because of the externality, the social marginal return function for use one lies below the private marginal return function. As a result, the socially efficient amount of land in use one (a_1^s) is less than the privately optimal amount (a_1^p).

While we have illustrated the role of externalities in the context of the simplest land allocation model, externalities exist in the more complex contexts as

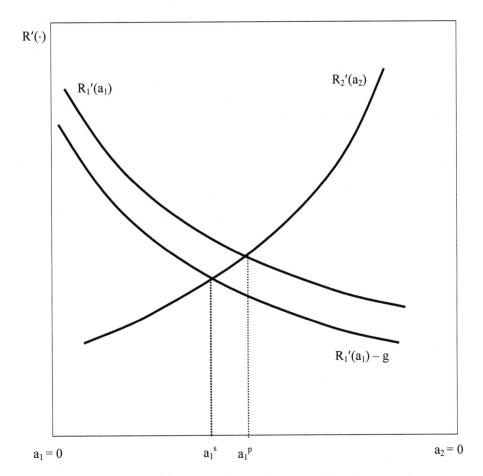

Figure 6.5 Privately and socially optimal allocation of land to uses a_1 and a_2 in the presence of a negative externality

well. For example, the external effect associated with a particular land use can depend on the quality or type of land. The extent to which pesticides or fertilizers from agricultural land use leach into surface or groundwater depends on soil characteristics (such as porosity) and land topology (including steepness). The role of land characteristics can be incorporated into the basic externality model by allowing the external effects to vary with land quality, i.e., by letting $g=g(q)$.

Intertemporal externalities exist when a land use creates a stock (rather than just a flow) of pollution that builds up in a water body over time, e.g. nutrient leaching that leads to surface water eutrophication. Likewise, an intertemporal externality can exist when use of the land requires irrigation for agricultural purposes that mines an exhaustible public groundwater resource. Benefits from forest carbon sequestration are a positive intertemporal externality since carbon dioxide is a stock pollutant. More generally, intertemporal externalities exist when current land uses generate future 'user costs' or benefits that are not reflected in the private returns from that use. In this case, g becomes $g(t)$.[23]

Finally, externalities can also be spatially- or location-dependent. For example, when a factory emits an air pollutant that decays over space or can be dispersed by the wind, then the external effect of that pollution will be different at different locations (air quality will vary with distance from the source, as in the spatial model discussed above). Likewise, runoff from a farm located farther from the water body will create less pollution damage than runoff from a farm near the edge of the water body. When the external effect of a land use depends on its distance from some receptor point, g becomes $g(z)$.

If the simple externality model is extended to incorporate externalities that vary over land characteristics, time or space, the same basic principle continues to apply. In each case, the effect of the externality is to create a difference between private and social costs and benefits, which causes private land allocation decisions to be socially inefficient (e.g., Goetz and Zilberman 1999). Whether private decisions lead to too much or too little land being devoted to a given use will depend on whether that use generates a positive or a negative external effect.

The Role of Public Policy

The economic theory of externalities holds that the divergence between private and social costs and benefits is caused by the lack of appropriately defined (or enforced) property rights (see, for example, Hanley et al. 2001). When property rights are not well-established, the party whose choice generates the external effect has no incentive to internalize that effect, i.e. factor that effect into their private land-use decisions. Policymakers have a number of policy instruments that can be used to influence land-use decisions in an attempt to correct the misallocation resulting from the existence of externalities, including various taxes (e.g., land use taxes, emissions taxes), regulations (e.g., zoning, easements, growth controls), and transferable development rights. Our purpose here is not to provide a comprehensive discussion of land-use policies. Rather, we provide a brief overview of some of the theoretical issues surrounding the design of optimal land use policies. For more extensive discussions of land-use policy, we refer the interested reader to van Kooten (1993).

Tax- or subsidy-based policies   It is well-known that, in the presence of externalities, efficient allocations can be achieved through the imposition of a Pigouvian tax (or subsidy), where the magnitude of the tax is set equal to the marginal external effect at the efficient allocation. In the context of the above model, this would require imposition of a per-unit tax τ on acreage in use one, where the magnitude of the tax is set equal to the dollar value of the external cost or benefit, i.e. $\tau=-g$. When faced with such a tax, private landowners would choose a_1 and a_2 to maximize $R_1(a_1)+R_2(a_2)-\tau a_1$, where the privately optimal land allocation must then satisfy the first-order condition:

(29) $R_1'(a_1) - \tau = R_2'(a_2)$.

This condition yields the same allocation as (28) when $\tau=-g$. Note that if g is negative, the tax rate is positive, while a positive g yields a negative tax, i.e., a subsidy. Thus, under this approach landowners are taxed for land uses that generate negative externalities and are subsidized for land uses that generate positive externalities. If the external effects change over time (due, for example, to changes in the demand for open space or environmental quality), then in the context of above model, g simply becomes $g(t)$ and efficiency requires that $\tau=-g(t)$, implying that the optimal tax or subsidy varies over time as well.

In practice, land-use taxes can be implemented through either property or income tax adjustments. For example, under use value assessment, property taxes are based on the private value of the land in its current use (such as agriculture or forestry) rather than the use with the highest private value (often development). The resulting reduction in the tax rate is effectively a subsidy for keeping the land in its current use, designed to encourage landowners to retain the current use. Similarly, income tax policies can provide credits or limit deductions related to particular uses of land in order to change the private returns and hence encourage or discourage those uses. For instance, U.S. tax policy prohibits the deduction of expenses for wetlands drainage, which effectively taxes the use of the land for any purpose that requires conversion from wetlands. If property and/or income tax incentives are designed to internalize the externalities created by certain land uses, they can achieve efficiency in some cases. For example, if the total subsidy under use value assessment reflects the external benefits from the acreage of land in the desired use (if the subsidy is set at the Pigouvian rate), then use value assessment can ensure efficient private land-use decisions.

The efficiency of land use taxes hinges, however, on a strong and often unrealistic assumption, namely, that the external effects depend only on the number of acres in that use. In many cases, the external effects stem not from the land use *per se*, but from the specific production practices used on that land or other landowner decisions. For example, the amount of water pollution from agriculture depends not only on the number of acres in agriculture (or even in any specific crop, such as corn) but also on the amount of polluting inputs (e.g., fertilizer and pesticide) used on those acres as well as the timing and method of application. Likewise, the external effects from an industrial land use depend on the abatement efforts undertaken by the landowner, which in turn determine emissions from the land. When pollution decays over space (as in the spatial model discussed above), distance or location is also an important factor. In such cases, the external effect will not depend directly on emissions, i.e., releases at the *source* – such as the smokestack or edge of field. Rather, it will depend on what Goetz and Zilberman (1999) term *immissions*, which refers to the pollution level at the *receptor point* (e.g., a nearby residential district or water body). If pollution decays over space, the amount of the pollutant that reaches the receptor point (the immissions level) will be less than the amount released at the source (the emissions level).

When external effects depend on immissions, as in the most general case, then the social objective function becomes:

(30) $R_1(a_1,p) + gp + R_2(a_2)$,

where p is level of immissions of the pollutant of concern.[24] In this case, in order to get an efficient outcome through taxation, the tax must ultimately be applied to immissions. This can be achieved through a tax applied directly to immissions, with total tax payments equal to $\tau \cdot p$, a result that holds even in the presence of intertemporal and spatial variation in returns (Goetz and Zilberman 1999). A uniform or constant per-unit tax on some other variable, such as acres in a particular land use or simply the quantity of a given input, will lead to efficient allocation only if there is a one-to-one correspondence between the taxed variable and immissions. In the absence of such a relationship, uniform land use (or acreage) taxes, input taxes, output taxes, etc., alone will not be efficient.[25]

It is possible, however, to ensure efficiency with a *non-uniform* tax applied to a variable other than immissions. To see this, let immissions be a function of total acreage in use one, location, land quality and the use of a potentially polluting input such as coal or fertilizer (denoted b), i.e., let $p=p(a_1,b,z,q)$. More specifically, let this function take the form $p=\gamma(z) \cdot \phi(a_1,b,q)$, where $\phi(a_1,b,q)$ represents emissions from the land and $\gamma(z)$ is a fate and transport function that determines the fraction of emissions that reach the receptor point. In this case, a spatially uniform tax on immissions, given by $\tau=-g$ would still yield efficiency. However, efficiency could also be achieved by a tax on emissions $(\phi(a_1,b,q))$, rather than immissions, provided the tax varies by location. More specifically, efficient private decisions could be induced by imposing a spatially-differentiated tax on emissions, where the tax rate τ is set equal to $-g\gamma(z)$ (see Hochman et al. 1977; Tietenberg 1995).[26]

Tax-based policies (applied to either immissions or emissions) internalize externalities by changing the marginal incentives (marginal benefits or marginal costs) faced by landowners. They can thus ensure efficiency of decisions that are based on a weighing of marginal costs and benefits. In some cases, however, landowners make non-marginal decisions, based on total rather than marginal returns. For example, the discrete land-use decisions characterized by (2) involve a comparison of returns per acre under two alternative land uses. In such cases, aligning private and social marginal returns (through a Pigouvian tax) is not necessarily sufficient to ensure efficiency. Since private decisions are based on total net returns, efficiency requires that total private net returns equal total social net returns. This, in turn, requires that total tax payments equal total external costs or benefits. In the simple case discussed above where G is linear, total external costs (ga_l or gp) will equal total tax payments (τa_l or τp) if the tax is set equal to marginal external effect ($\tau=-g$). However, when G is nonlinear, this condition no longer holds, and a Pigouvian tax alone can no longer ensure the efficiency of discrete land-use decisions.

Regulatory and other policies While taxes (or subsidies) can restore efficiency when externalities are present by appropriately modifying the marginal incentives of private landowners, in some cases efficiency can also be achieved through regulatory or other policies that control land uses more directly. These include zoning, transferable development rights (TDRs), growth controls, and easements. However, because these policies seek to induce or control particular land uses, but often do not directly control the specific production processes employed by the landowners under those uses (which can affect the magnitude of the external costs or benefits associated with those uses), they are unable to achieve the efficient outcome in all cases. Nonetheless, land-use policies have historically relied heavily on these approaches, and hence we provide a brief overview of these policies here. For more detailed discussion, we refer the reader to Fischel (1985) and Gustanski and Squires (2000).

Zoning places restrictions on the types of uses to which land can be put. These restrictions are site-specific and designed to prevent incompatible uses from occurring in close proximity to one another, which stem from the existence of negative spatial externalities among land uses. Thus, a landowner may be prohibited from building residential housing in an area that is zoned for commercial agriculture. In some cases, zoning can be used to dictate the efficient allocation of land that would be achieved through taxation. For instance, the solution to (28) could be achieved by zoning the appropriate sections of the land base for use two. Similar, though more complex, zoning policies would be needed to regulate externalities that vary with characteristics of the land and time. Because zoning limits the range of possible uses, rather than the externalities generated from the land, it does not provide an incentive for a landowner to modify the production processes employed under that land use. For example, zoning can ensure that industrial land will be located only within industrial zones, but it does not provide incentives for reducing emissions from the industrial land. Thus, zoning will not in general, ensure efficient landowner decisions.

A common criticism of zoning is that it results in an unequal distribution of wealth. For example, a landowner who is prevented from developing a parcel of agricultural land must forego the profits from development, whereas a landowner in an unrestricted area is allowed to reap the rewards from development. TDRs are designed to address this problem. A simple TDR policy would specify two zones, a preservation zone in which the density of land development is restricted and a development zone in which high-density development is allowed. Landowners in the preservation zone are allocated development rights, which landowners in the development zone must purchase in order to undertake land development. This approach facilitates a transfer of the profits from landowners in the development zone to those in the preservation zone.

In the simplest cases, it is clear that TDRs can achieve an efficient allocation of land. However, for more complex cases, land-use decisions under TDRs depend on how the programs are designed and the nature of the externalities involved. General conclusions regarding efficiency are difficult to reach (Carpenter and Heffley 1982). Mills (1980) examines two TDR programs designed to reduce externalities from developed land. In the first case, developed land uniformly reduces the value of land to users throughout the community and, in the second, site-specific public goods provide benefits to the community. A TDR program that controls the overall level of development is shown to restore efficiency in the first instance but not in the second.

Growth controls are policies that restrict or direct the population growth of a jurisdiction in some way, e.g. an urban growth boundary that delineates the area inside which urban development may occur. Growth controls are generally viewed as addressing negative externalities that are associated with the total population of a local jurisdiction. Engle, et al. (1992) use a basic monocentric model to consider several different cases, including congestion effects, in which transportation costs to the central business district depend on the total population within the city. With no growth controls, transportation costs increase when immigration occurs and the urban fringe boundary shifts out due to the population increase. With growth controls, total population does not increase, but rents are bid up due to new immigrants seeking to enter the city. While renters are indifferent between the two scenarios (since they either face increased commuting costs or increased rents), landlords of developed properties benefit from the growth controls and, because the urban fringe boundary does not expand outward with growth controls, landowners of undeveloped properties lose. Overall, because growth controls internalize the externality created by congestion, they can result in an efficient outcome if set at optimal levels. An alternative literature, which is largely empirical, views growth controls as suboptimal because they impose a supply constraint on housing and therefore result in a deadweight loss (for a literature review, see Fischel 1990). Implicit in this view is an assumption that there are no congestion effects or other sorts of negative externalities associated with total population levels.

Easements are a contractual agreement through which a third party (e.g., the government or a private conservation group) acquires a partial interest in a tract of land (Boyd et al. 1999). Easements are most often used to restrict the development of rural land. In this case, the landowner continues to own and manage the land in rural use, but, in exchange for payment, relinquishes the right to develop the parcel in the future. Easements are similar to zoning policies in that they involve restrictions on the uses to which land can be put. As such, easements can be used, in principle, to restore efficiency when externalities are present. Easements also provide compensation to landowners for relinquishing certain rights to their land, which makes them more attractive to landowners and more politically acceptable.

Conclusions

This chapter provides an overview of the economic analysis of land-use decisions. The discussion first seeks to understand decisions by private landowners. A basic premise underlying all economic models of land use is that landowners seek to maximize the net private returns from their land and hence make decisions based on a comparison of the net returns from alternative uses. When decisions can be made on an acre-by-acre basis, i.e., when returns depend only on the land use and not on how many acres are in that use, this implies that for each acre the landowner will choose the use with the highest return. When returns depend on the number of acres in that use, the landowner will allocate land among alternative uses in such a way that the return from putting an additional acre in each use, i.e., the marginal return, is equalized across uses. Only then will the landowner be unable to reallocate land so as to increase the total return.

While the basic principles embodied in these decision rules underlie all economic models of land use, the specification of net returns and the implications for land-use patterns will vary with the specific land-use context. For example, in some contexts returns from a given use will depend crucially on the land's characteristics or quality. In such cases, the optimal allocation decision will be different on lands with differing qualities. Similarly, if returns vary over time and current land-use decisions affect future returns, then net returns must be defined in terms of the present value of the stream of period-by-period returns, with adequate accounting of the impact of current decisions on future returns. In addition, the optimal allocation of land might vary over time. Land uses that are not currently optimal may become optimal at some later point in time, implying that land conversion would occur at that time. Finally, if location is important because of transportation costs or spatial externalities, then the returns to different uses will vary by location. In equilibrium, a comparison of returns will generally generate zones for different uses when location decisions are endogenous.

The land-use decisions that maximize private returns from the land will also maximize social returns if private and social costs and benefits from alternative uses coincide. However, many land uses generate externalities, which cause social and private costs or benefits to differ. In this case, private land-use decisions will not be efficient. In general, private decision making will lead to too much land in uses that generate negative externalities or external costs (in the absence of any other, offsetting market failures) and too little land in uses that generate positive externalities or external benefits. In such cases, there is a role for public policy to increase the social return from the land.

It is well-known that, in the presence of externalities, landowners can be induced to make socially efficient decisions through the use of taxes or subsidies linked to the magnitude of the external cost or benefit. Taxes will discourage certain activities or uses, while subsidies will encourage them. If the external cost or benefit varies with time or land quality, the corresponding tax or subsidy should vary as well.

However, in order to induce efficiency, the tax or subsidy should generally be levied on the factor that directly causes the external effect. If the external cost or benefit results from the extent of the land use *per se*, then the tax or subsidy should be based on the number of acres in that use. For example, the benefits from open space might depend primarily on the number of acres of open space provided. However, if the external costs stem from emissions of a pollutant and the emissions level can be altered without changing the basic land use (for example, the fertilizer runoff from agricultural land can be changed without taking the land out of agriculture or even changing the crop grown), then a tax on the land use will not create efficient incentives for reductions in emissions. In this case, the tax would have to be based on emissions. However, if pollution decays as it moves across the land or through the air, then the external cost depends on the pollution level at the receptor point (immissions) rather than the pollution level at the source (emissions) and the tax should be based on immissions instead. It is sometimes possible, however, to mimic the effect of one tax using another tax. For example, in some cases, the effect of a uniform tax on immissions can be mimicked by a spatially-differentiated emissions tax.

While tax or subsidy policies can be used to encourage efficient land-use decisions when those uses generate external costs or benefits, many actual land-use policies are based on a regulatory approach or restrictions on land use instead. Examples include zoning, tradable development rights, and easements. Although these policies can be effective at altering private land-use decisions, they will not generally yield efficiency if the external effects depend not only on the land use itself but also on the manner in which that use is undertaken (e.g., the specific production processes or the amount of polluting inputs used by the landowner).

The models and land-use principles discussed in this chapter are clearly based on a stylized representation of actual land-use decisions. Yet, they provide an organizing framework for understanding how land-use decisions are and should be made, and the factors that influence those decisions. An improved understanding of both the positive and normative dimensions of land use should contribute to an improved design of public policies aimed at increasing the social return from land resources.

Notes

1   Our approach has its roots in two long-standing theories of land use and location: the Ricardian model, in which rents accrue to land that is of higher quality (e.g. higher

soil fertility) and the von Thünen model, in which proximity to markets determines land use and intensity of use. For an overview of these models, see Randall and Castle (1985).

2 The extensions that are relevant may differ across applications, i.e., some extensions are more important in some contexts than others. For example, intertemporal issues would generally be more important in allocations between developed and undeveloped land (where irreversibility is important) than they would be in allocations between two crops such as corn and soybeans (where decisions are generally reversible), although intertemporal issues could be important in this context as well if crop rotations are used.

3 Since these factors are not important at this point of the discussion, for notational convenience we do not explicitly incorporate them in our notation. Nonetheless, the net returns should be viewed as functions of these variables.

4 This specification implicitly assumes that the land is currently not under any use or that the cost of converting land from one use to another is zero. In some cases, conversion is either not possible (i.e., some land-use decisions are irreversible) or very costly. Irreversibility is discussed below in the section on intertemporal models. For a discussion of the role of conversion costs, see, for example, Usategui (1990) and Stavins and Jaffe (1990).

5 When the returns are random from the researcher's point of view, then the allocation decisions of landowners become probabilistic. See, for example, Plantinga (1996) and the discussion of plot level data models in Chapter 5. A similar theory underlies random utility models of recreational site choice (e.g., Freeman, 1993, Ch. 13).

6 This assumes an interior solution. It is still possible to get a corner solution under diminishing marginal returns if the marginal return from one land use exceeds the marginal return from the other even when all land is devoted to that use.

7 For example, Goetz and Zilberman (1999) and Albers (1996) construct models of land use that simultaneously incorporate spatial and temporal variation. If the structure of the problem is recursive, then the different types of variation can be handled through a two-stage decision problem, where one first optimizes at a given point in time given spatial variation and then, given the optimal static response to spatial variation, optimizes over time.

8 This simplifies the presentation of the theoretical model. In principle, the model can be extended to allow for multiple characteristics that vary across land parcels, following the literature on microparameter distribution models (Hochman and Zilberman 1978). Empirical models of land use that incorporate land characteristics usually include a vector of characteristics in the estimating equations. See, for example, Wu and Segerson (1995) and Hardie and Parks (1997) and the related discussion in Chapter 5. Green, et al. (1996) present an empirical application to irrigation technology choice that uses micro-level data.

9 This assumes that a solution to (5) exists and is unique, which holds under appropriate restrictions on the returns function. See Stavins and Jaffe (1990) for consideration of how this result changes with explicit recognition of conversion costs.

10 Note, however, that this formulation assumes the returns to each use are realized with the same periodicity. If this is not the case, as, for example, with agriculture and forestry, then intertemporal land-use decisions are needed.

11 Partial irreversibility includes both the case where a reversal of the land-use decision can occur only over some time (e.g., the return of land to forestry) and the case where reversal is possible but costly.

12   It is analogous to the standard Faustmann rule for optimal timber harvest (see, for example, Conrad 2000).

13   For simplicity, we ignore the costs of conversion here. Inclusion of conversion costs reduces the net return to conversion. See Parks (1995) and Parks and Kramer (1995) for models with conversion costs.

14   Under a corner solution, if conversion is desirable, it would be desirable (although not feasible) to have conversion occur all at once, as in the previous model. If the problem were not linear in the control variable, then instantaneous conversion of all of the land would not generally be desirable either.

15   This specification assumes an infinite time horizon for the optimization problem. Alternatively, we could optimize over a fixed time horizon (e.g., from t=0 to t=T for some fixed T) and add the salvage value of the land at time T to the objective function. See, for example, Goetz (1997) and Goetz and Zilberman (1999).

16   Usategui (1990) has shown that this conclusion does not necessarily hold when there is uncertainty about the irreversibility of development.

17   This result follows from the convexity of the maximum operator and Jensen's inequality.

18   They assume that future income (and hence future urban land rent) is a Brownian motion process with positive drift.

19   These models assume that the household has a 'reservation' or fixed level of utility that it must always attain. This reservation level is determined by other alternatives available to the household, such as locating in a different city.

20   Goetz and Zilberman (1999) consider a model in which the net returns to both land uses (in their application, both industries) depend on location either directly through the production function or indirectly through location-specific input or output prices (due, e.g., to transportation costs). In their model, the location parameter can represent either distance (z) or soil quality. In the latter case, their model is analogous to the land allocation models that incorporate variation in land quality (e.g., Lichtenberg 1989). See the discussion above.

21   For a conceptual model that illustrates these effects, see Werczberger (1987). For empirical evidence of the presence of such effects and their impact on the pattern of development, see Irwin and Bockstael (2002).

22   This assumes that there are no other distortions in the land market. In the presence of other distortions, the effect of externalities must be analyzed within the theory of the second best.

23   This formulation can also be used to represent intratemporal externalities that affect intertemporal land-use decisions. For example, Anderson (1993b) uses a function of this form to incorporate the effect of the open space benefits from vacant land (which he assumes can vary over time) into a model of the optimal timing of development.

24   Note that the net return to the land use that generates the externality, here use 1, can in general depend not only on the number of acres in that use but also on the level of immissions, since returns can depend on the same production processes that determine immissions. Thus, here R_1 is written as a function of both acreage and immissions.

25   Efficiency may be restored by coupling one of these other taxes with a second policy instrument such as zoning.

26   While we have shown this result in the context of a very simple model specification, it continues to hold in more general models with endogenous entry/exit and endogenous land use zones, provided the transition equation for the spatial change in pollution satisfies certain reasonable assumptions. See Tomasi and Weise (1994).

References

Albers, H.J. 1996. 'Modeling Ecological Constraints on Tropical Forest Management: Spatial Interdependence, Irreversibility, and Uncertainty.' *Journal of Environmental Economics and Management* 30(1): 73–94.

Alonso, W. 1964. *Location and Land Use: Toward a General Theory of Land Rent.* Cambridge, Massachusetts: Harvard University Press.

Anderson, J.E. 1993a. 'Use-Value Property Tax Assessment: Effects on Land Development.' *Land Economics* 69(3): 263–69.

Anderson, J.E. 1993b. 'Land Development, Externalities, and Pigouvian Taxes.' *Journal of Urban Economics* 33: 1–9.

Arrow, K., and A. Fisher. 1974. 'Environmental Preservation, Uncertainty, and Irreversibility.' *Quarterly Journal of Economics* 88: 312–319.

Barbier, E.B., and J.C. Burgess. 1997. 'The Economics of Tropical Forest Land Use Options.' *Land Economics* 73(2): 174–95.

Boyd, J., K. Caballero, and R.D. Simpson. 1999. *The Law and Economics of Habitat Conservation: Lessons from an Analysis of Easement Acquisitions.* Discussion Paper ENR 99–32. Washington, District of Columbia: Resources for the Future.

Capozza, D.R., and R.W. Helsley. 1989. 'The Fundamentals of Land Prices and Urban Growth.' *Journal of Urban Economics* 26(3): 295–306.

Capozza, D.R., and R.W. Helsley. 1990. 'The Stochastic City.' *Journal of Urban Economics* 28: 187–203.

Carpenter, B.E., and D.R. Heffley. 1982. 'Spatial-Equilibrium Analysis of Transferable Development Rights.' *Journal of Urban Economics* 12: 238–61.

Conrad, J.M. 2000. *Resource Economics.* Cambridge: Cambridge University Press.

Conrad, J.M., and C.W. Clark. 1987. *Natural Resource Economics: Notes and Problems.* Cambridge, United Kingdom: Cambridge University Press.

Engle, R., P. Navarro, and R. Carson. 1992. 'On the Theory of Growth Controls.' *Journal of Urban Economics* 32: 269–83.

Fischel, W. 1985. *The Economics of Zoning Laws.* Baltimore, Maryland: The Johns Hopkins University Press.

Fischel, W. 1990. 'Do Growth Controls Matter? A Review of the Empirical Evidence on the Effectiveness and Efficiency of Local Government Land Use Regulation.' Lincoln Land Institute Working Paper (May).

Fisher, A.C., and W.M. Hanemann. 1987. 'Quasi-Option Value: Some Misconceptions Dispelled.' *Journal of Environmental Economics and Management* 14: 183–190.

Freeman, A.M. III. 1993. *The Measurement of Environmental and Resource Values.* Washington, District of Columbia: Resources For the Future.

Fujita, M. 1989. *Urban Economic Theory: Land Use and City Size.* Cambridge, United Kingdom: Cambridge University Press.

Goetz, R.U. 1997. 'Diversification in Agricultural Production: A Dynamic Model of Optimal Cropping to Manage Soil Erosion.' *American Journal of Agricultural Economics* 79 (2): 341–56.

Goetz, R.U., and D. Zilberman. 1999. 'The Economics of Land-Zoning.' Department of Economics working paper, University of Girona.

Green, G., D. Sunding, D. Zilberman, and D. Parker. 1996. 'Explaining Irrigation Technology Choices: A Microparameter Approach.' *American Journal of Agricultural Economics* 78(4): 1064–1072.

Gustanski, J.A., and R.H. Squires. 2000. *Protecting the Land: Conservation Easements: Past, Present, and Future.* Washington, District of Columbia: Island Press.

Hanemann, W.M. 1989. 'Information and the Concept of Option Value.' *Journal of Environmental Economics and Management* 16: 23–37.

Hanley, N., J.F. Shogren, and B. White. 2001. *Introduction to Environmental Economics.* Oxford: Oxford University Press.

Hardie, I.W., and P.J. Parks. 1997. 'Land Use with Heterogeneous Land Quality: An Application of an Area Base Model.' *American Journal of Agricultural Economics* 79(2): 299–310.

Henderson, J.V. 1985. *Economic Theory and the Cities.* New York, New York: Academic Press.

Hochman, E., and D. Zilberman. 1978. 'Examination of Environmental Policies Using Production and Pollution Microparameter Distributions.' *Econometrica* 46(4): 739–60.

Hochman, E., D. Pines, and D. Zilberman. 1977. 'The Effects of Pollution Taxation on the Pattern of Resource Allocation: The Downstream Diffusion Case.' *Quarterly Journal of Economics* 91(4): 625–638.

Irwin, E.G. 2002. 'The Effects of Open Space on Residential Property Values.' *Land Economics*, forthcoming.

Irwin, E.G. and N.E. Bockstael. 2002. 'Interacting Agents, Spatial Externalities, and the Evolution of Residential Land Use Pattern.' *Journal of Economic Geography* 2(1): 31–54.

Li, M. and J.H. Brown. 1980. 'Micro-Neighborhood Externalities and Hedonic Housing Prices.' *Land Economics* 56(2): 125–40.

Lichtenberg, E. 1989. 'Land Quality, Irrigation Development, and Cropping Patterns in the Northern High Plains.' *American Journal of Agricultural Economics.* 71(February): 187–94.

McFadden, D. 1974. 'Conditional Logit Analysis of Qualitative Choice Behavior.' In *Frontiers in Econometrics*, ed., P. Zarambka. New York, New York: Academic Press.

Miller, D.J., and A.J. Plantinga. 1999. 'Modeling Land-use decisions with Aggregate Data.' *American Journal of Agricultural Economics* 81(1): 180–194.

Mills, D.E. 1980. 'Transferable Development Rights Markets.' *Journal of Urban Economics* 7: 63–74.

Muth, R. 1969. *Cities and Housing.* Chicago, Illinois: University of Chicago Press.

Ogawa, H. and M. Fujita. 1980. 'Equilibrium Land Use Patterns in a Nonmonocentric Model.' *Journal of Regional Science* 20: 455–475.

Orazem, P.F., and J.A. Miranowski. 1994. 'A Dynamic Model of Acreage Allocation with General and Crop-Specific Soil Capital.' *American Journal of Agricultural Economics* 76(3): 385–395.

Parks, P.J. 1995. 'Explaining "Irrational" Land Use: Risk Aversion and Marginal Agricultural Land.' *Journal of Environmental Economics and Management* 28: 34–47.

Parks, P.J., and R.A. Kramer. 1995. 'A Policy Simulation of the Wetlands Reserve Program.' *Journal of Environmental Economics and Management* 28: 223–40.

Parks, P. and B. Murray. 1994. 'Land Attributes and Land Allocation: Nonindustrial Forest Use in the Pacific Northwest.' *Forest Science* 40: 558–75.

Plantinga, A.J. 1996. 'The Effect of Agricultural Policies on Land Use and Environmental Quality.' *American Journal of Agricultural Economics* 78(4): 1082–91.

Plantinga, A.J. 1999. *The Economics of Land Use: A Bibliography.* Maine Agricultural and Forest Experiment Station, University of Maine, Miscellaneous Publication 744 (December).

Plantinga, A.J., T. Mauldin, and D.J. Miller. 1999. 'An Econometric Analysis of the Costs of Sequestering Carbon in Forests.' *American Journal of Agricultural Economics* 81(4): 812–24.

Randall, A., and E. Castle. 1995. 'Land Resources and Land Markets,' In *Handbook of Natural Resource and Energy Economics, Volume II,* eds. A.V. Kneese and J.L. Sweeney. Amsterdam: Elsevier Science Publishers.

Stavins, R.N., and A.B. Jaffe. 1990. 'Unintended Impacts of Public Investments on Private Decisions: The Depletion of Forested Wetlands.' *American Economic Review* 80(3): 337–52.

Stavins, R.N. 1999. 'The Costs of Carbon Sequestration: A Revealed-Preference Approach.' *American Economic Review* 89(4): 994–1009.

Tietenberg, T. 1995. 'Tradable Permits for Pollution Control When Emission Location Matters: What Have We Learned?' *Environmental and Resource Economics* 5: 95–113.

Tomasi, T. and A. Weise. 1994. 'Water Pollution Regulation in a Spatial Model.' In *Nonpoint Source Pollution Regulation: Issues and Analysis,* eds. C. Dosi and T. Tomasi. Dordrecht: Kluwer Academic Publishers.

Usategui, J. M. 1990. 'Uncertain Irreversibility, Information, and Transformation Costs.' *Journal of Environmental Economics and Management* 19: 73–85.

Van Kooten, G.C. 1993. *Land Resource Economics and Sustainable Development: Economic Policies and the Common Good.* Vancouver: University of British Columbia Press.

Vickery, W. 1965. 'Pricing as a tool in coordination of local transportation,' in *Transportation Economics,* ed. J. Meyer. New York, New York: National Bureau of Economics Research.

Werczberger, E. 1987. 'A Dynamic Model of Urban Land Use with Externalities.' *Regional Science and Urban Economics* 17(3): 391–410.

Wu, J., and K. Segerson. 1995. 'The Impact of Policies and Land Characteristics on Potential Groundwater Pollution in Wisconsin.' *American Journal of Agricultural Economics* 77(4): 1033–45.

Chapter 7

Overview of Empirical Methods

Andrew J. Plantinga and Elena G. Irwin

Introduction

Empirical models of land use and land-use change are critical for testing theories of land use and informing policies aimed at managing land-use change. Empirical models have been used to identify the causes of a particular distribution of land use and the factors that drive land-use change. For example, these models can be used to test the extent to which net returns to alternative uses and physical characteristics of land (i.e., land quality) influence land-use decisions.

Empirical models of land-use change are based on the theoretical models reviewed in Chapter 6, which date back to von Thünen's (1826) spatial model of land use in the mid-19th century. Von Thünen's key insight, that differences in transportation costs are capitalized into land values and generate a spatially heterogeneous pattern of land rents, underlies the classic urban bid-rent model developed by Alonso (1964) and Muth (1969). Differences in urban land rents are explained by differences in households' costs of commuting to a centrally located employment center. Given that the costs of commuting to a central business district (CBD) are an important component of a household's budget, a household's net income decreases with increasing distance from the CBD and the rent the household is willing to pay will be lower at a location that is farther from the CBD than at a location nearer to the center. This generates the downward-sloping 'bid rent gradient,' in which urban land rents are hypothesized to decrease with distance from the CBD, that is a key component of empirical models of urban land use. Other theoretical models that also build on the von Thünen approach and that have provided a basis for empirical models include Barlowe (1958), Found (1971), and Capozza and Helsley (1989).

While empirical models of land use and land-use change have a common theoretical underpinning, the structure of the models varies according to the data used for estimation and the research question. For example, aggregate data of land use, e.g. at the county-level, are often times the only data available to a researcher and therefore the empirical model is oriented to explaining land use and land-use change at a regional level rather than at an individual parcel level. In other cases, randomly-sampled plot-level data may be necessary to explore plot-level determinants of land-use change, e.g. the importance of on-site physical characteristics such as soil type and slope as well as location features such as spillover effects from surrounding land uses. On the other hand, if the contiguous spatial pattern of land use is the primary research interest, then a complete dataset of the entire population of parcels within a geographic region – rather than just a random sample – would be important. These considerations suggest the following categorization of empirical models: (1) aggregate data models, (2) sample plot data models, and (3) parcel data models. In this chapter, we provide an overview of these models and a discussion of related econometric and modeling issues.

Aggregate Data Models

We begin the discussion of aggregate data models with a description of common sources of aggregate land-use data for the United States. We then present the basic aggregate land-use shares model that forms the centerpiece of econometric analysis with aggregate data. Next, we present a discussion of several econometric and modeling issues that arise with the basic model, including how to measure net returns to alternative uses, the importance of controlling for spatial differences in land quality, modeling of dynamic land-use decisions, and, finally, the estimation of disaggregated shares models.

Aggregate Data Sources

The majority of econometric land-use models have been estimated with aggregate data. One obvious appeal of using aggregate data is its low cost. As discussed in Chapters 2-5, a variety of federal government agencies collect data on land use in the U.S. with both times-series and cross-sectional observations. The U.S. Department of Commerce conducts the Census of Agriculture, which provides county-level data on farmer-owned land.[1] For instance, the Census of Agriculture reports the area of cropland (by crop type), pastureland, and woodland for each county and approximately each five years. Note, however, that Census of Agriculture data on forest area is incomplete since it only reports farmer-owned woodland. Many agricultural states (Iowa, Wisconsin, etc.) collect these data on an annual basis through state Agricultural Reporting Services.

The Forest Service, an agency within the U.S. Department of Agriculture, collects data on all forestland in the U.S. through its Forest Inventory and Analysis (FIA) unit. FIA inventories are conducted on a state-by-state basis and on a cycle that varies by state but is typically in the five to fifteen year range.[2] The inventories provide county-level estimates of forest area, disaggregated by owner, species, and additional forest characteristics. Due to the nature of their sampling design, the FIA does not collect detailed information on non-forest uses. Thus, in applications where non-forest uses are of interest, researchers often combine Census of Agriculture data on agricultural land uses with FIA data on forest land uses to yield an aggregate (county-level) data panel (e.g., Hardie and Parks 1997; Mauldin et al. 1999).

The Bureau of the Census produces estimates of urbanized land area based on the population census. Prior to 1990, only state-level estimates are reported. The

1990 and 2000 censuses, however, provide estimates at the county level. These estimates are not based on observed or reported land use but on population density within a specified geographic area. Thus, these estimates are not consistent with Census of Agriculture and Forest Service data because agricultural and forested land may be found within an area classified as urban. As an alternative, researchers often compute the area of land in urban and other uses as the difference between the total land area of a county and the agricultural and forest land areas.

The Basic Shares Model

The most common aggregate data model involves estimating the relationship between shares of land in alternative uses and hypothesized determinants of land use (e.g., Lichtenberg 1989; Parks and Murray 1994; Parks and Kramer 1995; Wu and Brorsen 1995; Wu and Segerson 1995; Hardie and Parks 1997; Mauldin et al. 1999; Plantinga et al. 1999). If county-level data is employed, then the land-use shares would be defined as the per cent of total county area devoted to given uses (e.g., the share of county land in agricultural use). The observed share for land-use k ($k=1,...,K$), in county i ($i=1,...,I$), and at time t ($t=1,...,T$) can be expressed as $y_{ikt}=p_{ikt}+\varepsilon_{ikt}$, where p_{ikt} is the expected share of land allocated to use k, and ε_{ikt} is a random error term with mean zero. The expected share, p_{ikt}, represents the optimal land allocation given economic and other conditions prevailing in time t. The actual land allocation observed at time t, y_{ikt}, may differ from the optimal allocation due to random occurrences such as bad weather or unanticipated price changes. These random events are assumed to have a zero mean, implying $E[y_{ikt}]=p_{ikt}$.

The expected shares are assumed to be a function of a vector of explanatory variables, X_{it}, and unobserved parameters to be estimated, β_k. From the theory in Chapter 6, aggregate land-use shares depend on the net returns to alternative uses as well as the distribution of land quality in the county, the measurement of which is discussed below. Roughly speaking, the βs measure the effect of the explanatory variables on the expected shares. Researchers frequently use the following logistic specification of the expected share,

$$(1) \quad p_{ikt} = \frac{e^{\beta_k' X_{it}}}{\sum_{s=1}^{K} e^{\beta_s' X_{it}}},$$

for all i, k, and t. This specification confines the land-use shares to the unit interval. Another advantage is that the model of observed shares can be transformed to yield an estimating equation that is linear in the parameters (see, for example, Chapter 19 in Judge et al. 1988). Specifically, the natural logarithm of each observed share normalized on a common and arbitrarily chosen share (below, y_{i1t}) takes the form,

$$(2) \quad \ln(y_{ikt} / y_{i1t}) = \beta_k' X_{it} + \mu_{ikt},$$

for $k=2,\ldots,K$, where μ_{ikt} is the transformed error term.[3] The model in (2) consists of $K-1$ equations that can be estimated using standard linear regression techniques. In each equation, the estimated parameters measure the marginal effects of the explanatory variables on the log of the normalized share. It is often more informative to estimate the marginal effect of each variable on the expected shares in (1) (see Greene 1999 for a discussion).

In many applications, the model in (2) is estimated with pooled times-series and cross-sectional observations. For instance, Lichtenberg (1989) assembles a panel of annual county-level observations of land-use shares for seven major crops in western Nebraska for the years 1966 to 1980. Regressors include crop prices, irrigation technology costs, and a land quality variable measuring countywide average water capacity of the soil. A quadratic specification is used to account for possible nonlinear relationships between the expected land-use shares and the explanatory variables. Hardie and Parks (1997) estimate a model using county-level observations of irrigated farmland, other farmland, and forestland shares for five states in the southeastern U.S. from 1982 and 1987. The independent variables include crop revenues and costs, timber prices and costs, land quality measures, and sociodemographic variables such as average age of landowners, population density, and per capita income. The latter variables are included to account for the diversion of land to urban and other uses. Plantinga (1996) and Miller and Plantinga (1999) estimate more general versions of the basic shares model in (2) that yield estimates of land-use shares by land quality class. For example, rather than estimating the share of land in forest for the entire county, forest shares are estimated for each land quality class within the county.

Econometric and Modeling Issues

Measurement of net returns   Theoretical and empirical evidence indicates that net returns are an important determinant of land-use decisions. In the context of the basic shares model, the manner in which net return measures are constructed is a function of the underlying decision problem. In many studies, the decision to allocate land to agricultural uses is viewed as a static problem. Landowners observe input costs at the start of the growing season, form expectations of prices for output they will receive at the end of the season, and allocate their land to the use yielding the highest expected net returns. Provided that capital investment decisions (e.g., investment in long-lived capital such as farm machinery and natural capital such as soil fertility) are independent of land-use decisions, the allocation problem is identical in each year and unrelated to allocation decisions in other years. In this case, researchers simply include net returns variables corresponding to the year of the land-use observation. For instance, Miller and Plantinga (1999) estimate crop share models for Iowa and include lagged crop prices (the lagged price is assumed to be expected price for the current year's crop) and current fertilizer costs.

When forestry is a feasible land use, the allocation decision involves a dynamic problem. Stavins and Jaffe (1990) and Plantinga (1996) present formulations of the individual's decision to allocate land to agriculture and forestry and solve the corresponding dynamic optimization problem. Plantinga (1996) presents sufficient conditions under which the allocation decision reduces to a simple comparison of the present discounted value of net returns from each use.[4] Present value measures of forestry and agricultural returns are included in econometric models estimated in Stavins and Jaffe (1990), Parks and Murray (1994), Plantinga (1996), and Mauldin et al. (1999).

In many applications, data on net returns to urban uses of land are not available and, instead, researchers include proxies for urban returns in shares models. Commonly-used proxy measures include population density and per capita income. The justification for these proxy measures is that pressures to develop land, and thus the returns to urban land, will be higher in locations with greater population densities and incomes. A potential shortcoming of the population density measure arises from the fact that population and urban land are simultaneously determined.[5] To avoid this problem, Lubowski (2002) develops a measure of the average net return to developed land for every county in the United States. This measure is formed as the difference between the average house price and the estimated value of structures. This residual is an estimate of the underlying value of the land. Hardie et al. (2000) show that parameter estimates in shares models are sensitive to alternative ways of modeling urban and rural land use.

Land quality When cross-sectional data are used, it is necessary to control for any systematic differences across observational units such as counties. Spatial differences in physiographic characteristics of the land are particularly important because land-use decisions are often closely tied to the quality of the land for particular uses. For example, high quality land is typically allocated to intensive agricultural uses such as row cropping, while low quality land is often put into forestry. Land-use shares for an individual county will, therefore, depend on the distribution of land quality within the county (see Chapter 6). In most applications, researchers include variables to characterize this distribution. For instance, Wu and Segerson (1995) include soil quality measures from the 1987 National Resources Inventory (see further discussion below), including the per cent of land in each county with erosion risk, medium- and fine-textured soils, a slope less than eight per cent, and so on. Stavins and Jaffe (1990) take an alternative approach. They treat the land quality distribution as unobservable, but assume that it takes a particular parametric form (log-normal). The parameters of the distribution are then recovered from the data as part of the econometric estimation.

The land quality distribution also provides a formal means of aggregating individual land-use decisions. In the static (dynamic) case, the rule is to allocate land to the use providing the highest expected profits (discounted stream of expected profits). In general, output yields and optimal input levels vary with the quality of the land, implying profits vary with land quality as well. Researchers often define land quality in terms of productivity and assume that profits from agricultural and forest uses are an increasing function of quality. In this case, profits from each use will exceed profits from all other uses over a compact range of land quality. As demonstrated in Chapter 6, by integrating the

118 Economics of Rural Land-Use Change

land quality distribution for the county over this range of land quality, one obtains an expression for the share of the county's land that is optimally allocated to that use.

Land-use dynamics An assumption implicit in the basic shares model is that landowners can change uses costlessly. While the cost of converting land from one row crop to another may be approximately zero, the costs of moving between agricultural, forest, and urban land uses are, in many instances, likely to be substantial. Modifying the shares model to account for conversion costs is difficult due to the aggregate nature of the data. The land-use observations reveal net changes in land use but provide no direct information on transitions between uses. For instance, over a given time period, one may observe a change in forest land area and an equal and opposite change in agricultural land area. This may be the outcome of a simple shift of land from agriculture to forest, but an infinite number of more complicated land-use transitions can produce the same result. Detailed studies of land-use change (e.g., Vesterby and Heimlich 1991) suggest that net change statistics often mask more complex sets of transitions. If this is the case, then the basic shares model will fail to capture the influence of conversion costs on land-use decisions and will provide an incomplete representation of land-use dynamics.

Even though land-use transitions are not directly observed in aggregate data, it is possible to model transitions explicitly using a modified version of the basic shares model (e.g., Plantinga and Miller 1997, Plantinga and Ahn 2002).[6] The basic insight underlying this approach is that the observed land-use share, y_{ikt}, can be expressed in terms of transitions from the full set of land uses. A general expression of this model is notationally complex, so a special case of the model involving two uses will be presented. Suppressing county subscripts, the shares of land in uses one and two can be written:

(3a) $\quad y_{1t} = s_{11t}\,y_{1t-1} + s_{21t}\,y_{2t-1}$,

(3b) $\quad y_{2t} = s_{12t}\,y_{1t-1} + s_{22t}\,y_{2t-1}$,

where s_{11t} is the share of land in use one in time $t-1$ that remains in use one, s_{12t} is the share of land in use two in time $t-1$ that is converted to use one by time t, and so on. Thus, $s_{11t}y_{1t-1}$ and $s_{12t}y_{2t-1}$ represent the contributions to the share of land in use one in time $t(y_{1t})$ of land that was in uses one and two in the previous time period. A similar interpretation applies to $s_{12t}y_{1t-1}$ and $s_{22t}y_{2t-1}$.

With aggregate data, only the land-use shares (y in Equations [3a,b]) are observed. The transition shares (s in Equations [3a,b]) are not observed. However, the transition shares may be parameterized in the manner of Equation (1). The share of land in use j ($j=1,2$) converted to use k ($k=1,2$) between $t-1$ and t is written:

$$(4) \quad s_{jkt} = p_{jkt} + \varepsilon_{jkt} = \frac{e^{\beta'_{jk} X_t}}{\sum_{s=1}^{2} e^{\beta'_{sk} X_t}} + \varepsilon_{jkt},$$

where, analogous to the basic shares model, p_{jkt} is the optimal transition share and ε_{jkt} is a mean-zero random shock. As in the basic model, p_{jkt} is expressed as a function of exogenous explanatory variables such as net returns and land quality measures (the Xs) and unobserved parameters to be estimated (the βs). In addition, measures of the costs of converting land from use j to k can be included in the set of explanatory variables. Substitution of Equation (4) into Equations (3a,b) yields the statistical model. Panel data (i.e., a combination of time-series and cross-sectional observations) can be used to estimate the βs in the resulting model.[7] With these results, estimates of the unobserved transition shares can be recovered. Specifically, p_{jkt} is computed using the estimated βs and the explanatory variables. Plantinga and Ahn (2002) use such estimates of the transition shares to analyze the relative costs of land conversion and land retention policies.

The presence of significant conversion costs raises the possibility that there may be option values associated with keeping land in its current use. In this setting, option values represent the expected value of delaying costly conversion decisions in order to obtain forthcoming information about the relative returns to different uses. Schatzki (1998) develops a theoretical model of a landowner's decision to allocate a parcel of land to agriculture or forestry. Costs of converting from one use to another are explicit and, in contrast to the deterministic formulations in Stavins and Jaffe (1990) and Plantinga (1996), the returns to forestry and agriculture are stochastic. This leads to a fundamentally different allocation rule than the one discussed above. Rather than simply comparing the discounted expected profits from each use, landowners monitor profits through time and convert land only when relative profits are high enough to overcome the value of the option to keep land in its current use and avoid incurring costs of conversion. An important implication of this result is that landowners – and, in the aggregate, land-use shares – may be unresponsive or slow to respond to changes in relative profits. Stavins and Jaffe (1990) allow for such incomplete responses to profit changes using a partial adjustment model of land use; actual changes in land use are only a fraction of what would be the optimal change in land use. Cho et al. (2001) include variables measuring the variance of net returns to capture potential effects of option values.

Sample Plot Data Models

For some land-use applications, researchers have access to sample plot data. These data typically come from an on-the-ground inventory of a randomly-selected collection of sample plots. The plots are usually small in size (less than one acre) and geographically dispersed.

Data and Model Specification

The most comprehensive set of plot-level land-use observations is provided by the National Resources Inventory (NRI). The NRI database provides detailed land-use and land quality information on approximately 800,000 randomly-selected plots at four points in time (1982, 1987, 1992, and 1997). The same plots have been surveyed in each of the four years, thus providing observations of land-use transitions. In addition, the aggregate data provided in the Forest Inventory Analyses (FIAs) conducted by the U.S. Forest Service (as discussed in the previous section) are based on plot-level surveys of private forests. Therefore, FIA data can be used in both aggregate and sample plot data models.

A natural way to model land-use decisions with sample plot data is to use a discrete choice model (e.g., probit or logit). Within this framework the researcher models the probability that a plot is allocated to a given land use. Specifically, with K possible land uses, the probability that plot i is allocated to use k in time t is given by:

$$(6) \quad \Pr(y_{ikt} = 1) = \Pr(V_{ikt} + \mu_{ikt} \geq V_{ijt} + \mu_{ijt})$$

for all $j=1,\ldots,K$, where y_{ikt} equals one if use k is selected and is zero otherwise, V_{ikt} is the deterministic value of allocating land to use k, and μ_{ikt} is a random variable that influences the value of use k but is unobserved by the researcher. V_{ikt} is often given the simple linear form

$$V_{ikt} = \beta_k' X_{ikt},$$

where X_{ikt} is a vector of variables explaining the allocation of land to use k (e.g., net returns) and β_k is a vector of unobserved parameters to be estimated. The right-hand side of Equation (6) can be rewritten

$$\Pr(\mu_{ijt} - \mu_{ikt} \leq \beta_k' X_{ikt} - \beta_j' X_{ijt}) \quad \text{for all } j.$$

Modeling the difference in the error terms, $\mu_{ijt} - \mu_{ikt}$, with a logistic (normal) cumulative distribution function leads to a logit (probit) model of land-use choice. If a time series of sample plot data is available, then (6) can be modified in a straightforward way to model land-use transitions (see the discussion of parcel data models for more details).

As an example, Kline and Alig (1999) use plot-level FIA data on broadly-defined land classes to estimate the probability that land changes from either farm or forest use to developed use in western Oregon and Washington. Independent variables include forest and farm rents, sociodemographic characteristics of the county in which the plot is located, and variables indicating the presence of zoning restrictions. Zoning restrictions may prohibit certain land uses and, thus, must be accounted for in the empirical analysis. A similar modeling approach is used by

McMillen (1989) to estimate the probability that land parcels in McHenry County, Illinois, are allocated to farm, residential use, or unimproved vacant lots. The data set consists of all parcels that were sold during the period 1979 to 1983. The independent variables include parcel characteristics such as size, neighborhood characteristics, and distances to important sites such as downtown Chicago. A number of recent applications make use of sample plot data from the NRI. Claassen and Tegene (1999) use NRI data for the Cornbelt region to estimate the probability that land is allocated to cropland, pasture, or the Conservation Reserve Program (CRP). Schatzki (1998) uses a similar approach to model CRP enrollment decisions in Georgia. Finally, Lubowski (2002) estimates a national-scale model of land use that examines transitions between cropland, forest, pasture, range, urban, and CRP lands.

Econometric and Modeling Issues

The structure of plot-level models is similar to that of aggregate data models and, indeed, the plot-level model is equivalent to the aggregate data model under certain restrictions.[8] From an econometric and land-use modeling perspective, however, there are advantages to using plot-level data. First, to the extent they are available, variables measuring plot-level characteristics such as land quality can be included in the econometric model. In aggregate data models, these characteristics must be represented using less precise aggregate variables. Second, if plots are resampled over time, observations of land-use transitions are provided and, in principle, these can be modeled explicitly. Time-series data are best suited to explaining changes in land use as the result of changes in the land-use determinants of interest (e.g., commodity prices). At present, the NRI and FIA databases provide relatively few observations over time. As more time-series observations are recorded, however, the relative advantage of using plot-level data will increase.

Parcel Data Models

If the contiguous pattern of land use within a region, and in particular the underlying spatial processes that generate these patterns, is of interest, then it is desirable to have data on the full population of land parcels within a region as opposed to a sampling of land plots (Bell and Irwin 2002). Note that aggregate data (e.g., county data) provide contiguous coverage of land use in a region but do not provide information on the spatial pattern of individual land uses. Thus, these data do not easily accommodate the exploration of spatial relationships between uses.

Data Sources

With the advent of Geographic Information Systems (GIS) to store and organize geographically-referenced data, land-use data of an entire population of parcels within a specified geographic area have become more readily available. Increasingly, county tax auditors, state planning agencies, emergency service agencies, and other governmental entities are collecting and storing detailed data on parcel and building characteristics in an electronic format that has made it possible for researchers to compile parcel databases for counties. Attribute information from local tax assessment databases typically includes market transaction price(s), assessed values, current land use, zoning, lot size, location, and structural characteristics of any house or building on the parcel. In addition to public sources, parcel data for metropolitan areas may also be purchased from several national real estate companies.

While these data make it possible to model land-use conversion at the level of the individual decision maker, acquiring and managing these data can be challenging. The availability of these data differs tremendously from state to state and, in many cases, from county to county. Often government agencies save only the most current information, so that changes over time in land use and other attributes are difficult to piece together. For example, local agencies do not always track a residential lot's subdivision history, so that the researcher must discern which subdivided lots comprise the original parcel. Because one county will typically contain tens, and sometimes hundreds, of thousands of parcels, management of these data requires a GIS to store and organize data and to generate spatial variables.

Other geographically-referenced data, including roads, cities and towns, recreational areas, soil quality, slope and elevation, school districts, etc., can also be acquired and overlaid with the parcel data, and GIS software can be used to generate a host of spatial variables to be included in econometric models. Again, availability of these data for a particular region varies greatly across states and sometimes across counties. Some of these data are available from federal government sources (e.g., the U.S. Bureau of the Census maintains Tiger Line files, from which roads, hydrology, Census tracts, and other geographic features can be extracted). Other federal government sources of GIS data include the US Geological Survey, the Environmental Protection Agency, and the U.S. Department of Housing and Urban Development. Data can increasingly be downloaded online from these agencies' websites or from other online data sources.[9]

Model Specification

Parcel data models of land use include those that explain land use, land values, and land-use conversion. All three types of models begin from the assumption that land is a heterogeneous good, comprised of a bundle of characteristics, and that the land use, value, or change can be estimated as a function of the parcel's characteristics. An advantage of using parcel data in modeling land-use change is that the data are at the same level of resolution as the economic agent who makes the land-use conversion decision. This avoids problems of aggregation and the need to assume a representative agent and allows for a much more detailed investigation of the land-use pattern and change. In addition, because data are available for a contiguous area, models can be estimated that account for spatial processes of land-use change and spatial interactions among nearby parcels. An important econometric issue that arises in the estimation of these models is the likely spatial autocorrelation of the error terms, which arises due to measurement error or unobserved variation that is positively correlated over space. This issue is discussed further in a later section.

Discrete Choice Models of Land Use

It is generally assumed that land is in a 'productive' use, implying that positive returns are generated from the use of the land (e.g. through agriculture or commercial forestry uses). Following Nelson and Hellerstein (1997), the net present discounted returns from productive land at parcel i in use k in period t can be written as:

$$(7) \quad R_{ikt} = \int (P_{ikT+t} Q_{ikT+t} - C_{ikT+t} X_{ikT+t}) e^{-rt} dt ,$$

where P is the output price, Q is the quantity of output, C is a vector of input prices, X is a vector of inputs, and r is the discount rate.

Assuming that the landowner will choose the land use that maximizes R_{ikt}, parcel i will be devoted to land use k if $R_{ikt} > R_{ijt}$ for all $j \neq k$. Given that not all factors that affect R are observable, this condition can be rewritten in a probabilistic framework in which the systematic and random portions of R are explicitly modeled, e.g. R_{ikt} could be written as an additive function of a systematic and a random term, $V_{ikt} + \mu_{ikt}$, and the land-use allocation decision would be expressed as in Equation (6). As above, assuming a distribution for the error terms and a functional form for the systematic portion, this model can be estimated using discrete choice methods.

Using land-use data generated from satellite imagery, Chomitz and Gray (1995) use this framework to estimate a model of land use in Belize and investigate whether road construction impacts deforestation. They find strong evidence that distance to roads and distance to markets via those roads influence the likelihood that land is in an agricultural use, although they recognize the potential endogeneity problem associated with the location of roads. Nelson and Hellerstein (1997) use a multinomial logit model to estimate the determinants of land use using 30 meter by 30 meter remotely sensed land cover data from satellite imagery of central Mexico. Road access is also found to be an important determinant of land-use choice.

Discrete Choice Models of Land Conversion

Economic models of land-use conversion are similar to models of land use, with the exception that they explicitly focus on explaining a *change* in land use, rather than the allocation of land to various uses at one point in time. While the underlying economic assumptions of individual behavior are the same – that individuals will choose a land use to maximize net returns – the focus is on the factors that cause a change in land use. Therefore, both the expected returns and the costs of conversion enter the decision (see the related discussion on modeling land-use dynamics with aggregate data). These models often start from the assumption that land-use conversion is a Markovian process, in which the probability of transition from one land use to another is a function of the parcel's current land use and a variety of exogenous parcel attributes. At the parcel level, data on land use is typically categorical and Markov transition probabilities between uses of land are estimated using a discrete choice, probabilistic approach. The simplest model, again based on profit maximization, is one in which parcel i, which is currently in state a, will be converted to state k in time t if:

(8) $R_{ikt|a} \geq R_{ijt|a}$ for all land uses $j = 1, ..., a, ..., J$,

where $R_{ikt|a}$ is defined as the net present value of the future stream of returns to parcel i in state k at time t, given that the parcel was in state a in time $t–1$ (Bockstael 1996). A discrete choice model of land-use conversion can be derived from Equation (8) using the same motivation as above for the discrete choice land use model laid out in Equation (6).

Using data on approximately 16,000 residential transactions that occurred during 1990 in a central Maryland region, Bockstael (1996) uses a two-step approach to estimating parcel-level conversions of land from agricultural or forest uses to residential use. First, a hedonic model of residential land prices is estimated in which the residual land price per acre is a function of lot size, accessibility to urban centers, public service dummy variables, and surrounding landscape variables. Parameter estimates from this model are used to predict the value of the developer's expected returns to converting a parcel to residential use, for all cells of the landscape that are considered developable in residential use in 1990. The land-use conversion model is then estimated as a function of the predicted residential price, predicted present value in agricultural use, and proxies for the costs of conversion.

Landis (1995) and Landis and Zhang (1998a, 1998b) use a reduced form approach to estimate a multinomial logit model of land-use change for the San Francisco Bay area, in which the probabilities of nine land-use change alternatives are estimated. They also estimate population and job growth for each jurisdiction, so that simulations of both the quantity and spatial location of land-use change are based on statistical models. The unit of observation for the land-use change model is a 100 square meter landscape 'cell,' rather than the land parcel itself, so that the estimation model does not directly correspond to the underlying behavior of an economic agent. One shortcoming of this approach is that neighboring effects (e.g., land-use externalities) cannot be distinguished from own-parcel effects, since it is unknown whether two adjacent cells belong to the same land parcel or not. This approach is often necessary because parcel-level land-use data are frequently not available and estimation of land-use change on a cell-by-cell basis is often employed.

Estimates from the land-use conversion models can be used to predict spatially-explicit land-use changes under different policy scenarios. For example, Bockstael and Bell (1997) use estimates from a residential land conversion model to predict the likelihood of development for each developable parcel in a future round of development under different policy scenarios. They calculate probability maps of development under different rural zoning policies and find that the predicted patterns are sensitive to the degree of differential zoning across counties.

Duration Models of Land Conversion

A limitation of the discrete choice framework as outlined above is the lack of temporal dynamics that enter the model. In high-growth regions, for example, the more interesting question may not be *whether* a parcel is converted, but rather *when* a parcel is converted. Duration models explicitly account for the timing of a qualitative change from one state to another and therefore are an appropriate way to capture the cumulative effects of explanatory variables on the transition probability. Given the nature of the land-use conversion problem in many areas, in which the timing of the conversion is often the question of interest, duration models offer an intuitively appealing approach.[10] The timing of an 'event,' defined as a qualitative change from one state to another, is viewed as a random variable, and the observed timing of events are treated as realizations of a random process. In turn, the distribution of durations associated with events (e.g., the duration of a land parcel in an undeveloped state) is described in terms of either a survival function or a hazard function.

The survival function is the probability that the event does not occur in period t and is equal to $1-F(t)$, where $F(t)=Pr(T \leq t)$, which is the cumulative distribution function of the random variable T, the duration length. The hazard function is the conditional probability that the event occurs between t and Δt, given that $T \geq t$ (i.e., given that the event has not yet occurred). This function is interpreted as the rate at which the event occurs and is usually written as:

$$(9) \quad h(t) = \lim_{\Delta t \to 0} \frac{\Pr\{t \leq T < t + \Delta t \mid T \geq t\}}{\Delta t}.$$

In the land-use conversion case, the hazard rate is usually the function of interest. In this context, the hazard rate can be defined as the conditional probability that a parcel is developed in period t, given that it has remained in an undeveloped state until time t. The hazard rate is typically modeled as a function of time and explanatory variables, some of which may be time-variant.

Different assumptions are possible regarding the distribution of durations. Fully parametric models, including the exponential, Weibull, log-normal, log-logistic, and complementary log-log models, can be specified. In addition, a semi-parametric approach, commonly referred to as the proportional hazards model or Cox regression model, is also possible. Irwin and Bell (Chapter 9) use this type of duration model to estimate a model of residential land conversion in which the influence of parcel-level characteristics and local growth management policies on the timing of a parcel's development are estimated.

Other examples from the literature include Hite, Sohngen, and Tempelton (2002), who use a duration model to study the factors influencing the suburbanization of agricultural land in a rural-urban county of Ohio. They find that property taxes have varying effects of the timing of the development of parcels with varying land quality. Irwin and Bockstael (2002) use a duration model to estimate the effects of neighborhood land use on the conversion timing of undeveloped parcels to residential use in exurban areas. Because the neighborhood land use variables vary over time as conversion occurs, a duration model is needed to capture the influence of these time-variant attributes on the conversion probability. Nickerson and Bockstael (2001a,b) model the landowner's decision to preserve land in a farmland preservation program that results in permanent protection, given that development represents a competing (and equally irreversible) land-use alternative. Duration modeling techniques are used to shed light on those factors that affect the timing of preservation and development decisions.

Spatial Econometric Issues

A major econometric issue that arises in estimating parcel data models is spatial dependence.[11] Spatial dependence refers to the notion that values associated with locations that are close-by are more correlated than values associated with locations that are farther apart. This condition may arise simply because neighboring sites tend to share many common features (e.g., they are both within close proximity to an urban center) or because of an underlying spatial process that causes neighboring sites to have similar values. For example, crime in one neighborhood may spillover into an adjacent neighborhood, causing both neighborhoods to experience high crime rates. Spatial dependence can also arise in aggregate and plot data models. However, in these cases, the scale of the data or the geographic dispersion of observations tends to mitigate the effects.

Depending on the type of spatial dependence, several different econometric problems arise. First, because spatial data is often measured according to boundaries that do not correspond to the geographic extent of the spatial dependence, measurement errors are frequently present. If so, the errors associated with neighboring locations will be correlated. This condition, referred to as spatial autocorrelation, can also arise due to spatially correlated omitted variables within an econometric model. In either case, ordinary least squares (OLS) is an unbiased, but inefficient, estimator. Spatial econometric techniques involve positing the form of the spatial autocorrelation and rewriting the model so that the error structure is independent and identically distributed (i.i.d.).

A second form of spatial dependence arises when values at different locations in space are interdependent (Anselin 1988):

(10) $y_i = f(y_1, ..., y_{i-1}, y_{i+1}, ... y_N)$,

where y_i is the observed value at location i and $i = 1,...,N$. As specified, this system is unidentifiable since it results in N^2-N parameters with only N observations. In this case, spatial econometric techniques are used to impose structure on the spatial process represented by f so that only a limited number of parameters need to be estimated. Spatial dependence of this form, if left uncorrected, will lead to biased OLS estimates due to the correlation between the spatially lagged dependent variable and the error term.

Established spatial econometric techniques are available for dealing with spatial autocorrelation and spatial lag structures for models with a continuous dependent variable. In both cases, a maintained hypothesis is made about the spatial structure (either of the errors or of the spatial lag) by means of an NxN spatial weights matrix. This matrix represents the researcher's best guess of how the values (or errors) associated with different locations are related. Each element of the matrix, w_{ij}, represents the assumed spatial dependency between locations i and j. A variety of different structures are possible. For example, in the case of a lag, the researcher may hypothesize that only nearest neighbors interact with each other, in which case a nonzero value would be assigned to all w_{ij} in which i and j are nearest neighbors and w_{ij} equals zero otherwise. Alternatively, the dependence may be assumed to be a decreasing function of distance between any two locations, in which the weights can be assigned by means of an inverse distance function, $w_{ij} = f(1/d_{ij})$, where d_{ij} is the distance between i and j.

Bell and Bockstael (2000) explore the consequences of spatial autocorrelation in a model of residential land values. The authors reason that this model is likely to suffer from an omitted variables problem that, in a spatial setting, will lead to spatial autocorrelation. Assuming that the form of the spatial autocorrelation is a first-order spatial autoregressive structure, the model is rewritten as:

(11a) $y = X\beta + \varepsilon$
(11b) $\varepsilon = \rho W \varepsilon + \mu$,

where y is a vector of residual residential land prices, X is a vector of parcel-level characteristics, ε is an error vector with a zero mean and a non-spherical variance-covariance matrix $\sigma^2(I-\rho W)^{-1}(I-\rho W)^{-1}$, where ρ is the spatial autoregressive coefficient, W is spatial weights matrix, and μ is i.i.d., with a variance-covariance matrix $\sigma^2 I$. Several different specifications of W are used in estimating the model using both Generalized Methods of Moments and Maximum Likelihood techniques. In addition, to avoid the economic interpretation problems that arise with row standardization of a distance-decay spatial weights matrix, a series of higher-order contiguity matrices are used to represent the spatial dependencies with a more flexible form. Results from these estimations show that parameter estimates are sensitive to row standardization and the specification of W and that significance levels of some of the coefficients change when the correction for spatial autocorrelation is applied.

While it is straightforward to apply these methods to estimating hedonic models of land values in which the dependent variable is a continuous variable, application of these methods to discrete choice land-use change models is much more challenging. In theory, the spatial error autocorrelation may take a similar form as in the continuous case illustrated in Equation (11). However, rather than a continuous dependent variable y, the discrete choice model contains a binary or categorical dependent variable indicating the discrete state of land use or land-use change associated with a parcel. Building on the model laid out in Equation (6), a discrete choice model with spatial error autocorrelation can be expressed as:

$$(12) \quad \Pr(y_{it} = 1 \mid y_{it-1}) = \Pr(V_{ikt} + \mu_{ikt} > V_{ijt} + \mu_{ijt}) = \Pr(\varepsilon_{it} < V_{ikt} - V_{ijt}),$$

where $\varepsilon_{it} = \mu_{ijt} - \mu_{ikt}$. The structure of the spatial error autocorrelation embedded in ε_t may take on any number of different forms, e.g., a first-order spatial autoregressive structure could be expressed as in Equation (11b). The result is a correlated error structure among neighboring observations: $corr(\varepsilon_{it}, \varepsilon_{ht}) > 0$, where parcels i and h are neighbors.

Even though the underlying spatial error structure may be the same in continuous variable and discrete choice models, the consequences of the resulting spatially correlated error covariance structure are more severe in a discrete choice setting. The added complexity arises because of the heteroskedasticity that is induced by the spatially correlated covariance structure that arises from spatial dependence. While heteroskedastic errors in a continuous model do not result in inconsistent estimates, they do lead to problems of inconsistency in discrete choice and duration models. As detailed by Fleming (2002), several approaches have been proposed for dealing with this problem in a discrete choice framework.[12] Pinske and Slade (1998) have proposed a Generalized Methods of Moments estimator for the binary probit model that corrects for heteroskedasticity arising from a first-order autoregressive specification of spatial error autocorrelation. However, this method only corrects the inconsistency problem; the resulting estimates are still inefficient. As a result, hypothesis testing is invalid. To obtain both consistency and efficiency, full spatial information must be incorporated into the estimation procedure. In this case, incorporating the non-zero covariance structure implies that the likelihood function must be expressed in terms of an N-dimensional integral. Evaluation of this N-dimensional integral is computationally difficult and often limited to datasets with a small number of observations (i.e., 500 or less). For a full discussion of these issues and a discussion of an alternative approach using a weighted non-linear least squares estimator, see Fleming (2002). Less complicated strategies have been employed by others in the literature. For example, Nelson and Hellerstein (1997) estimate a multinomial discrete choice model of land use in which they eliminate suspected spatial error autocorrelation by using a spatial sampling routine that randomly selects a sub-sample of data points where no two sites in the sub-sample are considered neighbors. In addition, they construct a normalized measure of vegetative cover from the dependent variable of the original neighbors of each observation in the sample and include this as an explanatory variable. In doing so, they attempt to control for spatial dependence that they surmise is due to the spatial lag effects associated with the vegetative cover variable.

Irwin and Bockstael (2002) take an alternative approach to estimating a land-use conversion model with spatial lag effects. They hypothesize that land-use externalities among neighboring sites create interdependence among the conversion decisions of agents. Due to correlation between spatially correlated errors and the spatial lag variable, an identification problem arises that cannot be solved simply by assuming a spatial structure for the error terms or the interaction effects. An identification strategy based on bounding the spatial interaction term from above is used, so that the effect is identified only if the estimated interaction parameter is negative. Evidence of negative interactions among land parcels converted to residential use is found, which the authors argue leads to a 'repelling' effect among residential subdivisions and explains the scattered pattern of residential development in their study area.

A second type of spatial effect that arises in models with spatial data is spatial heterogeneity, i.e., non-constant error variances across space. Correction for this type of nonstationarity can be carried out with the usual methods of correcting for heteroskedastic errors. However, in the case in which both spatial heteroskedasticity and spatial dependence occur, standard tests for heteroskedasticity may be misleading. With a single cross-section equation, spatial dependence and spatial heteroskedasticity may be observationally equivalent (Anselin 2001).

Conclusions

In this chapter we have reviewed the major types of empirical economic models of land use and land-use conversion and the modeling and data issues that arise in each case. While the review is intended to be comprehensive of empirical economic models, it is not comprehensive of empirical land-use models in general. Many 'non-economic' empirical models of land-use change exist, some of which may be considered reduced form models that are motivated by assumptions regarding underlying economic processes.[13] In addition, we have not reviewed simulation-based models of land use and land-use change. While some of these models are again outside of the realm of economic models, others have been developed based on economic theories of land use and land-use change. Examples of the latter include agent-based economic models of land-use change, in which the land-use behavior of profit-maximizing landowners is spatially distributed across a simulated landscape (for a review of these models, see Parker et al. 2001). Such models are useful for understanding the evolution of aggregate-level patterns of land use as a function of individual-level behavior in which interdependence among landowners (e.g., due to spatial externalities) is an important element. These models are a natural complement to empirical models because they offer a means to predict changes in aggregate-level land-use patterns using estimated parameters from an empirical model. By comparing these simulated predictions with observed patterns, it is possible to draw conclusions regarding the extent to which the estimated individual effects generate changes at a regional scale in the land-use pattern. For example, Irwin and Bockstael (2002) use the estimated parameters from a duration model of residential land-use conversion to simulate the predicted pattern of development under two scenarios: one in which the estimated negative effects from neighboring development were included (along with the other estimated parameters) and the other in which these effects were restricted to be zero. The results illustrate the extent to which the negative development externalities are predicted to lead to an increased sprawl of residential development.

Empirical models of land use and land-use change are critical for testing theories of land use. The evidence from the empirical literature strongly supports the notion that private land-use decisions are determined by the financial net returns to different land uses. As well, land quality is shown to consistently explain the aggregate distribution of land use. Less clear is the influence of private non-market benefits on land-use decisions. For example, a landowner may retain land in forest for recreational uses, even if it would be optimal to convert it to an alternative use based solely on market returns. Another issue deserving attention is the effect of uncertainty on land-use decisions. Given the conversion costs associated with switching land uses and uncertainty about future returns, one might expect there to be option values related to retaining land in its current use. Above, we cite several studies that have considered the influence of option values on land-use decisions, but this remains an open area for research.

Empirical land-use models are also useful for examining policies aimed at managing land-use change. For example, researchers can test whether land-use decisions are affected by existing land-use policies such as zoning restrictions (e.g., Kline and Alig 1999; Cho et al. 2001) or by variables that might be influenced by future policies. In the latter case, econometric land-use models have been used to simulate the effects of subsidies and taxes that modify the net returns to alternative land uses. Plantinga et al. (1999) and Stavins (1999) use econometric land-use models to simulate the effects of policies to promote carbon sequestration in forests. In a similar fashion, Plantinga and Ahn (2002) analyze the effects of hypothetical land-use conversion and retention subsidies. Econometric models are particularly suited to the analysis of land-use policies because they are based on historical data and, thus, have the potential to capture the actual decisions made by private landowners facing returns to alternative uses.

Notes

1   A website providing convenient access to Census of Agriculture, Bureau of Census, and other federal government data is http://govinfo.kerr.orst.edu.

2   For each state inventory, a report is published presenting basic statistics on the forest inventory, including forest area by county. For example, a recent inventory report for Wisconsin is Schmidt (1997). More detailed data can be obtained by accessing the raw inventory data. For eastern states, these data have been assembled in a consistent format referred to as the Eastwide Data Base.

3   The transformed error term is heteroskedastic. Hardie and Parks (1997) discuss one approach to adjusting the errors for heteroskedasticity.

4   The conditions include static expecations of future profits, an infinite time horizon, and bare land. Further, capital investment decisions are assumed to be independent of the land allocation decision.

5   From an econometric standpoint, failure to account for such endogenous relationships can lead to biased coefficient estimates.

6   See Stavins and Jaffe (1990) for a related application.

7   Estimation is more complicated in this case than with the basic shares model. The statistical model is non-linear in the parameters and the model has a complicated error structure. See MacRae (1977) for a detailed discussion of the econometric procedure and Plantinga and Ahn (2002) for an application.

8   The explanatory variables in the plot-level model are measured at the county level and there is no explicit recognition of plot-level changes in land use.

9   For example, ESRI, the largest GIS software company, maintains a website that allows free downloading of many of the Census geographic files and other geographic files: http://www.esri.com/data/online/index.html.

10 For additional details on the practical aspects of estimating duration models using SAS Statistical Software, see Allison (1995); for an overview of the modeling approach, see Greene (1999).

11 For a comprehensive treatment of spatial dependence and spatial heterogeneity in econometric modeling, see Anselin (1988).

12 To date, no one has considered potential solutions to the spatial dependency problem within a duration modeling framework.

13 For a partial review of these models, see Irwin and Geoghegan (2001).

References

Allison, P. 1995. *Survival Analysis Using the SAS System: A Practical Guide.* Cary, North Carolina: The SAS Institute.

Alonso, W. 1964. *Location and Land Use: Toward a General Theory of Land Rent.* Cambridge, Massachusetts: Harvard University Press.

Anselin, L. 1988. *Spatial Econometrics: Methods and Models.* The Netherlands: Kluwer Academic Publishers

Anselin, L. 2001. 'Spatial Econometrics,' in *A Companion to Theoretical Econometrics,* ed. B. Baltagi. Oxford, United Kingdom: Blackwell Publishers.

Barlowe, R. 1958. *Land Resource Economics.* Englewood Cliffs, New Jersey: Prentice-Hall.

Bell, K. and N. Bockstael. 2000. 'Applying the Generalized Methods of Moments Approach to Spatial Problems Involving Micro-Level Data.' *Review of Economics and Statistics* 82(1): 72–82.

Bell, K. and E.G. Irwin. 2002. 'Spatially Explicit Micro-Level Modeling of Land-Use Change at the Rural-Urban Interface.' *Agricultural Economics* 27: 217–232.

Bockstael, N.E. 1996. 'Modeling Economics and Ecology: The Importance of a Spatial Perspective.' *American Journal of Agricultural Economics* 78(5): 1168–80.

Bockstael, N. and K. Bell. 1998. 'Land Use Patterns and Water Quality: The Effect of Differential Land Management Controls,' in *International Water and Resource Economics Consortium, Conflict and Cooperation on Trans-Boundary Water Resources,* eds. R. Just and S. Netanyahu. Boston, Massachusetts: Kluwer Publishing.

Capozza, D.R. and R.W. Helsley. 1989. 'The Fundamentals of Land Prices and Urban Growth.' *Journal of Urban Economics* 26(3): 295–306.

Cho, S.H., J. Wu, and W.G. Boggess. 2001. 'Measuring Interactions Among Urban Development, Land Use Regulations, and Public Finance.' Department of Agricultural and Resource Economics working paper, Oregon State University.

Chomitz, K. and D.A. Gray. 1995. 'Roads, Land, Markets, and Deforestation: A Spatial Model of Land Use in Belize.' *World Bank Economic Review* 10: 487–512.

Claassen, R., and A. Tegene. 1999. 'Agricultural Land Use Choice: A Discrete Choice Approach.' *Agricultural and Resource Economics Review* 28(1): 26–36.

Fleming, M. 2002. 'A Review of Techniques for Estimating Spatially Dependent Discrete Choice Models,' in *Advances in Spatial Econometrics*, eds. L. Anselin and R. Florax, forthcoming.

Found, W.C. 1971. *A Theoretical Approach to Rural Land-Use Patterns*. London, United Kingdom: Edward Arnold.

Greene, W. 1999. *Econometric Analysis*, 4th ed. Englewood Cliffs, New Jersey: Prentice Hall Publishers.

Hardie, I. and P. Parks. 1997. 'Land Use with Heterogenous Quality: An Application of an Area Base Model.' *American Journal of Agricultural Economics* 79(2): 299–310.

Hardie, I., P. Parks, P. Gottleib, and D. Wear. 2000. 'Responsiveness of Rural and Urban Land Uses to Land Rent Determinants in the U.S. South.' *Land Economics* 76(4): 659–73.

Hite, D., B. Sohngen, and J. Templeton. 2002. 'Property Tax Impacts on the Timing of Land Use Conversion.' Department of Agricultural Economics manuscript, Mississippi State University.

Irwin, E.G., and N.E. Bockstael. 2002. 'Interacting Agents, Spatial Externalities, and the Evolution of Residential Land Use Patterns.' *Journal of Economic Geography* 2(1): 31–54.

Irwin, E.G., and J. Geoghegan. 2001. 'Theory, Data, Methods: Developing Spatially-Explicit Economic Models of Land Use Change.' *Journal of Agriculture, Ecosystems and Environment* 85(1-3): 7–24.

Judge, G.G., R.C. Hill, W.E. Griffiths, H. Lutkepohl, and T.C. Lee. 1988. *Introduction to the Theory and Practice of Econometrics*. New York, New York: John Wiley and Sons.

Kline, J.D., and R.J. Alig. 1999. 'Does Land Use Planning Slow the Conversion of Forest and Farm Lands?' *Growth and Change* 30(1): 3–22.

Landis, J. 1995. 'Imagining Land Use Futures: Applying the California Urban Futures Model.' *Journal of the American Planning Association* 61: 438–457.

Landis, J., and M. Zhang. 1998a. 'The Second Generation of the California Urban Futures Model. Part 1: Model Logic and Theory.' *Environment and Planning A* 30: 657–666.

Landis, J., and M. Zhang. 1998b. 'The Second Generation of the California Urban Futures Model. Part 2:Specification and Calibration Results of the Land Use Change Submodel.' *Environment and Planning B: Planning and Design* 25: 795–824.

Lichtenberg, E. 1989. 'Land Quality, Irrigation Development, and Cropping Patterns in the Northern High Plains.' *American Journal of Agricultural Economics* 71(1): 187–194.

Lubowski, R.N. 2002. 'Determinants of Land-Use Transitions in the United States: Econometric Analysis of Changes Among the Major Land-Use Categories.' PhD dissertation, Harvard University.

MacRae, E.C. 1977. 'Estimation of Time-Varying Markov Processes with Aggregate Data.' *Econometrica* 45(1): 183–98.

Mauldin, T.E., A.J. Plantinga, and R.J. Alig. 1999. 'Determinants of Land Use in Maine with Projections to 2050.' *Northern Journal of Applied Forestry* 16(2): 2–88.

McMillen, D.P. 1989. 'An Empirical Model of Urban Fringe Land Use.' *Land Economics* 65(2): 138–45.

McMillen, D. 1995. 'Selection Bias in Spatial Econometric Models.' *Journal of Regional Science* 35(3): 417–436.

Miller, D.J., and A.J. Plantinga. 1999. 'Modeling Land Use Decisions with Aggregate Data.' *American Journal of Agricultural Economics* 81(1): 180–194.

Muth, R.F. 1969. *Cities and Housing.* Chicago, Illinois: University of Chicago Press.

Nelson, G., and D. Hellerstein. 1997. 'Do Roads Cause Deforestation? Using Satellite Images in Econometric Analysis of Land Use.' *American Journal of Agricultural Economics* 79: 80–88.

Nickerson, C., and N. Bockstael. 2001a. 'Preservation or Development: Competing Uses over the Future of Farmland in Urbanizing Areas.' Selected paper presented at the American Agricultural Economics Association meetings, Chicago, Illinois, August 2001.

Nickerson, C., and N. Bockstael. 2001b. 'Farmland Preservation Programs: Implications for the Spatial Pattern of Preserved, Privately-Owned Farmland.' Selected paper presented at the Regional Science Association International meetings, Charleston, South Carolina, November 2001.

Parker, D., S. Mason, M. Janssen, M. Hoffman, and P. Deadman. 2001. 'Multi-Agent Systems for the Simulation of Land-Use and Land-Cover Change.' Center for the Study of Institutions, Population, and Environmental Change manuscript, Indiana University.

Parks, P.J., and R.A. Kramer. 1995. 'A Policy Simulation of the Wetlands Reserve Program.' *Journal of Environmental Economics and Management* 28(2): 223–240.

Parks, P.J., and B.C. Murray. 1994. 'Land Attributes and Land Allocation: Nonindustrial Forest Use in the Pacific Northwest.' *Forest Science* 40(3): 558–575.

Pinkse, J., and M.E. Slade. 1998. 'Contracting in Space: An Application of Spatial Statistics to Discrete-Choice Models.' *Journal of Econometrics* 85:125–54.

Plantinga, A.J. 1996. 'The Effect of Agricultural Policies on Land Use and Environmental Quality.' *American Journal of Agricultural Economics* 78(4): 1082–1091.

Plantinga, A.J., and S. Ahn. 2002. 'Efficient Policies for Environmental Protection: An Econometric Analysis of Incentives for Land Conversion and Retention.' *Journal of Agricultural and Resource Economics*, forthcoming.

Plantinga, A.J., T. Mauldin, and D.J. Miller. 1999. 'An Econometric Analysis of the Costs of Sequestering Carbon in Forests.' *American Journal of Agricultural Economics* 81(4): 812–24.

Plantinga, A.J., and D.J. Miller. 1997. 'Maximum Entropy Estimation of Land Use Shares and Transitions.' Maine Agricultural and Forest Experiment Station Technical Bulletin No. 166, University of Maine.

Schatzki, S.T. 1998. 'A Theoretical and Empirical Examination of Land Use Change Under Uncertainty.' PhD dissertation, Harvard University.

Schmidt, T.L. 1997. 'Wisconsin Forest Statistics, 1996.' U.S. Department of Agriculture Forest Service Resource Bulletin NC-183. St. Paul, Minnesota: North Central Forest Experiment Station

Stavins, R.N. 1999. 'The Costs of Carbon Sequestration: A Revealed-Preference Approach.' *American Economic Review* 89(4): 994–1009.

Stavins, R.N. and A.B. Jaffe. 1990. 'Unintended Impacts of Public Investments on Private Decisions: The Depletion of Forested Wetlands.' *American Economic Review* 80(3): 337–352.

Vesterby, M., and R.E. Heimlich. 1991. 'Land Use and Demographic Change: Results from Fast-Growth Counties.' *Land Economics* 67:279–91.

Von Thünen, J.H. 1826. *Von Thünen's Isolated State.* Translated by Carla M. Wartenberg, edited by Peter Hall, 1966. New York, New York: Pergamon Press.

Wu, J., and B.W. Brorsen. 1995. 'The Impact of Government Programs and Land Characteristics on Cropping Patterns.' *Canadian Journal of Agricultural Economics* 43(1): 87–104.

Wu, J., and K. Segerson. 1995. 'The Impact of Policies and Land Characteristics on Potential Groundwater Pollution in Wisconsin.' *American Journal of Agricultural Economics* 77(4): 1033–1047.

Chapter 8

An Application of the Land-Use Shares Model

Andrew J. Plantinga

Introduction

In Chapter 7, a land-use shares model that is commonly estimated with aggregate data was discussed. To provide more details on this approach, this chapter presents an application of the model to land use in Wisconsin. The material presented here is based on the models in Plantinga et al. (1999) and Plantinga and Wu (2002). Related applications are found in Lichtenberg (1989), Parks and Murray (1994), Parks and Kramer (1995), Wu and Segerson (1995), Hardie and Parks (1997), and Ahn et al. (2000).

The purpose of estimating land-use shares models is to quantify the relationship between the shares of land allocated to different uses and the hypothesized determinants of land use, such as the net return to a particular use. The estimation results indicate what land-use determinants are important in explaining land-use choices by individuals. Further, the results can be used to estimate how land use will change if the determinants of land use change.

Model Specification

The application presented in the next section employs county-level data for Wisconsin. In this case, the land-use share for a given use is defined as the per cent of total county area devoted to that use (e.g., the share of county land in agriculture). The observed land-use share for use k ($k=1,...,K$) in county i ($i=1,...,I$) at time t ($t=1,...,T$) can be expressed as $y_{ikt}=p_{ikt}+\varepsilon_{ikt}$, where p_{ikt} is the expected share of land allocated to use k, and ε_{ikt} is a random error term with mean zero. The expected share, p_{ikt}, represents the optimal land allocation given the economic and other conditions prevailing in time t. However, since decisions about land use must be made prior to time t, or at least at the beginning of period t, the actual land allocation observed at time t, y_{ikt}, may differ from the optimal allocation due to random occurrences such as bad weather or unanticipated price changes. These random events are captured in the term ε_{ikt} and are assumed to have a zero mean, implying that $E[y_{ikt}]=p_{ikt}$.

The expected shares are assumed to be a function of a vector of unobserved parameters to be estimated, β_k, and explanatory variables, X_{it}. Based on the theory presented in Chapter 6, aggregate land-use shares depend on the net returns to alternative uses as well as the distribution of land quality in the county, the measurement of which is discussed below. Researchers frequently use the following logistic specification of the expected share:

$$(1) \quad p_{ikt} = \frac{e^{\beta_k' X_{it}}}{\sum_{s=1}^{K} e^{\beta_s' X_{it}}},$$

for all i, k, and t. This specification confines the sum of land-use shares to the unit interval. If the shares account for all land in the county, then their sum must equal one, implying that one of the shares is redundant (since it can be computed from the other shares). Incorporating this additivity constraint, the expected share becomes:

$$(2) \quad p_{i1t} = \frac{1}{1 + \sum_{s=2}^{K} e^{\beta_s' X_{it}}}, \quad p_{ikt} = \frac{e^{\beta_k' X_{it}}}{1 + \sum_{s=2}^{K} e^{\beta_s' X_{it}}}, \quad (k=2,\ldots,K).$$

Another advantage of the logistic specification is that the model of observed shares can be transformed to yield estimating equations that are linear in the parameters. Following Zellner and Lee (1965), the natural logarithm of each observed share normalized on a common share (below, y_{i1t}) is approximately equal to

$$(3) \quad \ln(y_{ikt} / y_{i1t}) = \beta_k' X_{it} + \mu_{ikt},$$

for $k=2,\ldots,K$, where μ_{ikt} is the transformed error term.[1] The model in (3) consists of $K-1$ equations that can be estimated using standard linear regression techniques. In each equation, the estimated parameters measure the marginal effects of the explanatory variables on the log of the normalized share. As discussed below, it is often more informative to compute the marginal effect of each variable on an estimate of the expected share in Equation (1).

An Application of the Land-Use Shares Model to Wisconsin

We begin this section with a discussion of the data used in the application. Next, we present and discuss the results. Additional discussion of the model can be found in Plantinga et al. (1999) and Plantinga and Wu (2002), and an application to biodiversity is found in Matthews et al. (2002).

Data

The model in Equation (3) is estimated with data for Wisconsin counties at two points in time (1983 and 1996), corresponding to the dates of forest inventories conducted by the U.S. Department of Agriculture's Forest Service. County forest statistics are summarized in Spencer et al. (1988) and Schmidt (1997). Using these data, we measure y_{i2t} as the share of land (in county i at time t) that is classified as private timberland. The use of forestland in public ownerships (e.g., state and national forestland) is assumed to be determined by non-economic factors and is excluded from y_{i2t}. For the same reason, we exclude from y_{i2t} the small amount of private forestland in Wisconsin that is not classified as timberland due to low productivity. Data from the Census of Agriculture are used to measure the share of land in agricultural uses, denoted y_{i3t} (U.S. Department of Agriculture, National Agricultural Statistics Service). This measure includes all land in crop and pasture uses. We omit land enrolled in the Conservation Reserve Program because commodity production is prohibited on these lands. To compute y_{i3t} for 1983 and 1996, we must interpolate between Census observations for 1982 and 1987, and 1992 and 1997.

The area of land in urban and other uses (e.g., wetlands, corridors for electrical lines) is calculated as the difference between the total land area in the county and the areas of private timberland and agricultural land. Accordingly, the urban and other share is given by $y_{i1t}=1-y_{i2t}-y_{i3t}$. It would be cleaner to include only urban uses of land in this category. Unfortunately, data on urban land areas are not readily available. Beginning in 1990, the U.S. Bureau of the Census began reporting county estimates of urban land area in the Decennial Census of Population and Housing (U.S. Department of Commerce, Bureau of the Census). However, these figures are based on population statistics, rather than on direct observations of land use. With the rapid development of satellite imagery, the availability of data on urban land use has been increasing.

As indicated in the theory section (Chapter 6), the exogenous variables (X_{it}) in the land-use shares model include measures of the net return to each use and the distribution of land quality. In measuring net returns, one immediately faces a challenge posed by the differing periodicity of returns to agriculture and forestry. In most cases, returns to agriculture are realized on an annual basis while returns to forestry are realized periodically when a stand is harvested. To achieve consistency in the returns measures, one solution is to compute the present value of net returns to each use over an infinite time horizon.[2] Following this approach, net returns to forestry (W_{i2t}) and agriculture (W_{i3t}) are given by:

$$(4a) \quad W_{i2t} = \frac{\delta^{m_i}}{1-\delta^{m_i}} R_{i2t}$$

$$(4b) \quad W_{i3t} = \frac{1}{1-\delta} R_{i3t} ,$$

where δ is the discount factor equal to $(1+r)^{-1}$, r is the discount rate, R_{i2t} is the net return to forestry in county i that is realized every m_i years, and R_{i3t} is the annual return to agriculture in county i. The rotation length (m_i) has a county index to reflect the possibility that rotation ages may vary across counties due to differences in the tree species found there. Note, as well, that the net returns to forestry and agriculture are indexed by the current time t. This reflects an assumption that landowners consider only current returns in computing the present value of the stream of future returns.

In the Wisconsin application, W_{i2t} is measured as the present discounted value (five per cent discount rate) of an infinite stream of real timber net revenues per acre (1982=100). Revenue streams are calculated separately for major tree species in each county using species-specific stumpage prices (from assorted publications from the Wisconsin Department of Natural Resources), yield curves (from Birdsey 1992), and rotations corresponding to the Faustmann rotation for a five per cent discount rate.[3] Lagged (period t–1) prices are used to compute revenues since these are the prices observed by landowners when they make land-use decisions for period t. Timber management costs are ignored because there is little intensively managed forestland in Wisconsin. We lack complete data on tree planting costs and the data that are available (e.g., from the Conservation Reserve Program) suggest that these costs exhibit relatively little variation. Thus, we assume that tree planting costs (in real terms) are constant across space and time. In this case, the effects of planting costs will be measured in the intercept term included for the forestland share. County-level measures of average forestry returns are constructed as a weighted average of species-specific returns where weights reflect species composition within the county. Species weights are taken from the forest inventory reports mentioned above.

W_{i3t} is the present discounted value (five per cent discount rate) of an infinite stream of real annual per acre net revenues from crop and pastureland (1982=100). For each crop and pasture use (e.g., corn, soybeans, hay), annual net revenues are computed as the product of the average county price (in period t–1; see discussion above) and yield less variable production costs. Yield data is from the Wisconsin Agricultural Statistics Service and production cost data are from farm budgets developed by the University of Wisconsin Cooperative Extension Service. We assume that the fixed costs of agricultural production (e.g., machinery) are constant across crops, and that the fixed costs for holding land (e.g., property taxes) are constant across land-use alternatives. In this case, the effect of fixed costs is captured in the intercept term for the agricultural land-use share. A county average return is computed as a weighted average of crop and pasture net revenues, where weights correspond to crop and pasture shares in that county. The crop and pasture share data are from the Census of Agriculture.

The third land-use category includes urban and other uses. Due to data limitations, a measure of the average net return to developed land in a county is difficult to construct (see Lubowski 2002).[4] An alternative is to use a variable that proxies for these returns. One measure used frequently in shares models is population density, which indicates the pressures in the county for land development. In the Wisconsin application, population density is the total county population divided by total county land area and is denoted PD_{it}. Data are from the Census of Population and Housing and interpolation is used to form estimates for 1983 and 1996. To control for the distribution of land quality within each county, we develop three measures based on land capability class (LCC) data (U.S. Department of Agriculture 1973). LCC ratings are derived from parcel-level soil surveys and based on twelve soil characteristics (e.g., permeability, slope). The rating for a land parcel ranges from I to VIII, where class I land is the most productive for agriculture and class VIII land has practically no capacity for agricultural production. We measure the average land quality in each county (that is, the average LCC rating of parcels in the county) and denote this variable AQ_i. To reflect the variation of land quality within the county, we measure the proportion of highly quality land in the county (that is, land in LCC classes I and II), and the share of medium quality land (land in LCC classes III and IV). These variables are denoted HQ_i and MQ_i, respectively. The land quality variables are not indexed by time since land quality tends to remain constant over periods of decades.[5]

Econometric Estimation and Results

Corresponding to Equation (3), we compute the logarithm of forest and agricultural land-use shares normalized on the share of land in urban and other uses, that is, $ln(y_{i2t}/y_{i1t})$ and $ln(y_{i3t}/y_{i1t})$. Since our two equations have the same set of regressors, ordinary least squares applied separately to each equation is identical to seemingly unrelated regression, and we do not have to make an explicit adjustment for cross-equation correlation. The logarithmic transformation is known to induce heteroskedasticity in the error terms (see Zellner and Lee 1965). A standard adjustment for heteroskedasticity in shares models is described by Maddala (1983). This procedure, however, applies to grouped data. Grouped data is formed from a sample of n observations, where researchers observe the number of observations (n_k) in each category k. In the land-use context, one would observe the number of forest plots, agricultural plots, etc., from a sample of n plots. In our application, the land-use data is taken from different sources and, thus, do not conform to this sampling process. Accordingly, we use White's test to evaluate the null hypothesis of homoskedasticity under a general alternative hypothesis (see Davidson and McKinnon 1993). We fail to reject the null at the five per cent level in both equations. Finally, to determine if the parameters in our model are stationary, we test the null hypothesis of no change in the set of parameters over time, and for each equation fail to reject the null at the five per cent level.

Results are presented in Table 8.1. Estimates of the model parameters are reported in columns two and five. The effects of the regressors on individual land-use shares cannot be determined directly from the estimated equations because the dependent variables are a function of two shares. Alternatively, we can use Equation (2) to compute $\partial p_k/\partial X_l$, where X_l is the *l*th regressor, and evaluate the resulting expression at the estimated values of β_2 and β_3 and the mean values of the regressors. For example, the marginal effect of forestry returns (W_2) on the forest land-use share is:

$$(5) \quad \frac{\partial p_2}{\partial W_2} = \frac{e^{\hat{\beta}_2'\overline{X}}\hat{\beta}_{22} + e^{\hat{\beta}_2'\overline{X}}e^{\hat{\beta}_3'\overline{X}}[\hat{\beta}_{22} - \hat{\beta}_{23}]}{\left(1 + e^{\hat{\beta}_2'\overline{X}} + e^{\hat{\beta}_3'\overline{X}}\right)^2},$$

where β_{22} and β_{23} are the coefficients on forestry returns in the forestland and agricultural land equations, respectively, hats indicate estimated values, and bars indicate mean values. Estimates of the partial effects are reported in columns three and six of Table 8.1. The corresponding elasticities are given by $(\partial p_k/\partial X_l)(X_l/p_k)$ and evaluated in a similar fashion (columns four and seven). The partial effects and elasticities reported are nonlinear functions of all the model parameters, which complicates the estimation of standard errors for these expressions. For this application, we computed standard errors using the delta method described by Greene (2000).

The results largely conform to prior expectations. Considering the estimated partial effects, we see that the returns to forestry (W_2) have a positive and significant effect (at the five per cent level), all else equal, on the forest share, and a negative and significant effect on the agricultural share. The returns to agriculture (W_3) have the opposite effect, negatively influencing the forest share and positively influencing the agricultural share. Population density (PD) has a negative and significant effect on the forest share, but an insignificant effect on the agricultural share. This result suggests that urbanization primarily occurred on forestland during the period studied.

A higher average LCC rating (AQ) positively and negatively affects forest and agricultural shares, respectively. Recall that higher LCC ratings correspond to lower quality land. These results indicate that counties with lower average land quality have more forests and counties with higher average land quality have more agricultural land. The share of high quality land (HQ) is not found to have a significant effect on the forest or the agricultural shares. We would expected counties with more (less) high quality land to have more agricultural (forest) land. However, consistent with expectations, the share of medium quality land (MQ) is positively and significantly related to the agricultural share and negatively related to the forest share.

The estimates of the elasticities reveal that forest and agricultural land-use shares are much more responsive to agricultural returns than to forest returns. A one per cent increase in agricultural returns reduces the forest share and increases the agricultural share by approximately two per cent. In contrast, the land-use shares change by only about 0.15 per cent for a one per cent increase in forest returns. One possible explanation for this result is that landowners are less responsive to increases in forest returns because revenues from timber harvesting are realized periodically and often at a distant time in the future. In contrast, net revenues from agricultural production are typically realized on an annual basis. If landowners have limited access to capital markets, they may not be able to smooth lumpy revenue streams from forestry through borrowing and, thus, may prefer the more regular revenue stream from agriculture.

Table 8.1 Econometric results for the Wisconsin land-use model[a, b]

Variable	Forestland Equation			Agricultural Land Equation		
	Estimate	Partial	Elasticity	Estimate	Partial	Elasticity
Intercept	−1.30			−2.75*		
	(−1.89)			(−3.98)		
W_2	0.01	0.00*	0.15*	−0.01	−0.00*	−0.13*
	(1.07)	(2.01)	(2.01)	(−1.24)	(−2.02)	(−2.02)
W_3	−0.00*	−0.00*	−1.89*	0.00*	0.00*	2.09*
	(−2.16)	(−8.19)	(−8.19)	(8.57)	(10.69)	(10.69)
PD	−1.93*	−0.28*	−0.13*	−1.07*	0.01	0.00
	(−5.75)	(−4.03)	(−4.03)	(−3.16)	(0.09)	(0.09)
AQ	0.61*	0.15*	1.74*	−0.15	−0.12*	−1.05*
	(5.47)	(6.77)	(6.78)	(−1.30)	(−4.79)	(−4.79)
HQ	0.18	−0.01	−0.12	0.37	0.07	0.07
	(0.62)	(−0.21)	(−0.21)	(1.29)	(1.03)	(1.03)
MQ	0.12	−0.25*	−0.26*	2.02*	0.48*	0.37*
	(0.43)	(−4.37)	(−4.37)	(7.06)	(7.45)	(7.45)
R^2	0.65			0.64		

[a] *t*–ratios are in parentheses and * indicates significance at the five per cent level.
[b] Columns 3 and 6 give the partial effect of a variable on the forest and agricultural land-use shares and columns 4 and 7 give the corresponding elasticity. Partial effects and elasticities are computed at the mean values of the variables.

Table 8.2 Effects of the independent variables on the urban and other land shares[a, b]

Variable	Partial		Elasticity	
	Coefficient	t-ratio	Coefficient	t-ratio
W_2	0.0002	0.28	0.02	0.28
W_3	−0.0001*	−4.63	−1.09*	−4.63
PD	0.2700*	5.06	0.17*	5.06
AQ	−0.0500	−1.18	−0.10	−1.18
HQ	−0.2200*	−4.94	−0.30*	−4.94
MQ	−0.0300*	−1.93	−0.51*	−1.93

[a] * indicates significance at the five per cent level.
[b] Column two gives the partial effect of a variable on the urban and other land-use share and column three gives the corresponding elasticity. Partial effects and elasticities are computed at the mean values of the variables.

Using the definition of the expected share of land in urban and other uses (Equation [2]), we can compute the corresponding partial effects of the regressors and the elasticities (Table 8.2). The results show that higher returns to agriculture reduce the share of land in urban and other uses. However, no significant effect of forest returns is found. These results make sense if one considers that agricultural returns tend to be higher than forest returns and, thus, more competitive with returns to urban uses. As expected, the effect of urban returns (proxied for by population density) on the urban and other share is positive and significantly different from zero (five per cent level). Two of the three land quality variables have significant effects on the urban and other share. Higher proportions of medium and high quality land, all else equal, reduce the share of urban and other land. These results may reflect, as above, the competitiveness of agriculture with developed land uses. Counties with higher quality land will tend to have more agricultural land and less developed land since returns to agriculture increase with land quality. No significant effect of average land quality on the urban and other land share is found.

Discussion

In this chapter, we have used a land-use shares model to study the determinants of forest, agricultural, and urban and other land in Wisconsin. The estimation results strongly support the notion that land-use decisions are driven by net returns to alternative uses of the land. Furthermore, aggregate land allocations depend, for reasons indicated in Chapters 6 and 7, on the distribution of land quality within a county. These findings for Wisconsin are similar to the results of land-use share studies of other regions that consistently find that net returns and land quality variables influence the shares of land to alternative uses (see the references cited at the start of the chapter).

The results for Wisconsin have several implications for land-use policy. Consider, first, the finding that forest and agricultural land-use shares are less responsive to forest returns than to agricultural returns. A good deal of attention has been given to the possibility of converting agricultural land to forest in order to sequester carbon and mitigate the effects of climate change. Our results suggest that landowners will be less responsive to subsidies for forestry, which would increase forest returns, than they will be to taxes on agricultural land, which would decrease agricultural returns. Matters of political feasibility aside, it may be less costly to achieve a given amount of afforestation in Wisconsin with an agricultural tax, as compared to a forestry subsidy.

Another policy-relevant finding emerges from the estimated effects of forest and agricultural returns on the urban and other share (recall that agricultural returns were found to have a negative and significant effect and the effect of forest returns was insignificant). All 50 states have land-use policies designed to limit the conversion of rural lands to developed uses. For instance, through use value assessment programs, taxes are levied on agricultural and forestland according to the value of the land for agricultural and forest production rather than for potential (and often higher-valued) developed uses. Our results suggest that, at least in Wisconsin, such financial incentives are more likely to be effective at preventing the development of agricultural lands than forestlands.

A final policy implication relates to the estimated effects of land quality on forest and agricultural land-use shares. Stavins and Jaffe (1990) find that government flood control projects increased the rate of conversion of forested wetlands in the Mississippi Delta region by improving the quality of land for agriculture. Consistent with these results, we find for Wisconsin that higher land quality reduces forest shares and increases agricultural shares. As such, changes in land quality, resulting from government policies or deliberate actions on the part of landowners (e.g., installation of water drainage systems), can cause changes in aggregate land allocations, with corresponding effects on the environmental variables of interest (e.g., habitat for wildlife).

Two limitations of the analysis presented above should be mentioned. First, the estimated partial effects and elasticities are valid only for relatively small changes in the regressors. This suggests that our conclusions regarding land-use policies will only apply to policies that have relatively small effects on net returns and land quality variables. Larger policy effects can be evaluated by recomputing the expected shares in Equation (2) for each level of the policy variable. For instance, if we are considering a subsidy, S, for forestry, we would substitute W_2+S for W_2 in the expression for the expected forest share. This yields $p_2(S)$ and the effect of the subsidy on the forest share would be estimated as $p_2(S=S)-p_2(S=0)$. As with all predictions, the accuracy of these estimates will be higher if they fall within the range of the historical data (e.g., if W_2+S was observed historically).

A second limitation of the analysis relates to the use of shares models for estimating changes in land use. In estimating the shares model, we use data on the acres of land in each use. In other words, we estimated the model with data on *levels*. Using the results to then estimate *changes* in land use may not be appropriate if there are large costs associated with moving between uses. Such conversion costs cannot be incorporated into a shares model in any obvious way because changes in land use are not modeled explicitly in this framework. If conversion costs are negligible, or, put another way, the cost of moving from one land-use level to another is small, then a shares model can yield reliable estimates of changes in land use. Otherwise, an alternative modeling strategy that explicitly represents the dynamics of land-use change may be warranted.

Notes

1 See Zellner and Lee (1965) for more details on the error structure of the model.
2 This formulation implies that, at each point in time, landowners allocate their land to the use providing the largest present discounted value of net returns. Plantinga (1996) provides conditions under which this rule is the solution to an optimal intertemporal land allocation problem with net returns evaluated at current prices.

3   The Faustmann rotation is the rotation age that maximizes the present value of discounted timber revenues over an infinite time horizon (see Conrad 1999).
4   An even greater challenge is the measurement of net returns to other uses such as wetlands.
5   See the discussion of the potential effects of government policies on land quality.

References

Ahn, S., A.J. Plantinga, and R.J. Alig. 2000. 'Predicting Future Forest Land Area: A Comparison of Econometric Approaches.' *Forest Science* 46(3): 363–76.

Birdsey, R.A. 1992. 'Carbon Storage and Accumulation in United States Forest Ecosystems.' U.S. Department of Agriculture, Forest Service General Technical Report WO-59. Washington, District of Columbia.

Conrad, J.M. 1999. *Resource Economics*. New York, New York: Cambridge University Press.

Davidson, R., and J.G. MacKinnon. 1993. *Estimation and Inference in Econometrics*. New York, New York: Oxford University Press.

Greene, W.H. 2000. *Econometric Analysis*. Upper Saddle River, New Jersey: Prentice Hall.

Hardie, I.W., and P.J. Parks. 1997. 'Land Use with Heterogeneous Quality: An Application of an Area Base Model.' *American Journal of Agricultural Economics* 79(2): 299–310.

Lichtenberg, E. 1989. 'Land Quality, Irrigation Development, and Cropping Patterns in the Northern High Plains.' *American Journal of Agricultural Economics* 71(1): 187–194.

Lubowski, R.N. 2002. 'Determinants of Land-Use Transitions in the United States: Econometric Analysis of Changes Among the Major Land-Use Categories.' PhD dissertation, Harvard University.

Maddala, G.S. 1983. *Limited Dependent and Qualitative Variables in Econometrics*. New York, New York: Cambridge University Press.

Matthews, S., R. O'Connor, and A.J. Plantinga. 2002. 'Quantifying the Impacts on Biodiversity of Policies for Carbon Sequestration in Forests.' *Ecological Economics* 40(1): 71–87.

Parks, P.J., and R.A. Kramer. 1995. 'A Policy Simulation of the Wetlands Reserve Program.' *Journal of Environmental Economics and Management* 28(2): 223–40.

Parks, P.J., and B.C. Murray. 1994. 'Land Attributes and Land Allocation: Nonindustrial Forest Use in the Pacific Northwest.' *Forest Science* 40(3): 558–575.

Plantinga, A.J. 1996. 'The Effect of Agricultural Policies on Land Use and Environmental Quality.' American Journal of Agricultural Economics 78 (4): 1082–91.

Plantinga, A.J., T. Mauldin, and D.J. Miller. 1999. 'An Econometric Analysis of the Cost of Sequestering Carbon in Forests.' *American Journal of Agricultural Economics* 81(4): 812–24.

Plantinga, A.J., and J. Wu. 2003. 'Co-Benefits from Carbon Sequestration in Forests: Evaluating Reductions in Agricultural Externalities from an Afforestation Policy in Wisconsin.' *Land Economics* 79(1): 74–85.

Schmidt, T.L. 1997. 'Wisconsin Forest Statistics, 1996.' U.S. Department of Agriculture, Forest Service Resource Bulletin NC-183. St. Paul, Minnesota: North Central Research Station.

Spencer, J.S., W.B. Smith, J.T. Hahn, and G.K. Raile. 1988. 'Wisconsin's Fourth Forest Inventory, 1983.' U.S. Department of Agriculture, Forest Service Resource Bulletin NC-107. St. Paul, Minnesota: North Central Research Station.

Stavins, R., and A. Jaffe. 1990. 'Unintended Impacts of Public Investment on Private Decisions: The Depletion of Forest Wetlands.' *American Economic Review* 80(3): 337–52.

U.S. Department of Agriculture. 1973. 'Land Capability Classification.' Soil Conservation Service Agricultural Handbook No.210. Washington, District of Columbia.

U.S. Department of Agriculture, National Agricultural Statistics Service. *Census of Agriculture.* Retrieved from: http://govinfo.kerr.orst.edu.

U.S. Department of Commerce, Bureau of the Census. *Census of Population and Housing.* Retrieved from: http://www.census.gov.

University of Wisconsin Cooperative Extension Service. http://cf.uwex.edu/ces.

Wisconsin Agricultural Statistics Service. *Wisconsin Agricultural Statistics Publication.* Retrieved from: http://www.nass.usda.gov/wi/index.htm.

Wisconsin Department of Natural Resources. http://www.dnr.state.wi.us.

Wu, J., and K. Segerson. 1995. 'The Impact of Policies and Land Characteristics on Potential Groundwater Pollution in Wisconsin.' *American Journal of Agricultural Economics* 77(4): 1033–47.

Zellner, A., and T.H. Lee. 1965. 'Joint Estimation of Relationships Involving Discrete Random Variables.' *Econometrica* 33(Apr.): 382–94.

Chapter 9

Estimating a Spatially Explicit Model of Residential Land-Use Change to Understand and Predict Patterns of Urban Growth at the Rural-Urban Fringe

Elena G. Irwin and Kathleen P. Bell

Introduction

The ability to understand and predict changes in land-use patterns as the result of individuals' economic decisions is necessary for the effective design of environmental, public finance, and growth management policies. Changes in land-use pattern are the cumulative result of numerous individual decisions regarding the use of lands. Accordingly, the study of land-use change at a micro or individual scale provides for novel opportunities to understand the human behavior underlying these decisions and assess the effects of environmental, public finance, and growth management policies on these decisions. As many local and state governments in the U.S. grapple with increasing growth pressures, the need to understand the economic factors that influence individual choices regarding the use of land has taken on added urgency in recent years. In this chapter, we describe an empirical study of residential land-use change in Maryland at the rural-urban fringe. Our description focuses on the estimation of a micro-economic model of land-use change, giving particular attention to the spatial aspects of the model as well as its predictive capabilities.

The rural-urban fringe begins where suburbs end, and extends into rural areas. At the rural-urban fringe, changes in land use often coincide with transitions from traditional, rural communities to more developed, urban communities. Nelson (1992) and Daniels (1999) refer to these communities in transition as 'exurban' areas. Between 1960 and 1990, population in exurban counties increased by 60 million people, which accounted for over 25 per cent of the population growth within this time period (Nelson 1992). Coupled with this growth are evolving patterns of low-density development that have resulted in an increasingly low-density and sprawled land-use pattern. The pattern of land-use change in Calvert County, Maryland, one of the fastest growing exurban counties in Maryland, is typical of this growth. Between 1981 and 1997, this county experienced a 94 per cent increase in population and a 191 per cent increase in the number of acres in low-density residential use. Because exurban areas have outpaced urban and suburban areas in population growth for the last several decades, growth pressures are commonly observed at the rural-urban fringe. The rate and extent of development in these areas has raised public concerns regarding issues such as loss of open space and agricultural lands, traffic congestion, and crowding in schools. Models such as the one developed here provide a means to inform the development of policies aimed at managing these pressures by providing a tool to assess the effects of alternative policies and to ascertain the influence of different factors on land-use choices at the individual parcel level. In short, these models enable communities to consider 'what if' types of questions and to better anticipate the location and timing of future development.

In this chapter, we develop a spatially explicit economic model of land-use change suitable for addressing changes in land use at the rural-urban fringe. As their name suggests, spatially-explicit models emphasize spatial relationships. Hence, a spatially explicit model of land-use change devotes specific attention to the absolute and relative locations of land-use changes, variation in characteristics of the landscape over space, and potential interdependencies between decisions over space. Spatially explicit economic models were introduced in Chapter 7, which provides an overview of different empirical methods used to model land-use change. Recent advances in data and computing, notably Geographic Information System (GIS) data and modeling tools, have fostered the evolution of spatially explicit models in a variety of disciplines, and the evolution of spatially explicit models of land-use change will certainly be influenced by future advances in spatial computing and data availability. We use a duration modeling framework, as reviewed in Chapter 7, which allows us to better capture how the cumulative effects of changes in variables over time influence future land-use decisions and the timing of land conversion. Because the timing of land conversion is often of great interest to communities, the duration modeling framework offers an appealing perspective from which to model land-use change.

Our ability to address the spatial heterogeneity of the landscape over time is the direct result of having access to parcel-level land use data. These data enable us to track the characteristics of land parcels over time and space and permit a richer categorization of rural land-use change than that afforded by publicly available macro-scale land use data. We take a spatially disaggregated approach to modeling residential land-use change that accounts for the spatial heterogeneity of policies (e.g., zoning) and landscape features (e.g., slope, soil type, locational amenities) that influence individual land-use decisions. The residential land-use change model described here focuses on the conversion of undeveloped lands such as agricultural, forest, and open-space lands to residential use. This subset of land-use changes is of greatest concern for local and state policymakers interested in changes at the rural-urban fringe. We do not explicitly deal with commercial development, which makes up a relatively small proportion of developed uses in most exurban areas and typically follows residential development into these areas. However, we recognize that land-use changes associated with commercial development are also of interest to policymakers and citizens.

Spatially Explicit Models of Land-Use Change

As noted in Chapter 7, several varieties of spatially explicit models have been developed to examine the causes and consequences of land-use changes. Many of these models are developed to serve as predictive or forecasting tools. In practice, researchers typically gather data on land-use changes, estimate an empirical model of these changes, and then use the results of the model to characterize possible future land-use patterns. Specifically, the parameters from an estimated model are used to predict or forecast the spatial pattern of land use and land-cover change that could occur under different scenarios, where the scenarios involve simulating expected changes in explanatory variables or extending the time horizon of the modeling exercise. In general, spatially explicit models of land-use change are distinguished by the extent to which they are derived from an underlying conceptual framework that is based on individual landowner behavior.

Duration Model of Residential Land-Use Change

As noted in Chapter 7, a duration modeling approach is well-suited to the study of land-use change. The model described below was developed with the objective of characterizing the economic behavior underlying the conversion of agricultural, forest, and open lands to residential land use in Maryland at the rural-urban fringe. Accordingly, the model focuses on characterizing the returns to land in different uses at the rural-urban fringe, with an emphasis on how the returns in residential use compare to returns in other uses, such as agriculture or forestry, over time. As emphasized in Chapter 3, economic models of land-use change rely on the relative return of land in different uses to explain conversions of land from one use to another. The duration modeling framework permits explicit consideration of how these returns vary over time.

Conceptual Framework

We start from the viewpoint of a profit-maximizing landowner who owns an undeveloped land parcel and makes a discrete choice in every period regarding the subdivision of the parcel for residential use.[1] The individual landowner chooses either to convert the parcel by subdividing the parcel into multiple residential lots or to keep the parcel in an undeveloped use. Hence, conditional on the parcel being undeveloped in the present period, the individual's decision is a binary discrete choice of converting the parcel to residential use or keeping the parcel in an undeveloped use, such that the present discounted sum of all future expected returns from the land is maximized. Therefore, the individual faces a dynamic optimization problem in which he/she will choose to convert the parcel to residential use when the expected present discounted value of the parcel in residential use net of conversion costs and opportunity costs is maximized over an infinite time horizon. This optimization problem is consistent with the optimal timing model laid out in Chapter 6, Equation (7), in which the particular land-use change is from an undeveloped to a residential use and period D is the optimal time of conversion.

Let $V_{jrt|u}$ represent the net expected return from converting parcel j, which is currently in undeveloped land use u, to use r at time t, and δ is the discount rate. Rewriting the first order condition given in Chapter 7, Equation (8), in discrete time rather than continuous time yields the optimal decision rule:

$$(1) \quad V_{jrD|u} - V_{juD|u} > \delta V_{jrD+1|u} ,$$

which states that parcel j will be converted in period D only if the expected returns from converting, net the one-period opportunity cost of conversion, are greater than the discounted net returns from converting in period $D+1$. The landowner will convert the property in the first period if this relationship holds.

The conceptual model is further refined by recognizing that only a subset of the relevant parcel-level features are observable to researchers. Therefore, we adjust the expression of net expected returns to include a random portion, ε. These assumptions permit the expression of the land conversion rule for parcel j in probabilistic terms as:

$$(2) \quad P_{jrD|u} = \Pr\{V_{jrD|u} - V_{juD|u} + \varepsilon_{jD} > \delta V_{jrD+1|u} + \varepsilon_{jD+1}\} ,$$

where ε_{jD} and ε_{jD+1} represent the unobserved components associated with parcel j in time periods D and $D+1$, respectively, and P_{jrDu} is the probability that parcel j is converted from undeveloped use u to residential use r in time period D.

There are a variety of ways to model landowners' expectations of future returns from land conversion, $V_{jrt+1|u}$. Myopic expectations assume a lack of foresight such that the individual landowner uses information available in the current period to establish their expectations of returns in the next period. In this case, myopic expectations result in equating $V_{jrD|u}$ and $V_{jrD+1|u}$. Given this equality, and rearranging (2) yields:

$$(3) \quad P_{jrD|u} = \Pr\{\varepsilon_{jD+1} - \varepsilon_{jD} < (1-\delta)V_{jrD|u} - V_{juD|u}\} .$$

In further specifying the model, we hypothesize that net expected returns to maintaining a parcel in an undeveloped state as well as the net expected returns from developing a parcel will be a function of the current characteristics of the parcel. These include: physical features of the land parcel, e.g., soil type and slope, that influence the returns to the land in an undeveloped status as well as the costs of developing the parcel; characteristics related to the location of the parcel relative to features that alter the returns to development, e.g., distance to employment centers, shopping and recreational opportunities, and local land uses that generate spatial externalities; and policy variables that influence the returns and costs of developing land, e.g., the provision of public sewer and water to the parcel, the quality of public services, including schools, and zoning requirements that dictate the allowable land use and density of the parcel. For simplicity, let Z_jD represent the vector of these attributes of parcel j in period D and β the corresponding vector of parameters that denote the marginal effects of these variables on the probability of conversion. Then we can rewrite (3) as:

$$(4) \quad P_{jrD|u} = \Pr\{\omega_{jD} < f(Z_{jD};\beta,\delta\},$$

where $\omega_{jD} = \varepsilon_{jD+1} - \varepsilon_{jD}$. Expression (4) provides the conceptual foundation for the empirical model described in the subsequent section.

Empirical Model

While a variety of discrete choice methods are capable of empirically modeling the land-conversion decision rule shown above, we opt to employ a duration model because it is capable of describing both the temporal and spatial aspects of land conversion decisions. As explained in Chapter 7, duration models explicitly account for the timing of a qualitative change from one state to another and therefore are an appropriate way to capture the cumulative effects of explanatory variables on the probability of land conversion to residential use.[2] Given the nature of land-use changes in growing exurban areas, in which the timing of the conversion is often of great interest, duration models offer an intuitively appealing approach. In this case, we are interested in the timing of land conversion from an undeveloped land-use state to a residential land-use state.

As described in Chapter 7, events are the basis of duration models. The duration length (i.e., the time until an event occurs) is viewed as the realization of an underlying random process and therefore is treated as a random variable with a probability distribution. Models differ by their assumptions regarding the distribution of the duration length. Here, an event is the change from an undeveloped land-use state to a residential land-use state. Our empirical model begins with a sample of undeveloped land parcels and considers their duration in this state over several years. We define the survival function as the probability that the parcel is not developed in period t and the hazard rate as the conditional probability that a parcel is developed in period t, given that it has remained in an undeveloped state until time t. Varying assumptions are possible regarding the distribution of durations. We use the proportional hazards model (or Cox regression model) to estimate the land-use conversion model. This model is advantageous because it does not require a distributional assumption of the duration length. However, this comes at the cost of imposing a particular functional form that requires separability of the baseline hazard rate from the other variables of the model. Applying this model to the probability expression in (4), let λ_D represent the exponential of the baseline hazard rate and assume that the log of the hazard rate is linear in Z_{jD}, the vector of parcel j's attributes that are hypothesized to influence the expected returns to parcel j in residential and undeveloped states. This second assumption implies that we can write the hazard rate itself as a function of the exponential of $Z_{jD}{*}\beta$, where β is the corresponding parameter vector. Therefore, the hazard rate for parcel j can be expressed as:

(5) $h_{jD} = \lambda_d * \exp(Z_{jD}\beta).$

Cox's method is a semiparametric approach that relies on formulating the likelihood in terms of a ratio of the hazard functions, so that the baseline hazard, λ_D, drops out. Because only the baseline hazard is assumed to be a function of duration length D, which is the random process that is being modeled, an assumption of an error distribution for the resulting expression is unnecessary. However, because of the functional form assumption imposed on the model, the hazard rate that is estimated takes the form of a logistic function. This resulting expression is called the partial likelihood function, which gives the conditional probability that, given an event occurs in a particular time period, it occurs to a specific individual.[3]

Data

A variety of parcel-level landscape features, including policy attributes such as zoning, sewer provision, and proximity to roads, are assumed to influence the returns to converting a parcel to residential use. The model is estimated using parcel-level land-use change data from a central Maryland exurban region that surrounds the Washington, District of Columbia and Baltimore, Maryland metropolitan areas. By using the estimated parameters to then predict future changes in development patterns, it is possible to link the factors that influence parcel-level land-use changes with predictions of regional patterns of urbanization.

Data used to estimate the land-use conversion model include spatially defined, micro-level data on land parcels from the State of Maryland's Office of Planning's geo-coded tax assessment data base (MD Property View). The construction of this data set required merging data from several tax assessment data sources, some of which are not geo-coded, in order to compile a seven-year history of 'convertible' parcels within a five-county study area located in the exurban areas of Washington, District of Columbia and Baltimore, Maryland. These counties include Anne Arundel, Calvert, Charles, and Saint Mary's counties. The data set is comprised of all parcels that, as of January 1991, were large enough to accommodate a major subdivision of at least five houses given current zoning, and that could have been converted to residential use. The year of conversion for those that were converted during the period 1991 through 1997 is also included. This yields a total of 6,750 observations. The data set contains variables that pertain to the individual parcel, including lot size and land use. Because the centroids of the parcels are geo-coded, it was also possible to locate the parcels in space and, using a Geographic Information System (GIS), to generate a variety of additional spatial attributes associated with the individual parcels, including zoning, distance measures, and public sewer access.

The dependent variable is a binary variable that takes on the value of one in the first period that a parcel is converted from an undeveloped to residential use, which is referred to as an event; otherwise its value is zero. An event is defined here as the subdivision of an undeveloped parcel into residential lots in preparation for house construction. Any parcel that was not converted by 1997, the last year for which data are available, is censored. Based on this definition, the dataset contains 135 events and 6,615 censored observations, where events are parcels that were converted to residential use and censored observations are parcels that remained in undeveloped use from 1991 through 1997.

Because the empirical model is estimated using a reduced form approach, data on explanatory variables that would explain returns in residential use, undeveloped use, and the costs of conversion from undeveloped to residential use were sought. The following explanatory variables are included in the model. A soil quality indicator (GOODAG) is used as a proxy for agricultural profitability, which, all else equal is expected to delay the timing of a parcel's conversion. The soil quality variable equals one for all natural soils groups designated by the Soil Conservation Service as prime farmland and zero otherwise. The cost of converting a parcel is proxied using a dummy that measures a parcel's relative steepness of slope and soil suitability (COST). Specifically, this conversion cost dummy is equal to one for parcels that have steep slopes (more than 15 per cent) and/or poorly drained soils and zero otherwise. As the costs of conversion increase with poor soils and/or steeper terrain, the hazard rate is expected to decline.

A parcel's value in residential use is expected to be a function of its accessibility to major metropolitan areas, in this case Washington, District of Columbia and Baltimore, Maryland. Distances to both cities are measured via the roads network and are included in logarithmic form (LNDCDIST and LNBADIST). All else equal, parcels that are located within closer proximity to these urban areas are expected to have a higher hazard rate of conversion, implying that the expected sign of these coefficients is negative. A parcel's value in residential development is also expected to be influenced by the maximum allowable dwelling units per acre for which it is zoned, which determines the number of lots that can be developed on any given sized parcel. To capture potentially non-linear effects, it is specified in logarithmic form (LNDUPA). While in a static model we would expect this variable to have a positive effect on returns to development, the result is different in a dynamic framework as is modeled here. In a dynamic setting, in which returns to development increase over time, a decrease in the dwelling units per acre would be expected to accelerate the timing of development (increase the hazard rate) since developing at a higher density in the future is not possible and therefore there are no gains to postponing development.

Access to public sewer is also an important determinant of a parcel's value in residential use. A dummy variable, SEWER, is used to capture this and is coded one if the parcel is on public sewer and zero otherwise. The availability of public sewer is expected to have a positive effect on the hazard rate, since it reduces the cost of conversion. Finally, spillover effects from neighboring land uses are likely to influence a parcel's relative value as a residential location. We capture this using a relative measure of the amount of surrounding development within a 1,000 meter radius of the parcel centroid (NDEV). Development here is defined as all commercial, industrial, and residential uses for which a structure exists on the land parcel, excluding very low-density residential development (defined by a lot size of five acres or more). The sign of this neighborhood parameter is an empirical question. As Irwin and Bockstael (2002) discuss, both positive and negative development spillovers can be expected. The presence of positive spillovers would suggest that there are benefits from residential parcels being clustered together, e.g., a greater number of commercial services may be available. Alternatively, negative spillovers would indicate the presence of congestion costs that are generated by contiguous residential development. In all likelihood, both positive and negative spillovers exist and the sign of the parameter will depend on their net effect. Lastly, we include dummy variables for three of the four counties (SM, CH, and CA for St. Mary's, Charles, and Calvert counties, respectively) to control for the variety of policies and public goods that exist at the county level. These dummy variables are normalized on Anne Arundel County.

Empirical Results

Results from the proportional hazards model estimation are reported in Table 9.1. As expected, distances to the urban centers of Washington, District of Columbia (LNDCDIST) and Baltimore, Maryland (LNBADIST) have a negative effect on the hazard rate. A negative estimate indicates that the time until conversion of parcels that are located further away from these urban centers will be longer. This result is consistent with the basic urban bid rent model, which predicts a negative land rent gradient. The zoning variable (LNDUPA), which dictates the maximum allowable density of development, is found to depress the hazard rate up to a certain point. Parcels located in areas where the maximum allowable densities are one house per acre or less have a higher survival length. On the other hand, being located in areas where more than one dwelling unit per acre is permitted decreases the survival length of the parcel. Access to public sewer (SEWER) is found to be positive and significant. This is consistent with our expectations that the provision of public sewer to parcels shortens their time until conversion because public sewer access reduces conversion costs. The proxy for the opportunity cost of conversion (GOODAG) is found to be negative, but insignificant. This suggests either that this variable is not a good proxy for the agricultural profitability of a land parcel or that these returns do not significantly influence a parcel's timing of conversion. As expected, the dummy variable capturing higher costs of conversion (COST) is found to have a negative effect on the hazard rate of land conversion.

The estimated coefficient for the measure of surrounding development (NDEV) is negative and significant at the ten per cent level. This is consistent with earlier findings presented by Irwin and Bockstael (2002) and indicates that as the

Table 9.1 Results of the empirical model of land conversion[a, b]

Variable	Estimate	(Standard Error)
NDEV	−1.2647*	(0.7303)
LBADIST	−4.6481**	(0.8469)
LDCDIST	−1.1213**	(0.4669)
GOODAG	−0.3936	(0.4056)
COST	−1.4853**	(0.3022)
LNDUPA	−1.6664**	(0.2219)
SEWER	0.9034*	(0.5335)
SM	5.6025**	(1.1333)
CH	7.8194**	(1.1015)
CA	4.3234**	(0.9668)

[a] Dependent variable equals one if conversion occurred at $T=t$; otherwise equals zero; N=6750.
[b] ** and * indicate significance at the five and ten per cent levels, respectively.

amount of development within a parcel's neighborhood increases, the time until its eventual development increases. However, as discussed by Irwin and Bockstael (2002), these estimates are biased in a positive direction due to problems of spatial error autocorrelation. Because the estimated effect is negative, the direction of the effect is identified (negative), but due to the upward bias of the parameter estimate, the magnitude is not. The negative sign implies that surrounding development generates a net negative effect due to some type of congestion externalities.

Lastly, three of the four estimates associated with the county-level dummy variables are found to be positive and significant (only Howard County is insignificant). All else equal, the hazard rates of parcels located in St. Mary's, Calvert, or Charles counties will be higher relative to the rates of parcels located in Anne Arundel County. This result is somewhat surprising, since Anne Arundel County is relatively well-off and has, on average, the highest quality of public services. However, it is also, on average, the most developed of all the counties and has the highest average cost of living. Thus, the positive coefficients may simply reflect the preferences of those households that are moving to these exurban locations. In short, individuals may prefer less urban areas that have a lower cost of living, including lower taxes.

Predicted Patterns of Land-Use Change

As mentioned previously in this paper, many spatially explicit economic models of land-use change are developed to serve as predictive tools. In this section, we present such an application using the parameter estimates from the duration model shown in Table 9.1. Predicted survival functions are estimated using these parameter estimates for the 6,615 remaining parcels in the dataset that, as of the end of 1997, were not yet converted (e.g., the censored observations). These estimates can be interpreted as the probability that a currently undeveloped parcel will survive in its undeveloped state for an additional seven years (i.e., until 2004, since 1997 is the last year of the sample).

A visual description of the spatial pattern of the estimated survival probabilities is shown in Figure 9.1 for a selected county, Charles County. The spatial distribution of the survival probabilities reveals that many of the parcels with the lowest survival probabilities (i.e., those that are predicted to be converted sooner) are located in the northern portion of the county, which is just south of Washington, District of Columbia, and the eastern portion of the county, which is where the majority of the county's recent growth has occurred.

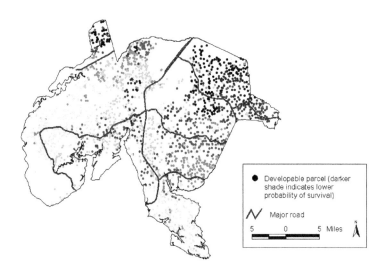

Figure 9.1 Baseline predicted probabilities of land conversion*

*Estimated survival probabilities for undeveloped parcels in Charles County, Maryland.

To illustrate the utility of this modeling approach in predicting changes under an alternative regime, we consider the effect of a smart growth policy that seeks to concentrate development in areas that are adjacent to existing development through the provision of public sewer to these areas. All other areas are treated as areas in which public sewer will not be provided in the foreseeable future. For example, areas that are too far from existing sewer lines or whose topography does not allow for easy extension of sewer lines would be designated as such. To gauge the impact of this hypothetical policy on the predicted pattern of development, we consider a growth scenario in which 500 additional parcels are developed in Charles County under both the baseline and smart growth policy scenarios. Figure 9.2 illustrates the results of this exercise. A visual comparison of the spatial pattern of development under the two scenarios reveals that the predicted baseline pattern of development is somewhat more scattered than the smart growth predicted pattern. In particular, development is more concentrated in the north central area of the county under the smart growth policy, which is where the hypothetical public sewer extension is largely concentrated. While this public sewer extension is predicted to reduce the scattered development in the central portion of the county that occurs in the baseline scenario, the overall effect of the smart growth policy on the predicted pattern of development is relatively minor.

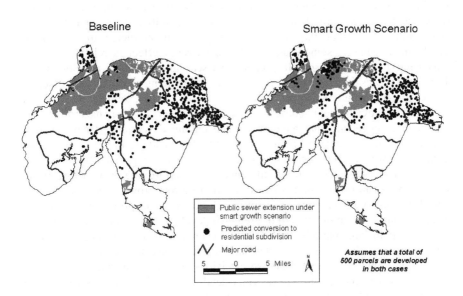

Figure 9.2 Comparison of predicted development pattern under baseline and smart growth scenarios

Conclusions

An improved understanding of the forces that contribute to the changes in regional growth and urbanization patterns will inform the development of a myriad of public policies including public finance, environmental, economic development, and land-use planning policies.   Because the regional pattern of land-use conversion is the cumulative result of many individual decisions distributed over space, it is important to understand how policies are likely to influence individual behavior and in turn, how these behaviors that are distributed across space influence changes in the regional pattern of development.   Spatially explicit microeconomic models of land-use change enable the prediction of effects from a change in a policy variable, e.g., a change in zoning, on individuals' conversion decisions.   In turn, these models allow for the cumulative result of individual responses to a policy change to be predicted in a spatially explicit manner. Therefore, these models provide a means to link policy changes to predicted changes in the regional pattern of land use.

Our results indicate the relative importance of several policy variables that are found to heavily influence the expected returns to development. These include the zoning variable, which determines the maximum allowable density of residential development for any given parcel, and the presence or absence of public sewer. By using the estimated parameters from the land-use conversion model, we are able to predict how a policy that only indirectly influences land-use conversion is expected to alter individuals' behavior and the resulting development pattern. Our results show that the smart growth policy is predicted to concentrate development patterns somewhat, but that the overall effect is relatively minor. This suggests that smart growth policies that seek to concentrate development in designated places may only be partially successful in doing so because of offsetting effects that moderate the impacts of such policies. For example, we find that surrounding development confers a negative effect on the hazard rate of conversion, suggesting that attempts to concentrate development may result in creating congestion that will reduce the desirability of living in the targeted area. In addition, we find that the quality of public services, as proxied by the county dummy variables, is a very strong influence on the hazard rate. Competing effects such as these can offset policymakers' efforts to direct growth. Nonetheless, we find that a policy of directing growth through public sewer provision does have a moderate influence on the pattern of predicted development in our study area.

In conclusion, spatially explicit micro-economic models of land-use change have numerous advantages over other land-use modeling approaches. First, these models are able to model land-use decisions at an organizational unit that corresponds with the spatial unit at which land-use decisions are made (e.g., land parcels). Second, by design, these models are easily able to capture the spatial heterogeneity of the landscape. Third, these models lend themselves to applied policy applications: individual responses to policies can be modeled, predictive scenarios can be simulated, and the results of the estimation and simulation exercises can be summarized easily using spatial visualization tools such as maps. However, there are notable disadvantages to this approach as well. Spatial data is not available at the parcel level in many areas, though the availability of GIS data is steadily improving throughout the United States. As a result, micro-scale models are not feasible in some areas. In addition, the reduced form approach summarized here describes the likelihood of conversion, not the amount of conversion. Hence, the empirical results must be combined with data such as forecasts of housing demand for a fuller understanding of growth and urbanization pressures at a regional level.

Notes

1   Because the underlying decision model and the resulting optimal conversion rule is developed in full in Irwin and Bockstael (2002), we provide only a sketch of it here.
2   See Gourieroux and Jasiak (2001) for a basic description of how duration models are applied by economists.
3   For additional details on the practical aspects of estimating a proportional hazards model using SAS, see Allison (1995).

References

Allison, P. 1995. *Survival Analysis Using the SAS System: A Practical Guide*. Cary, North Carolina: The SAS Institute.

Berry, M., B. Hazen, R.L. MacIntyre, and R. Flamm. 1996. 'LUCAS: A System for Modeling Land-Use Change.' *IEEE Computational Science and Engineering* 31: 24–35.

Bockstael, N.E. and K.P. Bell. 1998. 'Land-use patterns and Water Quality: The Effect of Differential Land Management Controls,' in *International Water and Resource Economics Consortium, Conflict and Cooperation on Trans-Boundary Water Resources*, eds. R. Just and S. Netanyahu. Norwell, Massachusetts: Kluwer Publishers.

Burchell, R., N. Shad, D. Listokin, H. Phillips, A. Downs, S. Seskin, J. Davis, T. Moore, D. Helton, and M. Gall. 1998. *The Costs of Sprawl – Revisited*. Transportation Cooperative Research Program Report 39. Washington, District of Columbia: National Academy Press.

Daniels, T. 1999. *When City and County Collide*. Washington, District of Columbia: Island Press.

Flamm, R. and M. Turner. 1994. 'Alternative Model Formulations for a Stochastic Simulation of Landscape Change.' *Landscape Ecology* 9: 37–46.

Gourieroux, C. and J. Jasik. 2001. 'Durations,' in *A Companion to Theoretical Economics*, ed. B. Baltagi. Malden, Massachusetts: Blackwell Publishing.

Hazen, B.C. and M.W. Berry. 1997. 'The Simulation of Land-cover Change Using a Distributed Computing Environment.' *Simulation Practice and. Theory* 5: 489–514.

Irwin, E.G. and N.E. Bockstael. 2002. 'Interacting Agents, Spatial Externalities, and the Endogenous Evolution of Residential Land-use pattern.' *Journal of Economic Geography* 2: 31–54.

Irwin, E.G. and J. Geoghegan. 2001. 'Theory, Data, Methods: Developing Spatially-Explicit Economic Models of Land-use change.' *Journal of Agriculture Ecosystems and Environment* 85(1–3): 7–24.

Ladd, H.F. 1992. 'Population Growth, Density, and the Costs of Providing Public Services.' *Urban Studies* 29(2): 273–295.

Landis, J. 1995. 'Imagining Land Use Futures: Applying the California Urban Futures Model.' *Journal of the American Planning Association* 61: 438–457.

Landis, J. and M. Zhang. 1998a. 'The Second Generation of the California Urban Futures Model. Part 1: Model Logic and Theory.' *Environment and Planning A* 30: 657–666.

Landis, J. and M. Zhang. 1998b. 'The Second Generation of the California Urban Futures Model. Part 2: Specification and Calibration Results of the Land-use Change Submodel.' *Environment and Planning B*. 25: 795–824.

Nelson, A. 1992. 'Characterizing Exurbia.' *Journal of Planning Literature* 6(4): 350–368.

Veldkamp, A. and L. Fresco. 1996. 'CLUE-CR: An Integrated Multi-scale Model to Simulate Land-use change Scenarios in Costa Rica.' *Ecological Modeling* 91: 231–248.

Veldkamp, A. and L. Fresco. 1997. 'Exploring Land Use Scenarios: An Alternative Approach Based on Actual Land Use.' *Agricultural Systems* 55: 1–17.

PART III
CONSEQUENCES OF
LAND-USE CHANGE

Chapter 10

Land-Use Change and Ecosystems: Anticipating the Consequences of Private and Public Decisions in the South Florida Landscape

J. Walter Milon

Introduction

Public debate about the consequences of land-use change and 'urban sprawl' raise important challenges for social and natural scientists. From a social science perspective, land-use change is often viewed as an economic process in which landowners determine land use based on the economic rents from alternative activities, as described in Chapter 6 (Muth 1961; Alonso 1964). While this simple atomistic framework provides useful insights, it is often criticized for treating land as uni-dimensional and ignoring the private and public externalities associated with land uses (e.g., Bockstael 1996). On the other hand, natural scientists concerned with land-use change attempt to determine the consequences of land conversion from natural to developed states for species diversity and the provision of ecological services. As discussed in Chapter 6, these externalities and environmental effects may extend beyond the boundaries of the converted land and contribute to the negative impacts of urban sprawl. A fundamental message from these different perspectives is that land-use change decisions, driven by the invisible hand of private property incentives, may not lead to socially optimal land-use patterns (Brueckner 2000; Daily 1997; Douglas 1994).

This tension between private and social interests in land-use decisions creates an important research agenda for social and natural scientists. The broad objectives of this agenda were succinctly expressed by Jane Lubchenko, past president of the American Association for the Advancement of Science, in her prospectus on the role of scientists in the 21st century:

> The current and growing extent of human dominance of the planet will require new kinds of knowledge and applications from science – knowledge to reduce the rate at which we alter the Earth systems, knowledge to understand Earth's ecosystems and how they interact with the numerous components of human-caused global change, and knowledge to manage the planet (Lubchenko 1998, p.495).

Specifically, for land-use change, knowledge of the local and global effects of land uses on the functional and structural components of ecosystems is necessary for informed policy decisions. These decisions may range from the choice of policy instruments used to guide private land-use decisions to public investment in infrastructure such as roads and community services (U.S. Environmental Protection Agency 2001).

One approach to better understand the types of knowledge needed for land-use decision-making is to consider two interrelated questions. How were past land-use changes influenced by the state of knowledge at the time of the decision? And, how might these decisions have differed if the present state of knowledge had been available for past decisions? This *ex post facto* approach may not provide an explicit agenda for future research on land-use change. But, it does provide a basis to compare the growth of knowledge about the effects of land-use changes over time and the role of scientific knowledge in land-use change decisions.

To implement this approach, we consider the case of land-use change associated with the Central and Southern Florida Project (C&SFP). The C&SFP was initially authorized by the U.S. Congress in 1948 to implement flood control and water management for the lower half of the Florida peninsula. It led to one of the most extensive transformations of a natural ecosystem to agricultural and urban land uses anywhere in the U.S. In response to the ecological impacts caused by the C&SFP, Congress recently authorized an eight billion dollar, 20-year ecosystem restoration initiative for the region that has been described as the most ambitious and expensive restoration effort undertaken anywhere in the world.[1]

The remainder of this chapter provides a review and evaluation of the economic rationale and scientific knowledge that informed the initial 1948 decisions on the C&SFP. Because the C&SFP was authorized under the Flood Control Act,[2] a relatively complete analysis of the expected benefits and costs of the initial and subsequent Congressional authorizations is part of the historical record. We then consider how scientific knowledge about the region and the environmental impacts of land-use decisions have changed in the past half-century and how that knowledge contributed to recent efforts to undertake ecosystem restoration. We also address the question of whether the initial 1948 decision to authorize the C&SFP might have been different if this current knowledge had been available.

This retrospective assessment illustrates some of the difficult issues involved in land-use change decisions and the limits of present knowledge about the consequences of land-use change. It also highlights the problem of ecological and social 'surprises' in land-use change dynamics and how these surprises may lead to irreversible outcomes. These issues can be considered in the context of evaluating potential land-use changes in other areas.

The Central and South Florida Project and Land-Use Change

Re-Development Conditions and the 1948 Authorization

Land use and water management have been inextricably intertwined in Florida since statehood in 1845. Under the Swamp and Overflowed Lands Act of 1850 (the 'Swamp Lands Act'), the U.S. Congress transferred ownership of 24.2 million acres to the State of Florida for the exclusive purpose of making them productive by draining the wetlands. The Act stipulated that the sale of lands to private interests should finance reclamation (Blake 1980). This region, a mosaic of freshwater wetlands and upland areas, extended from north of Lake Okeechobee to the southern tip of Florida (Figure 10.1). The heart of the region was the Everglades, a shallow sawgrass-dominated wetland in which surface water gradually flowed from Lake Okeechobee to what is now Everglades National Park. The entire Everglades area was just a few feet above mean sea level, so seasonal and inter-annual changes in rainfall led to the expansion and contraction of flooded wetland areas (Light and Dineen 1994). The Everglades were bordered on the east by a coastal ridge, five to ten miles in width, where the natural elevation (from ten to 25 feet above sea level) inhibited direct flooding from the Everglades.

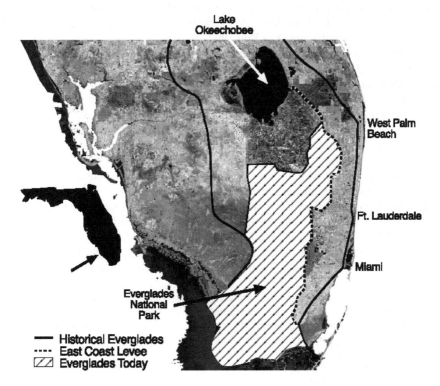

Figure 10.1 The Everglades/South Florida region: past and present

Subsequent to the Swamp Lands Act, the State of Florida entered into several land sale agreements that would transfer land to private ownership if the land was drained. A number of projects prior to 1900 attempted to drain parts of the area south of Lake Okeechobee but these were unsuccessful and financial disasters. It was not until the State of Florida initiated efforts in 1906 to dig five canals (varying in length from 42 to 85 miles) from Lake Okeechobee to outlets along the southeast Florida coast that drainage efforts showed some initial success. By the early 1920s these canals were completed and agricultural development began on the reclaimed lands south of Lake Okeechobee. At the same time, a private railroad was constructed along the eastern coastal ridge to Miami, thereby linking South Florida with the rest of the state.

These events prompted a major influx of new inhabitants and land-use changes in the South Florida region. Population increased from about 2,000 people in 1900 to 230,000 in 1930, one of the highest growth rates recorded in the U.S. (Chapman 1991; Solecki 2001). Most of the urban development and population growth at this time was confined to three coastal cities (Miami, Fort Lauderdale, and West Palm Beach). These cities were within a few miles of the Atlantic Ocean on the narrow coastal ridge. Approximately 100,000 acres of natural lands were converted to agricultural uses during this period. Agricultural land use was concentrated in the area immediately south of Lake Okeechobee (in what would later be known as the Everglades Agricultural Area [EAA]) and around Miami (DeGrove 1958; Snyder and Davidson 1994).

These developments were dramatically altered by a subsequent series of events. In 1926 and 1928, hurricanes caused the loss of more than 2,500 lives due to flooding directly south of Lake Okeechobee (Carter 1974). This led to the first formal involvement by the federal government in the region since the Swamp Lands Act to construct a dike around the southern end of the lake. During the Great Depression of the 1930s, many small drainage districts that had been established throughout the region went bankrupt and failed to complete or maintain water control structures. Then in September and October of 1947, two hurricanes contributed to annual rainfall of more than 100 inches (nearly double the average). The accumulated rainfall once again flooded the area south of Lake Okeechobee and caused extensive flooding in the western areas of the coastal cities where new agricultural and urban development bordered the Everglades. These areas remained flooded for several months (U.S. Army, Chief of Engineers 1948).

In response to pleas from local and state officials, the U.S. Army Corps of Engineers quickly developed a comprehensive plan for the region to:

> ...afford a high degree of flood protection throughout this area; it would provide for removal of excess waters in wet seasons, and for their control, storage, and use in maintaining water levels during dry periods. Adequate control of water levels is essential for agricultural use of lands in this area and for maintenance of municipal water supplies. The comprehensive plan would benefit in varying degrees over 2,300,000 acres of land, as well as numerous cities and towns (U.S. Army, Chief of Engineers 1948, p.2).

The key element in this plan, which would be authorized as the Central and Southern Florida Project (C&SFP), was the construction of a north-to-south levee and canal system paralleling the coastal ridge that provided flood control and helped to prevent saltwater intrusion into the local aquifer. The levee and canal system was constructed approximately 20 to 25 miles inland from the coast (Figure 10.1) and permitted new agricultural and urban development on several hundreds of thousands of acres along the east coast that were subject to flooding as part of the Everglades (Carter 1974). Areas to the west of the levee would become water conservation areas for aquifer recharge and prevention of salinity encroachment. Also, the plan provided for additional canals and pumping structures in the Everglades Agricultural Area to expand the amount of arable land from about 140,000 acres in the late 1940s to over 700,000 acres (Snyder and Davidson 1994).

Table 10.1   Estimated annual benefits, costs and benefit-cost ratios for the Central and Southern Florida Project by year of study (in thousands of 1999$)*

Category	1948	1957	1968	1999
Flood Damage Reduction	61,552.5	86,790.3	n/a	n/a
Increased Land Use	118,278.3	192,938.5	n/a	n/a
Navigation				
Commercial	1,313.0	−33.6	n/a	n/a
Recreational	n/a	342.8	n/a	n/a
Fish and Wildlife	2,170.9	1,713.8	n/a	n/a
Water Supply				
Agricultural	n/a	n/a	20,550.0	1,990.0
Urban	n/a	n/a	25,100.0	27,200.0
Recreation	n/a	n/a	21,500.0	n/a
Total Benefits	183,314.7	281,751.8	67,150.0	29,190.0
Total Costs	89,094.8	77,082.3	24,054.0	402,292.0
Benefit-Cost Ratio	2.1	3.7	2.8	n/a

*n/a refers to data that are not applicable or not estimated.

Source: U.S. Army, Chief of Engineers (1948).

The economic logic for the C&SFP is evident in the benefits and costs estimated for the project in the initial Congressional authorization in 1948. Table 10.1 presents the estimated average annual benefits by category for the project and the aggregate benefits and costs along with the benefit-cost ratio.[3] The benefit estimates show that the proposed flood control measures would prevent the significant economic damages that had plagued the region during the 1947 floods. The $61.5 million estimate (expressed in 1999 dollars) reflected the expected annual average damages if the C&SFP was not constructed, and accounted for the frequency of flooding in the region (U.S. Army, Chief of Engineers, 1948). These large flood control benefits, however, were still approximately 50 per cent less than the increased land-use benefits of $118.3 million. The bulk of these land-use benefits (65 per cent) were attributed to new and enhanced production in the Everglades Agricultural Area with the remainder along the lower east coast. In light of the estimated project costs of $89.1 million, it is evident that the C&SFP, authorized in 1948, would not have been a viable flood control project (i.e., one with a benefit-cost ratio greater than one) without the added benefits of increased agricultural land use throughout the region. Note also that other benefit categories, such as project impacts on navigation and fish and wildlife, were considered an insignificant source of benefits (or costs) in the 1948 assessment.

Another important aspect of the initial C&SFP assessment is the consideration of water flows to Everglades National Park (Figure 10.1). Local efforts in South Florida to create a national park on two million acres in the southern part of the region date back to the 1920s. However, the land that would have been transferred back to federal ownership to create a park had already been deeded to railroad and drainage interests. Despite significant opposition, Congress authorized the creation of Everglades National Park in 1934. Continuing disputes about the park boundaries and land ownership delayed the dedication until 1947. Final boundaries were not settled until 1958; these boundaries encompassed approximately 60 per cent of the area initially proposed (Carter 1974).

The 1948 assessment of the C&SFP briefly mentions Everglades National Park citing the short time it had been established. The assessment states, however, that the plan

> ...would not damage or interfere with this great national park as the purposes of the comprehensive plan are aimed at restoring and preserving natural conditions over areas which appear unsuited to agriculture...[I]t is believed that this comprehensive water-control plan and the national park plan are complementary features of Federal activity necessary to restore and preserve the unique Everglades region (U.S. Army, Chief of Engineers 1948, p.57).

In contrast, the Department of Interior (responsible for administration of the Park) commented on the C&SFP assessment that,

> The Everglades National Park has been established so recently that the National Park Service has had neither time nor resources to make studies of the actual effect of the project on the park or as to the best means whereby the project may be made to

contribute to the preservation of the park in its natural state, in accordance with the expressed will of Congress...[I]t is felt imperative that plans of operation should be the subject of negotiated agreements between the Corps of Engineers and the National Park Service prior to construction and so recognized in authorizing legislation for the project (U.S. Army, Chief of Engineers 1948, pp.ix–x).

These concerns of the Department would not be addressed in the 1948 authorization but would become an important issue as government scientists and others sought to evaluate the effects of water control and land-use change in the region.

The 1954 and 1968 Reauthorizations

The first phase of the C&SFP authorized in 1948 consisted mostly of projects necessary to provide flood protection to the urban areas along the lower East Coast and the Everglades Agricultural Area south of Lake Okeechobee. The second phase, authorized in 1954, provided funding to complete the original plan by including flood control in the Kissimmee River basin north of Lake Okeechobee. But, the large share of total benefits attributable to increased land use in the 1948 assessment led to:

...[s]ome questions in Congress as to whether this was, in fact, mainly a reclamation rather that a flood-control project, and whether the degree of local cooperation required by authorizing law was consistent with that required for western land-reclamation projects (U.S. Army, Chief of Engineers 1957, p.13).

These questions led to a new assessment of the benefits and costs of the C&SFP. The new assessment completed in 1957 noted that,

The speed required in preparing the original report made it impossible to fully determine all the sources of benefits; consequently, large benefits sources were omitted...The interim period has given experience on which to evaluate economic trends and the necessary time for detailed study and investigation... *The best experts and publications on population-growth trends, agricultural production, marketing, and production costs have been exhaustively consulted* (emphasis added)(U.S. Army, Chief of Engineers 1957, p. 53).

The annual benefits and benefit-cost ratio from the 1957 assessment are also shown in Table 10.1. The major differences in the 1948 and 1957 assessments were the large increase in both flood damage reduction and increased land-use benefits that were attributed to more rapid economic development of the region than anticipated:

Since both in and outside the project area the rate of actual development without project incentive has far exceeded the most optimistic forecasts of 1947, it is understandable that shifts in land use have taken place. In numerous areas along the lower east coast, the decisive trend is toward urban land development which in 1947 appeared to have either permanent or long-term agricultural use (U.S. Army, Chief of Engineers 1957, pp.53–4).

As a result of higher land values for the areas protected from flooding, benefits from the C&SFP increased and the benefit-cost ratio for the project increased from 2.1 to 3.7. This new assessment did not mention the effects of the project on fish and wildlife in the region nor was there any discussion of water deliveries to Everglades National Park.

While the initial impetus for the C&SFP was the region-wide flooding of 1947, an extended drought in the early 1960s led to calls for a new assessment of the project. By this time, most of the flood protection measures included in the original 1948 plan had been completed or deleted as not essential for the project. In 1968, a new report to Congress by the U.S. Army Corps of Engineers concluded that the C&SFP would not be able to meet the water resource needs of the region after the mid-1970s. Rapid population growth, increased agricultural irrigation, and a newfound recognition of the water needs of Everglades National Park created unanticipated water demands. The report from the District Engineer stated:

> There are impending shortages of water to meet projected demands fully at all times. The days of plentiful water and indiscriminate use cannot be sustained. The problems of conflicting demand for water and the restoration and preservation of natural values, while permitting the full expansion of the population and economy, require solution (U.S. Army, Chief of Engineers 1968, pp.52–3).

The report noted that population growth estimates for the year 2000 were more than three times the original projections. Urban water demands were expected to more than double between 1970 and 2020 while agricultural water demand was expected to increase by 50 per cent. Moreover, the transmittal letter from the Chief of Engineers acknowledged that "...preservation of Everglades National Park is a project purpose and that available water should be provided on an equitable basis with other users" (U.S. Army, Chief of Engineers 1968, p.1).

As in earlier assessments, the 1968 report sought to present the best scientific information available. The report noted that, 'A number of specialists were engaged to assist the Corps of Engineers' in the analysis and went on to list the services of water resource systems analysts, fishery biologists, meteorologists, hydrogeologists, and botanists (U.S. Army, Chief of Engineers 1968, p.17). Moreover, in one of the first attempts to scientifically link water flows and ecological impacts in Everglades National Park, the report observed:

> Investigations have been made of historical flows through the park...Park research biologists are currently developing water-need criteria based on a study of nesting success of birds under various conditions of rainfall and flow across Tamiami Trail. Since conditions leading to successful rookeries are generally good for the overall ecology of the park, it has been proposed to use nesting success as an indicator of ecological well-being (U.S. Army, Chief of Engineers 1968, p.53).

Even though water supply had never been included in prior benefit assessments of the C&SFP, the 1968 assessment determined that modifications to water control structures to increase water storage could satisfy the new water demands. The benefit estimates from the 1968 assessment presented in Table 10.1 indicate relatively equal benefits for urban and agricultural users. Moreover, nearly a third of the total benefits would accrue from enhanced recreational opportunities at existing facilities. The benefit-cost ratio of 2.8 once again indicated that the expenditures were economically justified, but no estimates of potential benefits or costs to Everglades National Park were included in the assessment.

Perhaps the most significant indicator of how the C&SFP had been transformed from flood control to a water supply project was the determination that, 'Flood-damage-reduction benefits are considered incidental and not of sufficient magnitude to warrant their evaluation in this report' (U.S. Army, Chief of Engineers 1968, p.78). Nevertheless, modifications to the C&SFP to increase water storage and supply for the growing population of urban and agricultural users were authorized as part of the Flood Control Act of 1968. The water needs of Everglades National Park were addressed in a subsequent 1970 federal 'guarantee' of water deliveries to the Park despite vocal protests from the Florida Congressional delegation (Carter 1974, pp.122–4).

The Restudy and the Water Resources Development Act of 2000

In the ensuing decades from the 1970s to the turn of the century, a number of significant forces continued to drive land-use changes in South Florida. Most notable is the population influx that swelled the number of residents in the region from 2.4 million in 1970 to over six million in the 2000 Census (U.S. Bureau of the Census 2001). This population growth was fueled by a continuing migration of new residents from northern states and a sudden influx of people from Caribbean and Latin America nations who sought improved political and economic conditions in South Florida (Boswell and Curtis 1991).

Accompanying this population growth was a continual conversion of natural lands to agricultural and urban uses. As illustrated in Figure 10.2, population growth and land-use change were closely linked in South Florida. Prior to the 1950s, less than ten per cent of the total land area in the region was converted from natural lands. Between 1950 and 1970, population growth from 760,000 to 2.4 million residents led to the conversion of more than 1.4 million acres of natural land, with nearly three-fourths of this land converted to agriculture. This was one of the most rapid rates of land conversion and population growth anywhere in the U.S. (Solecki and Walker 2001). From 1970 to 1990, the population grew to more than 4.6 million residents, resulting in the conversion of an additional 654,800 acres, of which the majority was to urban uses. By 1990, more than 40 per cent of the natural land area within the region was converted to other uses (*Ibid.*). The southeast coastal ridge along with the former Everglades wetlands that had been drained by the C&SFP levee and canal systems became a continuous strip of urbanized land extending from the coast to the levees. The remaining agricultural land was confined to the EAA and the area southwest of Miami.

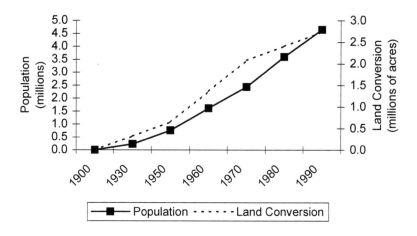

Figure 10.2 Population and land-use changes in South Florida

The rapid urbanization of South Florida was largely responsible for pioneering legislation to establish comprehensive growth management in Florida during the 1970s and 1980s. These laws were intended to reduce urban sprawl and to create maps to define allowable land uses within the jurisdiction of all local governments (Colburn and deHaven Smith 1999). Yet, many critics of these laws contend that they actually exacerbated urban expansion and sprawl by failing to provide adequate transportation infrastructure in rapidly growing areas (e.g., Holcombe 2001). Perhaps the most significant achievement of the C&SFP was that the East Coast levee became a *de facto* urban growth boundary that defined limits for land conversion that would not have existed otherwise (Ding, Knaap, and Hopkins 1999).

By the early 1990s, growing concern about the transformation of the South Florida landscape led to a series of Congressional resolutions and directives to reevaluate the C&SFP, '… to determine whether modifications are advisable at the present time, in the interest of environmental quality, water supply and other purposes' (U.S. Army Corps of Engineers 1999, p.1). The ensuing reevaluation concluded that,

> The remaining Everglades and other natural ecosystems in South Florida no longer exhibit the functions, richness, and spatial extent that defined the predrainage systems. There have been substantial and irreversible reductions in the spatial extent of the wetland systems (including an approximately 50 per cent reduction in the extent of the true Everglades) and in the total water storage, timing, and flow capacities of these systems. These systems will not recover their defining characteristics under current conditions and will not be sustained into the future (U.S. Army Corps of Engineers 1999, p.iii).

To address these problems, a study team involving 30 federal, state, and local agencies, and tribal governments participated in a multi-year planning effort. Over 160 specialists from these agencies and academia developed and evaluated alternative plans to modify the existing C&SFP (U.S. Army Corps of Engineers 1999, Section 7). In the process, a suite of state-of-the-art hydrological and ecological models were developed to inform the planning process (Sklar et al. 2001). This included models to simulate changes in hydrology, land use, and species abundance under alternative restoration scenarios. The resulting Comprehensive Everglades Restoration Plan (CERP) provided recommendations for an extensive restoration plan containing more than 60 major components that would take more than 20 years to implement, at an estimated cost of $7.8 billion (U.S. Army Corps of Engineers 1999). Specific land-use components in the CERP include: (1) the conversion of agricultural land around Lake Okeechobee and the EAA to water storage and treatment areas, (2) public acquisition of the few remaining natural areas along the western boundary of the urbanized coastal ridge, and (3) extensive modifications to the existing structure of canals and levees.

The CERP report also provided information about expected economic benefits that are summarized in Table 10.1. The total annual benefits of $29.2 million included only water supply benefits, and no aggregate benefit-cost analysis was developed, as in past C&SFP assessments. This occurred because the initial Congressional authorization for the CERP in the Water Resources Development Act of 1996 (P.L. 104–303) directed that restoration activities:

(A) are justified by the environmental benefits derived by the South Florida ecosystem in general and the Everglades and Florida Bay in particular; and
(B) shall not need further economic justification if the Secretary determines that the activities are cost-effective (P.L. 104–303, Section 528).

As a result, the CERP planning effort concluded that, 'Many of the benefits afforded by the alternative plans are environmental in nature and were not converted to monetary units for evaluation,' and that, 'economic benefits were not used to "justify" ecosystem restoration plans' (U.S. Army Corps of Engineers 1999, pp.7–46, 7–48). This lack of information about economic benefits created numerous questions about the cost-sharing and distributional implications of the plan (Milon and Hodges 2000). Nevertheless, Congress subsequently authorized pilot projects and programmatic authority for the CERP in the Water Resources Development Act of 2000 (P.L. 106–541).

A Critique of the Assessments and Implications for Land-Use Planning

The history of the C&SFP and land-use change in South Florida provides some important insights about the role, and limits, of scientific information in land-use decisions and planning. First, public concern about health, safety and economic welfare will typically lead to infrastructure investment to address threats to these fundamental values. In the case of the C&SFP, loss of human life and property destruction due to flooding were the stimulus for federal and state investments during the 1940s to the 1970s in drainage systems and other structures designed to control the natural hydrological processes of the region. Scientific assessments through benefit-cost analyses for the C&SFP provided an economic rationale for public assistance to reinforce private incentives for land-use change. Public values associated with natural systems were recognized through the preservation of specific areas such as Everglades National Park. But the assessments were fraught with errors of omission due to a lack of foresight to anticipate the consequences of these public infrastructure investments on broader social and economic values associated with the natural systems of the region. Thus, the primary focus on health and safety led to an incomplete accounting of the social consequences of flood prevention infrastructure.

A second important insight is that scientific assessments are not immune to the 'surprises' associated with dynamic social and natural systems. The initial assessments of the C&SFP recognized the potential for population growth in South Florida. But no one could realistically anticipate that flood controls would facilitate land-use changes that would make it possible for the population to grow from approximately one-half of a million people in the region in the mid-1940s to over six million people by 2000. It was not until the late 1960s, when population growth and drought began to stress the region's natural systems, that the extent of future population changes could be recognized. Even then, however, the primary public and scientific focus was the provision of agricultural and municipal water supplies rather than the potential consequences of population growth on land-use changes within the region. Similarly, scientific research did call attention to the effects of changes in water flows to Everglades National Park. However, no research addressed the broader impacts of land-use changes on the hydrological structure and ecosystems within the South Florida landscape.

A third insight comes from the recent development of new scientific models to evaluate the hydrological and ecological responses of natural systems in the region in response to alternative restoration plans. As described by Sklar et al. (2001), these state-of-the-art scientific models provide a level of detail and scope that has never been available before to evaluate changes in the South Florida landscape. Yet, while these models are necessary for any meaningful evaluation of restoration plans, their complexity is also a source of uncertainty about their predictive capability. These models seek to replicate conditions within the region that have not existed for decades and for which there are no accurate records. Even the CERP report cautions that, 'Simply stated, the pre-drainage Everglades is as much a vision created by opinion as by fact' (U.S. Army Corps of Engineers 1999, pp.5–36). Moreover, as with most natural systems models, there is no simple way to 'ground truth' the models because responses in the natural systems can be influenced by many events, encompass a large spatial scale, and occur slowly over time (Oreskes, Shrader-Frechette, and Belitz 1994).

A closely related concern is the inherent uncertainty of scientific models. Their predictive uncertainty is exacerbated by the current state of knowledge about ecological discontinuities and thresholds that can cause abrupt and unexpected changes in natural systems (Muradian 2001; Rosser 1995). Given that land-use changes have reduced the spatial extent of the original Everglades by approximately 50 per cent, it is not unrealistic to question whether the region's natural systems can be restored as envisioned in the CERP. As Kahn and O'Neill (1999) point out, small gradual changes in land use and stresses to the environment may indirectly lead to unanticipated irreversibilities. The subsequent state of nature may be stable but it cannot recover to its original condition. The irreversibility of past land-use changes and scientific uncertainty about future states was acknowledged in the CERP report's observation that,

> Because the pre-drainage Everglades cannot be recreated in its original form, the restoration goal is to create a "new" Everglades, one which will be different from any system that existed in the past, and one which will be substantially healthier than the current system...It is too early in the south Florida ecosystem restoration process to state with certainty what the "endpoint" for the restored Everglades should become. It is likely that the length of time required to implement the restoration projects, and the varying time lags in ecological responses, will mean that the current, managed system will evolve into a "new" Everglades over long time scales. Thus, the point at which restoration is achieved, and the precise characteristics of that "restored" system, represent questions that are not completely answerable at present (U.S. Army Corps of Engineers 1999, pp.5–36, 5–37).

Finally, economists and other social scientists should note the explicit neglect of economic valuation of land use and environmental changes in the CERP evaluation process. Despite the objective of the CERP to enhance environmental quality within the region, economic and social analysis was confined to accounting for the engineering and land acquisition costs of the restoration effort and measuring the benefits of enhanced water storage for agricultural and municipal water supplies. With the Congressional directive, in the Water Resources Development Act of 1996, that restoration would be justified solely by whether a plan to achieve environmental benefits for the South Florida ecosystem was cost-effective, the planning agencies made no effort to monetize expected environmental benefits. While there are several possible explanations for the Congressional directive, it is difficult to avoid the conclusion that Congress believed that economic valuation measures would add little to a scientific assessment of restoration alternatives. Part of this belief may have been the product of ongoing debate among economists about the merits and credibility of environmental valuation methods (e.g., Portney 1994). It is more likely, though, that Everglades ecosystem restoration was deemed a worthy social objective regardless of the cost. Economic valuation data, however, would facilitate decisions between alternative restoration processes and goals. However, valuation would be seriously compromised by the inability to predict restoration end-points.

Summary and Discussion

Since the initial formulation of the C&SFP more than 50 years ago, significant progress has been made in scientific understanding of the environmental processes that accompany land-use change. Natural scientists can model the physical properties of natural systems and adaptations of species to changes in these systems. Social scientists have developed methods to assign economic values to changes in landscapes for other purposes than land development. Given the development of these methods and models that are capable of predicting the consequences of land-use change in South Florida, one could ask, 'If this information had been available in the late 1940s, would state and federal governments have proceeded to alter the regional drainage and water management systems and encourage land-use change throughout the region?'

Certainly one could point to the high cost of attempting to restore the damaged Everglades ecosystem (Table 10.1) as justification for a different response to the flooding damages of the late 1940s. Moreover, these restoration costs understate the true costs of the drainage systems in South Florida because they do not account for other foregone ecological benefits from land-use changes in developed areas to the east of the protective levee. Yet, despite the magnitude of these costs, this simple comparison obscures the underlying social processes that influenced land-use change in the region. A speculative counterfactual – what would have happened if the C&SFP had not been undertaken – would be that the region would nevertheless have undergone a dramatic transformation of land use. The powerful drivers of population growth in the region would have resulted in more isolated attempts by private landowners to protect and enhance the economic value of their land at the expense of ecological values that do not accrue to the landowner. From this perspective, the urban growth boundary created by the C&SFP protective levee may have actually reduced the potential ecological damages and made it possible to initiate restoration in the remaining undeveloped portions of the Everglades ecosystem. This alternative perspective suggests that scientific information, no matter how complete, can never fully resolve the inherent conflict between private and public values in land. Knowledge of potential changes in public values for land must compete in the arena of public debate with democratic ideals of private property ownership.

An illustrative microcosm of these inherent conflicts in contemporary land-use planning in South Florida is provided by the ongoing controversy over the '8½ square mile area (8½ SMA)' to the southwest of Miami in southern Dade County. As shown in Figure 10.3, the 8½ SMA lies to the west of the East Coast levee that was constructed as part of the original C&SFP during the 1950s and directly to the east of Everglades National Park (ENP). With elevations ranging from six to eight feet above sea level and no drainage outlet, the area floods easily during the wet season (April-October). Despite the low elevation, the area was not included in the boundaries of Everglades National Park and agricultural activities were initiated on a limited scale in the late 1950s and 1960s. By the 1970s, residential development began to expand into the area even though there was no flood protection and Dade County enacted regulations to severely restrict residential land use in the area. Nevertheless, from the 1970s to the mid-1990s, the number of residences in the area increased from a few dozen to over 350 fixed structures and over 100 house trailers. Because of the land-use regulations for the 8½ SMA,

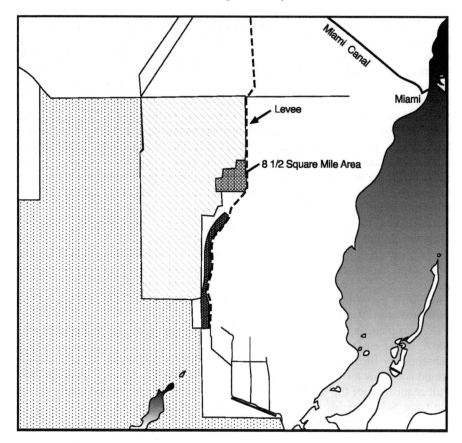

Figure 10.3 The 8½ Square Mile Area in Dade County, Florida

Dade County maintained only a few miles of roads so access to the area became very limited during heavy rains and many roads and residences remained flooded for weeks following tropical storms and hurricanes (Office of the Governor, State of Florida 1995, pp.5–15).

Following scientific studies of hydrological problems in ENP in the 1980s, Congress authorized the Everglades National Park Protection and Expansion Act of 1989 (P.L. 101–229) to enhance hydrological conditions in the park. This would occur by extending the boundaries of the park eastward through acquisition of land west of the protective levee (Figure 10.3). The 8½ SMA was not designated for acquisition, but it was stipulated that the area would be provided with a flood protection system if the Corps of Engineers determined that future water levels in the expanded ENP would adversely affect the area (P.L. 101–229, Section 104(b)). In 1992, the Corps proposed a canal and levee system for the 8½ SMA at a cost of $31 million.

In 1994, however, Congress amended the ENP Protection and Expansion Act to provide funds for acquisition of land in the 8½ SMA following recommendations for acquisition by a federal science advisory group (Science Sub-Group). In December of 1998, the Governing Board of the South Florida Water Management District (the local sponsor for the C&SFP) voted unanimously to initiate acquisition of the entire area at a cost of $22 million more than the Corps' proposed canal system (U.S. General Accounting Office 1999). This decision, however, was met with strong opposition from landowners in the 8½ SMA and a lawsuit filed by the Miccosukee Tribe alleging that the decision lacked proper public notice and violated Florida's Sunshine Law. The District subsequently voted to delay acquisition plans and requested that the Corps prepare a new evaluation of flood mitigation alternatives for the 8½ SMA. The Corps completed the reevaluation in July 2000 and noted that, 'The need to reevaluate this plan can be attributed to enhanced modeling capabilities and an expanded scientific understanding of the ecosystem function and structure that was not available during the preparation of the 1992 plan' (U.S. Army, Corps of Engineers 2000, p.ES–4). The Corps' report recommended a modified canal and levee system for a smaller portion of the 8½ SMA, and the acquisition of western portions of the 8½ SMA. The plan's estimated cost was $88.1 million; the cost of full acquisition was estimated at $179 million.

This plan was viewed as an acceptable compromise by landowners in the 8½ SMA. Eight environmental groups led by the Natural Resources Defense Council subsequently filed a lawsuit, however. These groups alleged that the Corps' plan would not allow for full restoration of hydroperiods in the eastern portion of ENP. Full acquisition of the 8½ SMA was the only alternative to prevent extinction of the Cape Sable seaside sparrow, an endangered species, whose habitat had been damaged by the change in hydroperiods (Daerr 2000).

This land-use conflict illustrates the interplay of public values, scientific information, and private property rights in contemporary land-use decisions in South Florida. The quantity and quality of scientific information about the social and ecological consequences of land-use change is vastly superior today to what it was 50 years ago. Yet, the availability of this enhanced information is only a necessary condition for inclusion in public debate about land-use alternatives. Other imperatives for the protection of private property interests and public safety will continue to be of equal or greater importance in the land-use decision process.

Notes

1   Further information on the Everglades restoration is available at www.evergladesplan.org.
2   The Flood Control Act of 1936 required the Corps of Engineers to evaluate whether the 'benefits to whomsoever they may accrue, are in excess of the estimated cost' for all federal projects. The techniques to implement this principle would be more fully developed in subsequent decades (e.g., Eckstein 1958; U.S. Water Resources Council

1973) but basic concepts were relatively well-developed at the time of the initial C&SFP authorization.

3   The approach to benefit-cost analysis used by the Corps was based on a 50-year time frame in which benefits and costs were averaged over the entire period to derive an annualized value. The total benefits and costs over the time period were not reported.

References

Alonso, W. 1964. *Location and Land Use: Toward a General Theory of Land Rent.* Cambridge, Massachusetts: Harvard University Press.

Blake, N. 1980. *Land Into Water – Water into Land: A History of Water Management in Florida.* Tallahassee, Florida: University Presses of Florida.

Bockstael, N. 1996. 'Modeling Economics and Ecology: The Importance of a Spatial Perspective.' *American Journal of Agricultural Economics* 78: 1168–80.

Boswell, T. and J. Curtis. 1991. 'The Hispanization of Metropolitan Miami,' in *South Florida: The Winds of Change*, ed., T. Boswell. Miami, Florida: Association of American Geographers.

Brueckner, J. 2000. 'Urban Sprawl: Diagnosis and Remedies.' *International Regional Science Review* 23: 160–71.

Carter, L. 1974. *The Florida Experience: Land and Water Policy in a Growth State.* Baltimore, Maryland: Johns Hopkins University Press.

Chapman, A. 1991. 'History of South Florida,' in *South Florida: The Winds of Change*, ed. T. Boswell. Miami, Florida: Association of American Geographers.

Colburn, D. and L. deHaven Smith. 1999. *Government in the Sunshine State.* Gainesville, Florida: University Press of Florida.

Daerr, E. 2000. 'Lawsuit Filed to Save Sparrow.' *National Parks* 74: 13–14.

Daily, G., ed. 1997. *Nature's Services: Societal Dependence on Natural Ecosystems.* Washington, District of Columbia: Island Press.

DeGrove, J. 1958. 'The Central and Southern Florida Flood Control Project: A Study in Intergovernmental Cooperation and Public Administration.' Ph.D. dissertation, University of North Carolina.

Ding, C., G. Knaap, and L. Hopkins. 1999. 'Managing Urban Growth with Urban Growth Boundaries: A Theoretical Analysis.' *Journal of Urban Economics* 46: 53–68.

Douglas, I. 1994. 'Human Settlements,' in *Changes in Land Use and Land Cover: A Global Perspective,* eds. W. Meyer and B. Turner. Cambridge, England: Cambridge University Press.

Eckstein, O. 1958. *Water Resource Development: The Economics of Project Evaluation.* Cambridge, Massachusetts: Harvard University Press.

Holcombe, R. 2001. 'Growth Management in Action: The Case of Florida,' in *Smarter Growth: Market-Based Strategies for Land Use Planning in the 21st Century*, eds. R. Holcombe and S. Staley. Westport, Connecticut: Greenwood Press.

Kahn, J. and R. O'Neill. 1999. 'Ecological Interaction as a Source of Economic Irreversibility.' *Southern Economic Journal* 66: 391–402.

Light, S. and J. Dineen. 1994. 'Water Control in the Everglades: A Historical Perspective,' in *Everglades: The Ecosystem and Its Restoration*, eds. S. Davis and J. Ogden. Delray Beach, Florida: St. Lucie Press.

Lubchenco, J. 1998. 'Entering the Century of the Environment: A New Social Contract for Science.' *Science* 279: 491–7.

Milon, J.W. and A.W. Hodges. 2000. 'Who Wants to Pay for Everglades Restoration?' *Choices*, Second Quarter: 12–16.

Muradian, R. 2001. 'Ecological Thresholds: A Survey.' *Ecological Economics* 38: 7–24.

Muth, R. 1961. 'Economic Change and Rural-Urban Land Conversions.' *Econometrica* 29: 1–23.

Office of the Governor, State of Florida. 1995. 'East Everglades 8.5 Square Mile Area Study Committee.' Tallahassee, Florida.

Oreskes, N., K. Shrader-Frechette, and K. Belitz. 1994. 'Verification, Validation, and Confirmation of Numerical Models in the Earth Sciences.' *Science* 263: 641–6.

Portney, P. 1994. 'The Contingent Valuation Debate: Why Economists Should Care.' *Journal of Economic Perspectives* 8: 3–18.

Rosser, B. 1995. 'Systemic Crises in Hierarchical Ecological Economics.' *Land Economics* 71: 163–72.

Science Sub-Group, South Florida Management and Coordination Working Group. 1993. 'Federal Objectives for the South Florida Restoration.' Miami, Florida.

Sklar, F., H. Fitz, Y. Wu, R. Van Zee, and C. McVoy. 2001. 'The Design of Ecological Landscape Models for Everglades Restoration.' *Ecological Economics* 37: 379–401.

Snyder, G. and J. Davidson. 1994. 'Everglades Agriculture: Past, Present, and Future,' in *Everglades: The Ecosystem and Its Restoration*, eds. S. Davis and J. Ogden. Delray Beach, Florida: St. Lucie Press.

Solecki, W. 2001. 'The Role of Global-to-Local Linkages in Land Use/Land Cover Change in South Florida.' *Ecological Economics* 37: 339–56.

Solecki, W. and R. Walker. 2001. 'Transformation of the South Florida Landscape,' in *Growing Populations, Changing Landscapes: Studies from India, China, and the United States*, ed. U.S. National Academy of Sciences. Washington, District of Columbia: National Academy Press.

U.S. Army, Chief of Engineers. 1948. *Comprehensive Report on Central and Southern Florida for Flood Control and Other Purposes.* 80th Congress, 2nd Session, House Document No. 643. Washington, District of Columbia: Government Printing Office.

U.S. Army, Chief of Engineers. 1957. *Central and Southern Florida Project – Local Cooperation in the Part of the Project Authorized by the Flood Control Act of 1954.* 85th Congress, 1st Session, House Document No. 186. Washington, District of Columbia: Government Printing Office.

U.S. Army, Chief of Engineers. 1968. *Central and Southern Florida Project – Local Cooperation in the Part of the Project Authorized by the Flood Control Act of 1968* 90th Congress, 2nd Session, Public Law No. 483. Washington, District of Columbia: Government Printing Office.

U.S. Army, Chief of Engineers. 1999. *Central and Southern Florida Project Comprehensive Review Study.* Final Integrated Feasibility Report and Programmatic Environmental Impact Statement. Jacksonville, Florida.

U.S. Army, Chief of Engineers. 2000. *General Reevaluation Report and Final Supplement to the 1992 Final Environmental Impact Statement on the Modified Water Deliveries to Everglades National Park Project for the 8.5 Square Mile Area.* Jacksonville, Florida.

U.S. Bureau of the Census. 2001. *Statistical Abstract of the United States: 2001.* Washington, District of Columbia: Government Printing Office.

U.S. Environmental Protection Agency. 2001. *Our Built and Natural Environments.* Development, Community, and Environment Division, EPA 231-R-01-002. Washington, District of Columbia.

U.S. General Accounting Office. 1999. *South Florida Ecosystem Restoration: An Overall Strategic Plan and a Decision-Making Process are Needed to Keep the Effort on Track.* GAO/RCED-99-121. Washington, District of Columbia.

U.S. Water Resources Council. 1973. *Principles, Standards and Procedures for Water and Related Land Resource Planning.* Federal Register 38, No. 174, Part III.

Chapter 11

Conserving Biodiversity by Conserving Land

Stephen J. Polasky and Christian A. Vossler

Introduction

Land management decisions on public and private lands affect important ecosystem processes and functions with potentially far-reaching and long-term consequences. Humans are now managers of much of the habitable land of the earth. Over half of all land that is not tundra, ice, boreal, desert, or rock is devoted to agriculture (Tilman et al. 2001). Including managed forests, the majority of habitable land on earth is actively managed for human uses. The expected increase of two to three billion people over the next 50 years will further increase human land-use needs.

In a recent book, biologist Simon Levin states: 'the central environmental challenge of our time is embodied in the staggering loss, both recent and projected, of biological diversity...' (Levin 1999, p.1). Though other factors, such as the introduction of exotic species, over-harvesting, pollution, and climate change, contribute to the loss of biodiversity, habitat loss is thought to be the primary reason for the loss of terrestrial biodiversity (Ehrlich and Ehrlich 1981; Wilson 1988). In fact, a common method biologists use to predict the number of species present in a given land area is through construction of a 'species-area curve,' which is based on empirical evidence linking the amount of habitat and the number of species found in the habitat (MacArthur and Wilson 1967). Several studies have found that the current rate of species extinction is several orders of magnitude above the 'natural' or background rate of extinction (National Research Council 1995; Pimm et al. 1995). Given land conversion trends, projections into the future are for even higher extinction rates (Wilson 1988).

In the U.S., the Endangered Species Act has focused attention on the relationship between land use and species conservation. Under the Endangered Species Act, otherwise lawful land uses may be prohibited if they would result in harm to a species listed as endangered or threatened. Included in activities that cause harm are land uses that significantly modify habitat in ways that kill or injure listed species or interfere with essential activities such as breeding, feeding or sheltering. A number of recent high-profile endangered species cases have highlighted actual and potential restrictions on various land uses, including timber harvesting and urban development. These cases include timber harvest restrictions to protect the spotted owl and marbelled murralet in the Pacific Northwest, potentially wide-ranging restrictions on urban and rural land use to protect salmon from Washington to California, restrictions on land development in Southern California to protect the California gnatcatcher, Stephens' kangaroo rat and other species, and timber harvest restrictions in the Southeast to protect the red-cockaded woodpecker.

As the Endangered Species Act examples demonstrate, society faces difficult choices over whether to allow habitat conversion for economic gain versus conserving habitat to protect biodiversity. In each of the cases mentioned above, there is a tradeoff between economic activity (e.g., timber harvest, housing development, etc.) and conserving the habitat of threatened and endangered species on certain lands. Because the conservation of biodiversity and the material well-being of the human population are both important goals, it is important to set conservation priorities intelligently and to minimize the reduction in other goals from pursuing conservation. In this chapter, our objective is to ensure that the maximum amount of biodiversity is conserved for any given level of cost. We illustrate our approach to this problem using land-value data, and taxonomic and geographical distribution data for breeding bird species in Oregon.

In the next section, we present a general framework for cost-effective conservation decision-making that was first described by Solow et al. (1993). The framework requires specifying a biodiversity measure as an indicator of the relative worth of possible conservation outcomes, the probabilities of various outcomes occurring under a given set of management actions, the cost of these management actions and the conservation budget. We then discuss in more depth biodiversity measures and management actions. We apply our framework to a practical problem of selecting biological reserves under a budget constraint to maximize two measures of species diversity using taxonomic information, geographical distribution data of bird species, and land values in Oregon. The final section contains concluding comments.

A Conservation Decision-Making Framework

We begin by explaining the conservation decision-making framework of Solow et al. (1993). In this framework, the goal is to maximize expected biodiversity conserved under a budget constraint. There are three important components to this framework. First, what is the definition of biodiversity? In other words, what is the objective of conservation? For example, the definition of biodiversity could be the total number of species conserved or it could be a measure of the value of ecosystem services provided. In order to proceed with the analysis, however, there must be a clearly defined objective. In the applications that follow we will use two different biodiversity measures based on presence or absence of species: (1) the total number of species present (species richness), and (2) a measure of phylogenetic diversity of the conserved species.

Second, how do various management actions affect biodiversity? A wide range of management actions can be considered in this framework. Management actions could include such things as setting aside habitat as biological reserves, alternative pesticide application or tillage practices on agricultural land, or alternative timber harvest rotations in forests. Management actions could also include consideration of public policies such as zoning laws that restrict allowable land uses on certain parcels, or decisions on where to put infrastructure, such as roads or sewers, which will affect the pattern of future development activities. Since habitat decline is probably the single most important cause of biodiversity decline, land-use and land management decisions are particularly important to analyze. In the application to follow, we focus on the conservation strategy of setting aside land for biological reserves. Once it is decided what management actions to consider, there must be some way to assess the biological consequences of implementing those management actions. In practice, there may be limited ecological knowledge on which to base this assessment. At present, lack of ecological understanding is a key limiting factor in our ability to make intelligent choices regarding conservation. In the reserve-site selection problem we will consider the typical assumptions made are that species that are represented in those land areas selected in reserves will be conserved while those outside of any reserve area will be lost.

Third, what are the costs of various management actions? At a very general level, these costs represent sacrifices in other goals that must be made in order to further conservation. In the application to follow we measure these costs in dollar terms. For example, if a public land management agency decides to prohibit timber harvesting or grazing on public land in order to protect habitat for certain species, the cost of this restriction would be the foregone income that could have been earned had timber harvesting or grazing been allowed. It is important to note that these costs are what economists would call opportunity costs in that they represent the costs of foregone opportunities to society that are required for conservation. Opportunity costs are not necessarily the same thing as the budgetary consequences for an agency or landowner. Prohibiting logging in order to protect an endangered species may not require any budgetary outlay but it does impose an opportunity cost in terms of lost income from timber operations.

Formally, the conservation decision-making problem combining these three elements can be written as:

$$(1) \quad Max \sum_{s \in S} D(s) P_x(s),$$

subject to

$$C(x) \le B,$$

where $D(s)$ is the measure of the biological diversity outcome, S is the set of possible outcomes, $P_x(s)$ is the probability that outcome s will occur under conservation strategy x that describes what management actions will be taken, $C(x)$ is the opportunity cost of implementing conservation strategy x, and B is the conservation budget. By varying the budget, one can trace out the maximum achievable level of biodiversity conservation for various budget levels. In other words, following this procedure one can establish the cost curve for biodiversity conservation.

Biodiversity Measures, Species Richness, and Phylogenetic Diversity

Before turning to the application, we discuss in more detail biodiversity measures, specifically focusing on measures based on species presence and absence, and management actions, focusing on the reserve-site selection problem. What is referred to as 'biodiversity' can mean many different things. For example, one heavily referenced definition of biodiversity is the following:

> Biodiversity is the variety of life and its processes. It includes the variety of living organisms, the genetic differences among them, the communities and ecosystems in which they occur, and the ecological and evolutionary processes that keep them functioning, and yet ever changing (Keystone Center 1991).

Virtually anything in the field of study of biological sciences can fit into this definition. It is important to have a clear statement of the objective for any optimization or priority-setting exercise. For purposes of concreteness in what follows, we focus on measures of diversity that depend upon the survival or extinction of species, which we will refer to as measures of species diversity. Prior work on measure of species diversity includes Vane-Wright et al. (1991), Weitzman (1992, 1993), Faith (1992, 1994), Solow et al. (1993), Solow and Polasky (1994). Of course, we do not intend to imply that these measures capture all of the importance or value of biodiversity.

The simplest measure of species diversity is species richness. For species richness, $D(s)=N$, where N is the number of surviving species in outcome s. Using species richness as the objective means that one implicitly assumes that all species have equal conservation value. Further, it implicitly assumes the value of conserving any individual species is independent of what other species survive or go extinct: the marginal value of a species is constant regardless of what other species are conserved or extinct.

A measure of phylogenetic diversity takes into account the dissimilarity among species and gives higher value to species that are relatively unique among the set of surviving species. Phylogenetic diversity for a set of species is defined as the branch length of the phylogenetic tree for those species. A phylogenetic tree represents the pattern of evolution among species, indicating when species took divergent paths from a common ancestor. Assuming a constant rate of DNA changes along all branches, the branch length connecting any two species is proportional to the genetic dissimilarity between the species. Conserving a species that does not have closely related surviving species adds more to phylogenetic diversity than conserving a species that does. In this sense, phylogenetic diversity

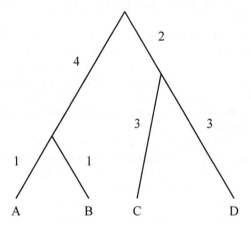

Figure 11.1 Example phylogenetic tree for a set of four genera

places a premium on genetically unique species. Under phylogenetic diversity, the marginal value of a species is not constant but rather depends upon the phylogenetic distance to the nearest surviving species.

Figure 11.1 shows a simple example with four species. The measure of phylogenetic diversity for the set of all four species is the entire branch length of the phylogenetic tree shown in Figure 11.1, or 14. If species A is lost but B, C, and D remain, the measure drops to 13. However if both A and B are lost, then the whole left hand branch is lost and diversity falls to eight. The marginal value of conserving species A, which is defined as the change in phylogenetic diversity when species A goes extinct, depends upon whether species B is conserved or not. If B is conserved then the marginal value of conserving A is only one, because diversity declines from 14 to 13. If B is not conserved then the marginal value of A is five, because the diversity of species A, C, and D is 13 while that of C and D alone is eight.

Measures of species diversity as described above are measured in biological terms. Another approach is to try to monetize the value of various biological outcomes. The advantage to doing so is that when $D(s)$ is specified in dollar terms then the decision-making framework can be simplified to one of maximizing net benefits:

$$(2) \quad Max \sum_{s \in S} D(s) P_x(s) - C(x).$$

Here, $D(s)$ is expressed in monetary units (dollars) to represent the species conservation benefits. In economic terms, Equation (2) represents a cost-benefit approach. In comparing across different sets of management actions, the preferred choice is one that results in the greatest difference between benefits and costs (i.e., maximum net benefits).

On the other hand, Equation (1) represents a cost-effectiveness approach. One cannot directly compare biological benefits with dollar value costs. Instead, the approach is to get the greatest biological return for any specified level of cost. A cost-effectiveness approach can be used to find the best strategy given a budget, but cannot be used to find the optimal conservation budget. The cost-benefit approach can be used to find the optimal conservation strategy including the optimal size of the conservation budget.

Valuing conservation outcomes in dollar terms presents a number of daunting challenges. Much of the value of biodiversity conservation may be non-use values. Survey methods are the only tools available for measuring such values. Even if the biology is totally understood, the multi-dimensional species or land valuation problem requires presenting a great deal of information to survey respondents. Klauer (2000) states that 'people cannot be expected to analyze the behavior of ecosystems when making economic decisions. Preferences of individuals do not reflect everything scientists find out about the functioning of ecosystems.' An added complexity to this valuation problem is the uncertainty surrounding ecosystem changes $(P_x[s])$ (Barbier 1994; Bingham et al. 1995; Bockstael et al. 1995; Suter 1995; Toman 1997). Bockstael et al. (1995) state: 'By evaluating only those components of the ecosystem that have immediate values to individuals, and focusing on short term changes, this practice ignores the fact that changes in ecosystems play out over time and space and may indeed be irreversible.' Besides the difficulties with incomplete information and the assimilation of information, many people find difficulty in, or fundamentally object to, making tradeoffs between conservation and money (see, for example, Spash and Hanley 1995).

Because of the difficulty of estimating values in dollar terms, cost-effectiveness analysis, rather than cost-benefit analysis, is often used when analyzing biodiversity conservation. The valuation question, however, cannot be avoided entirely even when one sticks to biological measures. Trying to maximize a measure of species diversity may require value judgments about the relative worth of different species, e.g., all species have equal value. Likewise, a measure of ecosystem function may require value judgments about the relative importance of different ecosystem functions.

Management Actions: The Reserve-Site Selection Problem

As stated in the introduction, conserving biodiversity is largely a matter of conserving habitat. In other words, the most important management actions for conservation of biodiversity are largely land-use decisions. One particularly simple format for considering land-use decisions is the reserve-site selection problem. In the reserve-site selection problem, a conservation planner chooses a set of sites to select as biological reserves under a budget constraint to maximize a measure of biodiversity, in our case either species richness or phylogenetic diversity. Species that are present in at least one selected site are assumed to survive. Those species not present in any selected site are assumed to go extinct.

When species richness is the measure of biodiversity, the reserve network selection problem is an integer-programming problem and can be written formally as:

(3) $\quad Max \sum_{i=1}^{m} y_i$,

subject to

(4) $\quad \sum_{j \in N_i} x_j > y_i, \quad i = 1, 2, ..., m$,

and

(5) $\quad \sum_{j=1}^{n} c_j x_j \leq B$,

where x_j equals one if site j is chosen, zero if not, and $j=1, 2, ..., n$; y_i equals one if species i is covered, zero if not, and $i=1, 2, ..., m$; and N_i is the set of candidate sites that contain species i, c_j is greater than zero and is the opportunity cost of choosing a reserve at location j, and B is greater than zero and is the conservation budget. The objective function in Equation (3) is to maximize the number of species included in the network. The m constraints represented in Equation (4) ensure that species i is not counted as included if no site in which it occurs is selected. The budget constraint is given in Equation (5).

When the objective is phylogenetic diversity, the objective function in Equation (3) is replaced by:

(6) $\quad Max\ P(y_1, y_2, ..., y_m)$,

where $P(y_1, y_2, ..., y_m)$ is the measure of phylogenetic diversity given that the species that survive are those for which y_i equals one.

Integer-programming problems can be quite difficult to solve, especially if many sites can be chosen from a large number of potential sites. In other papers, we have used methods from operations research to solve for the optimal set of sites to maximize species richness under a budget constraint (Ando et al. 1998; Polasky, Camm, and Garber-Yonts 2001). These papers used species richness as the objective function. Maximizing phylogenetic diversity makes the integer-programming problem much harder to solve. To date, the problem of maximizing phylogenetic diversity has not been solved optimally for large problems. In the application that follows, we follow the lead of Polasky et al. (2001) who used the 'greedy algorithm' to find a good, though not necessarily optimal, solution for this

Table 11.1 Example where the greedy algorithm fails to pick optimally

	Potential reserve sites		
	A	B	C
Species identification number	1 2 3 4	1 2 5	3 4 6
Total number of species:	4	3	3

problem. In the greedy algorithm, the first site chosen is the site that has the largest diversity per dollar. For example, with species richness as the objective, the first site chosen would be the one with the highest ratio of number of species present to site cost (c_i). Beyond the first site, sites are added sequentially by choosing the site that adds the greatest increment to the objective function per dollar spent. Sites are added in this fashion until the budget is exhausted.

The greedy algorithm has great intuitive appeal in that each site chosen gives the largest return per budget outlay of any site that could be added to existing sites. Though the greedy algorithm generally finds good solutions, it does not necessarily pick an optimal solution. A simple example illustrates this point. Suppose that only two sites may be protected out of three potential reserve sites (labeled A-C in Table 11.1). Species (labeled one through six) inhabit various sites, as shown in Table 11.1. The optimal choice in picking two sites to maximize species diversity is to choose sites B and C, which together cover all six species. However, the greedy algorithm begins by selecting site A since it contains four species while the other sites only contain three. At the second step, either site B or C would be added to A. Either way, only five of the six species are covered. This limitation should be kept in mind when interpreting the results from the empirical example below.

Application: Conserving Bird Genera in Oregon

In this section we illustrate the application of the approach for selecting which sites to include in a biological reserve network to maximize conservation given a budget constraint. We begin by describing the biological and economic data and then describe the results of the cost-effectiveness analysis.

Data

The study area for this application is roughly the western two-thirds of the state of Oregon. This is the area for which we had both information about land values and biological information about species ranges. The study area was partitioned into 289 potential biological reserve sites by overlaying a hexagonal grid. Each hexagonal grid has an area equal to 635 km^2.

Following Polasky, Camm, and Garber-Yonts (2001), the opportunity cost of designating a site as a biological reserve is assumed to be the average per acre land value at the site. In theory, the price of land equals the net present value that accrues from land ownership. In other words, the land value captures the stream of income that the land generates over time, all discounted to the present. For public lands, we estimated the potential net present value of income generated either from timber harvesting or livestock grazing. We used data on forest inventory, forest site productivity data, timber prices and harvest costs to generate the present value of timber income. We used data on livestock forage productivity by site, as well as livestock prices and costs, to generate the present value of grazing. Establishing a biological reserve presumes that no economic activity will occur on that land so that the land price (or the present value of income from economic activity) represents a measure of the opportunity cost of selecting the site as a reserve. Wilderness areas and national parks for which society has decided that conservation is the highest value use are assumed to have no opportunity costs for being set aside as reserves. Of course, there are some values such as recreation or ecosystem service values that may be enhanced by preserving the site in its natural condition. These values are not captured in this study. Details of the assumptions, methods, and data sources for the land value figures are described in Garber-Yonts and Polasky (1998) and in Polasky, Camm, and Garber-Yonts (2001).

Figure 11.2 shows average per acre land values for the 289 potential reserve sites. Land values are high west of the Cascade Range, where forestry and agriculture are productive and most of the population of Oregon resides, in the Willamette Valley, particularly on the outskirts of the Portland metropolitan area, in the Rogue River Valley, along the Pacific Coast, and near the city of Bend in central Oregon. With the exception of the Bend area, land values are low east of the Cascades.

We record the presence or absence of each of 248 bird species that occur in the study area for each of the 289 potential reserve sites. The data on species presence/absence by site were compiled from records of the Nature Conservancy's Natural Heritage Program. A detailed description of this data set is given in Master et al. (1995). In the original data, each species at each site was placed into one of four categories: (1) confident – a verified sighting of the species at the site had occurred in the past two decades; (2) probable – the site contains suitable habitat for the species and there have been verified sightings nearby; (3) possible – no verified sightings have occurred at the site and the site is of questionable suitability for the species; (4) not present – habitat is unsuitable for the species. We assume that a species is present at a site if and only if it was in the 'confident' or 'probable' categories. In Polasky et al. (2000), Arthur et al. (2002), and Camm et al. (2002), the problem with uncertainties about presence/absence are analyzed. In these papers, probabilities are assigned for the 'probable' and 'possible' categories and the objective is to maximize expected coverage in a site-constrained problem.

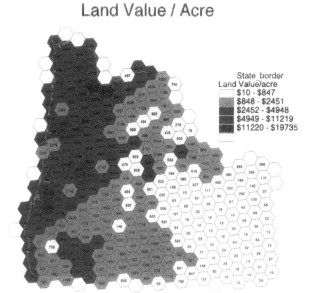

Figure 11.2 Land value per acre by reserve site

Figure 11.3 Genus richness by reserve site

Sibley and Ahlquist (1990) provide phylogenetic distances between numerous bird species of the world based on a measure of DNA-DNA hybridization (T50 H values). This work was most concerned with higher-order phylogeny and taxonomy and did not report many of the interspecific distances within a genus. For more complete coverage we use genus rather than species as the unit of analysis. The data for intergeneric distances were taken from branch lengths of UPGMA phylogenetic trees of birds reported in Sibley and Ahlquist (1990, pp.838–70).

Figure 11.3 shows the number of genera that occur in each potential reserve site. There are a total of 104 genera present in the study area. Genus richness tends to increase in a southerly direction. High pockets of genus richness occur in the Klamath Lake region in southern Oregon (an area noted for its large number of bird species), along the southern central coast, the Steens Mountain area of eastern Oregon and in the Willamette Valley. The high desert areas in the eastern part of the study area contain the fewest genera. Figure 11.4 shows the phylogenetic diversity across the potential reserve sites. The geographic pattern of phylogenetic diversity is similar to the pattern of genus richness.

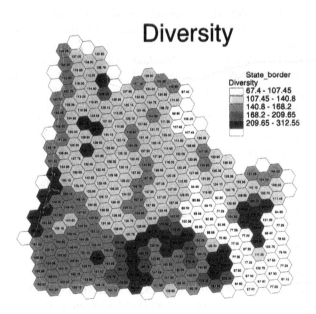

Figure 11.4 Diversity by reserve site

Results

To generate results, we apply the greedy algorithm to the reserve-site selection problem, where the objective is to maximize either the number of genera represented or phylogenetic diversity of represented genera, given a budget constraint. We vary the size of the budget in order to trace out how much coverage can be obtained for varying levels of cost. By doing so we can trace out a cost curve for biodiversity conservation.

Two cost curves – one chosen to maximize richness per dollar spent, the other to maximize diversity per dollar spent – are presented as Figures 11.5 and 11.6, respectively. In these figures, costs reported are the sum of the per acre land value for each site chosen as a reserve. Costs reported here should be interpreted in a relative sense only. To accurately calculate the total costs of setting up the reserve network, one would have to multiply the cost per acre by the number of acres included in the reserve. For example, if reserves were 10,000 acres each, one would multiply all of the cost number reported here by 10,000 to get total cost. The numbers on the curves, labeled one to 16, show how many sites have been included in the reserve network to get to that level of coverage. For example, in Figure 11.5, the cost of covering 70 genera, which can be achieved by selecting eight sites, is $180.

As illustrated in Figure 11.5, inclusion of the first site, which is quite inexpensive, covers 52 genera. Including sites two through nine is also inexpensive, but only covers an additional 20 genera. All of the first nine sites chosen are located east of the Cascade Mountains where land values are low. At this point there is almost complete coverage of all genera east of the mountains. In order to get more coverage some sites west of the Cascades must be included. The tenth site chosen has much higher land value but adds 14 genera to what had been represented previously. Beyond this point, adding additional reserve sites generally adds one genus at a time from increasingly expensive land. Adding in the eleventh to sixteenth sites yields large increases in costs for little increase in coverage.

A similar pattern emerges in Figure 11.6 where the horizontal axis measures phylogenetic diversity rather than genus richness. In both cases, the cost accumulation (total cost) curves for conservation are relatively flat until near complete coverage when they become quite steep. In other words, it is relatively inexpensive to conserve the majority of representative genera (either in terms of richness or diversity), but the costs of obtaining complete coverage are substantial. For example, when our objective is to maximize richness per dollar spent, conservation costs are $180 for 70 genera ($2.57/genus), $5,235 for 99 genera ($52.88/genus) and $16,061 for all 104 genera ($154.43/genus). In this regard, our results are similar to others reported in the literature (Montgomery, Brown, and Adams 1994; Ando et al. 1998; Montgomery et al. 1999; Polasky, Camm, and Garber-Yonts 2001). For example, Ando et al. (1998) find that conserving 50 per cent of endangered species in the U.S. costs less than ten per cent of the total cost of covering all endangered species.

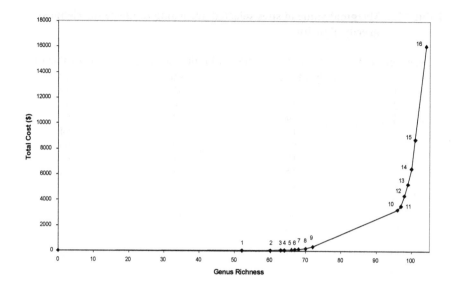

Figure 11.5 Richness cost accumulation curve

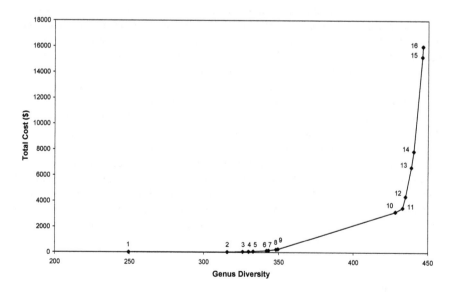

Figure 11.6 Diversity cost accumulation curve

**Table 11.2 Marginal value of sites selected according to the genus richness –
greedy algorithm**

Order selected	Value if it were the only site selected*	Marginal value of site	Total value of sites
1	52	52	52
2	42	8	60
3	19	3	63
4	12	1	64
5	54	2	66
6	12	1	67
7	12	1	68
8	53	2	70
9	21	2	72
10	60	14	96
11	26	1	97
12	54	1	98
13	24	1	99
14	58	1	100
15	21	1	101
16	63	3	104

*In this context, value only refers to the number of genera represented by a given site.

Table 11.2 shows the contribution of sites selected in order of selection when genus richness is the goal. Table 11.3 gives analogous information about sites when phylogenetic diversity is the goal. The second column shows the number of genera/phylogenetic diversity that occurs at that site. The third column, labeled 'marginal value of site', shows the number of genera/phylogenetic diversity that inclusion of this site adds that had not been previously conserved at other included sites. The final column shows the total or cumulative genus richness/phylogenetic diversity of including all sites up to that point. Except for the initial site selected, the contribution of the site by itself and the marginal values of each site differ substantially. For example, the fourteenth site selected when genus richness is the goal has a value of 58 if it was the only existing site, but contributes only one genus to the reserve network given that 13 other sites are included in the reserve network. What a particular site contributes to the overall conservation goal is that portion of diversity not covered elsewhere, which is what generates its marginal value. In general, the marginal value of each site depends heavily on the degree of substitutability or complementarity with other sites.

Conclusions

As discussed in the introduction, conserving biodiversity is an important environmental policy objective. The decline of habitat, which is directly related to

**Table 11.3 Marginal value of sites selected according to the genus diversity –
greedy algorithm**

Order selected	Value if it were the only site selected*	Marginal value of site	Total value of sites
1	249.45	249.45	249.45
2	286.95	66.30	315.75
3	246.95	10.30	326.05
4	81.15	3.90	329.95
5	83.65	3.10	333.05
6	284.65	8.80	341.85
7	78.55	1.30	343.15
8	243.75	5.05	348.20
9	289.40	1.25	349.45
10	307.45	78.70	428.15
11	167.95	4.90	433.05
12	154.35	2.00	435.05
13	134.50	3.90	438.95
14	305.90	1.60	440.55
15	306.95	5.45	446.00
16	293.00	0.35	446.35

*In this context, value only refers to the number of genera represented by a given site.

land-use decisions, is the leading cause of the decline of biodiversity, whether measured at the genetic, species, or ecosystem level. Species and habitat conservation considerations already factor into many land-use and land management decisions. In the future, attention to conservation considerations in land use and land management is likely to increase as conflicts between human uses and species and habitat conservation increase. Given this, the academic and policy communities should be developing tools that land managers can use to navigate these conflicts as they try to pursue both profitable economic activities and conservation.

In this chapter we have discussed methods for trying to simultaneously pursue both human land-use and conservation objectives. The methods we used combine ecological and economic information to maximize biodiversity conservation for a given cost. We illustrated the approach using land value data, taxonomic information, and the geographic distribution data of bird species in Oregon. This illustration illuminates several points that we think are relevant for conservation policy generally. First, while some degree of conflict between pursuit of economic activity and conservation may be inevitable, much of biodiversity can be conserved with minimal disruption to the economy. In our results, and those of other studies, a large fraction of biodiversity conservation can be accomplished at low cost. This result occurs because there are rural areas that contain a large number of species or important habitat that are of marginal value for economic activities. Conserving those places that have high conservation value and low economic value results in protection of a large fraction of biodiversity at very low cost.

Second, complete protection of all biodiversity is likely to be expensive. Some species have limited ranges that occur on land for which high-value economic activity could occur. In our study, the protecting the last few bird genera entailed greater expense than protecting the other 90 to 95 per cent of the genera. Cases where conservation entails high cost represent difficult policy choices for society. To date we have not successfully established a policy course for making tradeoffs between conservation and economic activities. In theory, the Endangered Species Act prohibits harm to listed species, which includes adverse habitat modification. The law would seem to imply that conservation should occur regardless of how high the costs might be. In practice, however, political pressures, inadequate funding, and lack of knowledge often lead to conservation taking a back seat to economic activity despite what is written in the Endangered Species Act.

Finally, coordinating land-use plans that allow pursuit of both economic activity and conservation objectives requires both a broad perspective and attention to local details. Predicting whether a species can survive in a location depends upon detailed knowledge of local conditions. How important it is that a species survives in that locale depends in large part on whether it is one of many populations or the last remaining population of the species. If there are large, relatively safe populations of the species that exist in other locations, then it is less important to safeguard the species in this particular locale. However, it would be of great importance to conserve a species, if losing this population causes the overall extinction of the species. Similarly, a case can be made that species with no close genetic relatives may be of greater conservation importance than species with close genetic relatives, as losing the former will result in a greater loss of unique genetic material. Understanding the marginal contribution of particular species or particular habitats can only be done with knowledge of the bigger picture, including what other habitats and species are likely to be conserved. One challenge to conservation planning is to successfully coordinate the big picture with local detailed information and local land managers responsible for land-use and land management decisions on their land.

References

Ando, A., J. Camm, S. Polasky, and A. Solow. 1998. 'Species Distributions, Land Values, and Efficient Conservation.' *Science* 279: 2126–8.

Arthur, J.L., R.G. Haight, C.A. Montgomery, and S. Polasky. 2002. 'Analysis of the Threshold and Expected Coverage Approaches for the Probabilistic Reserve Selection Problem.' *Environmental Monitoring and Assessment* 7(2): 81–9.

Barbier, E.B. 1994. 'Valuing Environmental Functions: Tropical Wetlands.' *Land Economics* 70(2): 155–73.

Bingham, G. 1995. 'Issues in Ecosystem Valuation: Improving Information for Decision Making.' *Ecological Economics* 14(2): 73–90.

Bockstael, N., R. Costanza, I. Strand, W. Boynton, K. Bell, and L. Wainger. 1995. 'Ecological Economic Modeling and Valuation of Ecosystems.' *Ecological Economics* 14(2): 143–59.

Camm. J.D., S.K. Norman, S. Polasky, and A.R. Solow. 2002. 'Nature Reserve Selection to Maximize Expected Species Coverage.' *Operations Research* 50(6): 946–55.

Ehrlich, P.R. and A.H. Ehrlich. 1981. *Extinction: The Causes and Consequences of the Disappearance of Species.* New York, New York: Random House.

Faith, D.P. 1992. 'Conservation Evaluation and Phylogenetic Diversity.' *Biological Conservation* 61: 1–10.

Faith, D.P. 1994. 'Genetic Diversity and Taxonomic Priorities for Conservation.' *Biological Conservation* 68: 69–74.

Garber-Yonts, B., and S. Polasky. 1998. *Oregon Land Values Dataset Manual.* Oregon Multiscale Biodiversity Conservation Project, Oregon Fish and Wildlife Department.

Keystone Center. 1991. *Final Consensus Report of the Keystone Policy Dialogue on Biological Diversity on Federal Lands.* Keystone, Colorado: The Keystone Center.

Klauer, B. 2000. 'Ecosystem Prices: Activity Analysis Applied to Ecosystems.' *Ecological Economics* 33(3): 473–86.

Levin, S.A. 1999. *Fragile Dominion: Complexity and the Commons.* Reading, Massachusetts: Perseus Books.

MacArthur, R.H., and E.O. Wilson. 1967. *The Theory of Island Biogeography.* Princeton, New Jersey: Princeton University Press.

Master, L., N. Clupper, E. Gaines, C. Bogert, R. Solomon, and M. Ormes. 1995. *Biodiversity Research Consortium Species Database Manual.* Boston, Massachusetts: The Nature Conservancy.

Montgomery, C.A., G.M. Brown, Jr., and D.M. Adams. 1994. 'The Marginal Cost of Species Preservation: The Case of the Northern Spotted Owl.' *Journal of Environmental Economics and Management* 26: 111–28.

Montgomery, C.A., R.A. Pollak, K. Freemark, and D. White. 1999. 'Pricing Biodiversity.' *Journal of Environmental Economics and Management* 38: 1–19.

National Research Council. 1995. *Science and the Endangered Species Act.* Washington, District of Columbia: National Academy Press.

Pimm S.L., G.J. Russell, J.L. Gittleman, and T.M. Brooks. 1995. 'The Future of Biodiversity.' *Science* 269: 347–50.

Polasky, S., J. Camm, A. Solow, B. Csuti, D. White, and R. Ding. 2000. 'Choosing Reserve Networks with Incomplete Species Information.' *Biological Conservation* 94(1): 1–10.

Polasky, S., J. Camm, and B. Garber-Yonts. 2001. 'Selecting Biological Reserves Cost-Effectively: An Application to Terrestrial Vertebrate Conservation in Oregon.' *Land Economics* 77(1): 68–78.

Polasky, S., B. Csuti, C.A. Vossler, and S.M. Meyers. 2001. 'A Comparison of Taxonomic Distinctness versus Richness as Criteria for Setting Conservation Priorities for North American Birds.' *Biological Conservation* 97: 99–105.

Sibley, C.G., and J.E. Alhquist. 1990. *Phylogeny and Classification of Birds: A Study of Molecular Evolution.* New Haven, Connecticut: Yale University Press.

Solow, A.R., and S. Polasky. 1994. 'Measuring Biological Diversity.' *Environmental and Ecological Statistics* 1: 95–107.

Solow, A., S. Polasky, and J. Broadus. 1993. 'On the Measurement of Biological Diversity.' *Journal of Environmental Economics and Management* 24(1): 60–68.

Spash, C.L., and N. Hanley. 1995. 'Preferences, Information, and Biodiversity Preservation.' *Ecological Economics* 12(3): 191–208.

Suter, G.W. 1995. 'Adapting Ecological Risk Assessment for Ecosystem Valuation.' *Ecological Economics* 14(2): 137–41.

Tilman, D., J. Fargione, B. Wolff, C. D'Antonio, A. Dobson, R. Howarth, D. Schindler, W.H. Schlesinger, D. Simberloff, and D. Swackhamer. 2001 'Forecasting Agriculturally Driven Global Environmental Change.' *Science* 292: 281–4.

Toman, M.A. 1997. 'Ecosystem Valuation: An Overview of Issues and Uncertainties,' in *Ecosystem Function and Human Activities: Reconciling Economics and Ecology.* New York, New York: Chapman and Hall.

Vane-Wright, R.I., C.J. Humphries, and P.H. Williams. 1991. 'What to Protect? Systematics and the Agony of Choice.' *Biological Conservation* 55: 235–54.

Weitzman, M. 1992. 'On Diversity.' *Quarterly Journal of Economics* 107: 363–406.

Weitzman, M.L. 1993. 'What to Preserve? An Application of Diversity Theory to Crane Conservation.' *Quarterly Journal of Economics* 108: 157–83.

Wilson, E.O. ed. 1988. *BioDiversity.* Washington, District of Columbia: National Academy Press.

Chapter 12

Land-Use Changes and Regulations in Five Western States of the United States

JunJie Wu

Introduction

This chapter describes land-use changes and regulations in five western states of the United States (Oregon, California, Idaho, Nevada, and Washington). There is a significant variation in the degree of government involvement in land-use planning and regulations in these five western states. State and local governments in Oregon and Washington are actively involved in land-use planning and regulation, while governments in Nevada and Idaho impose few land-use regulations. State and local governments in California are moderately involved in land-use planning and regulations. Thus, the study region offers an excellent 'laboratory' to study the effect of land-use regulations on land-use changes. However, to my knowledge, there is no economic study that provides a comprehensive survey of local land regulations at the regional or national level.

While the federal government monitors trends in land-use conversions, state and local governments impose most land-use controls. The federal government has yet to articulate anything close to a clear vision of land-use policy (Daniels 1999). Despite the fact that land-use regulations are largely a local issue, relatively few studies have focused on local land-use regulations because of a lack of data. Those that do focus on land-use policies tend to be case studies of specific programs in specific areas. For example, Henderson (1991) compares the effectiveness of zoning laws, price regulation, and the shifting of fiscal burdens between existing residents and developers. He finds that traditional instruments, such as zoning, are not efficient. In a world of perfect certainty, price controls and creative fiscal arrangements produce efficient outcomes. With uncertainty over future prices, only by restructuring fiscal arrangements can the community efficiently control the developer. McMillen and McDonald (1993) examine the circumstances under which land-use zoning can increase land values and find that a necessary condition for the assignment of a block exclusively to residential use to increase land values is that residential land values rise as the proportion of the block that is in residential use increases. Their empirical results imply that the land-use zoning system could not have brought about a general increase in land values. Kline and Alig (1999) analyze Oregon's land-use planning program with regard to how effective it has been in protecting forests and farmland from development. Daniels (1998) examines the purchase of development rights as a tool of farmland protection in Lancaster County, Pennsylvania. The Proceedings of the 1998 National Conference on the Performance of State Programs for Farmland Retention, held in Columbus, Ohio, provide a review and evaluation of current farmland retention programs in several states (Libby et al. 1998). Daniels and Bowers (1997) describe the many challenges in farmland protection and explain how to create a package of techniques to meet those challenges. Other examples that focus on local regulations include Pfeffer and Lapping (1994), who examine programs based on the exchange of development rights in the northeastern United States, and Lang and Hornburg (1997), who analyze urban growth management in Portland, Oregon. A common characteristic of these studies is that they focus on a specific program in a specific region. However, because many regulations share common objectives and are implemented simultaneously, it is difficult to isolate the effect of a specific program on land development.

Economic studies on land use along the rural-urban fringe are also limited, despite the fact that the accelerated loss of farmland and open space to development has generated strong public support for growth management in the U.S. In the 1998–2000 U.S. elections, hundreds of local and statewide initiatives for growth management were put on ballots, and a majority of these initiatives were passed. These reactions were hardly surprising given the strong sentiment against sprawl. It is claimed that sprawl is ugly, that it eats up farmland, reduces amenities and open space, increases public service costs and taxes, causes traffic jams, increases urban runoff and flooding, and reduces wildlife habitat and water quality. Sprawl is even blamed for causing obesity, apathy, and antisocial behavior.

In stark contrast to this emotionally-charged indictment of sprawl, many economists believe that urban spatial patterns are a result of a market process that allocates land between urban and agricultural uses. For example, Brueckner (2000) argues that urban spatial expansion is mostly benign. After all, people like big houses, large yards, proximity to amenities, the convenience of shopping malls, and other benefits associated with sprawl. Thus, to a large extent, sprawl is a result of consumer choices.

The stakes are high in this debate on the costs and benefits of urban sprawl. Policy measures designed to curb urban sprawl will ultimately affect a key element of American lifestyle, the consumption of a large amount of living space at affordable prices (Brueckner 2000). To fully understand the costs and benefits of urban sprawl and the nature of any anti-sprawl policy, we must first understand the causes of urban sprawl. Despite the importance of this issue, there is no convincing economic theory for explaining fragmented, leapfrog development in the rural-urban fringe. Mills (1981) examines sprawl in a monocentric city and attributes it to landowner decisions to preserve a ring of undeveloped land for future use. The Mills study, however, does not capture the complexity of urban sprawl and the phenomena that has been characterized as 'an economic system gone awry.' Brueckner (2000) argues that urban spatial expansion results mainly from a growing population, rising income, and falling commuting costs, as has been discussed in earlier chapters. However, as with other studies on urban spatial structures, he does not provide an explanation for leapfrog development in the rural-urban fringe. Landis (1995) and Landis and Zhang (1998) develop empirical models to predict land development at the individual parcel level based on economic and/or location variables, but do not explain the endogenous process of the formation of urban spatial structure.

Below, we first describe the land-use changes in the five western states examined, followed by a discussion of land-use regulations in the region. Results on the interactions between land-use changes and regulations in the five western states are then presented. The last section contains concluding remarks.

Data

The data on land-use regulations used in this study were obtained from a comprehensive survey of local land-use regulations conducted at Oregon State University between August and October of 1999. The survey was sent to all county land-use planning directors in five western states. Respondents were asked to report whether or not a particular type of land-use regulation (29 in all) was in use in their counties, and to evaluate the effectiveness of each of the regulations. The survey was conducted following Dillman's *Total Design Method* (Dillman 1978). The questionnaire was designed after an extensive literature review and was pre-tested by a few selected county land-use planning directors. The questionnaire was revised based on their comments, and the revised questionnaire was sent to all county land-use planning directors in five western states. Two postcard reminders were sent to those who did not respond by two and four weeks. Telephone calls were made to those who did not respond. The overall response rate was 69 per cent. Counties of Washington had the highest response rate (87 per cent), followed by Oregon (78 per cent), Nevada (65 per cent), California (60 per cent), and Idaho (57 per cent). There were a total of 194 counties in the five western states.

The data on land use were taken from the 1982 and 1992 National Resource Inventories (NRI). The NRI collected land-use data at 800,000 randomly selected sites across the continental United States and divided land use into eleven major categories (cultivated cropland, non-cultivated cropland, pastureland, rangeland, forestland, urban and built-up land, and five other categories). In this study, cultivated cropland, non-cultivated cropland, pastureland, and rangeland are categorized as farmland, and urban and built-up land is categorized as developed land. The NRI recorded land use at each site in 1982 and 1992. By comparing the land use in 1982 and 1992 at each NRI site, we estimate land-use changes over that period. Each NRI site is assigned a weight (called the expansion factor) to reflect the acreage it represents. The sampling design of the NRI ensures that inferences at the national, regional, state, and sub-state levels are made in a statistically reliable manner.

Land-Use Changes

Table 12.1 summarizes the land-use changes between 1982 and 1992 in the five western states. The last column of Table 12.1 shows the total acreage loss for each major land-use category, and the last row of Table 12.1 shows the total acreage gain. The differences between the gains and the losses give the net gains or net losses for the seven major land-use categories. There were a total of 83.9, 44.0, and 5.6 million acres of farmland, forestland, and urban land, respectively, in the five western states in 1982. By 1992, the total acreages of farmland and forestland fell to 79.4 and 43.6 million acres, respectively, while the total acreage of urban land increased to 6.7 million acres. Farmland had the largest reduction in total acreage, with about three million acres of net loss in cropland and 1.5 million acres of net loss in rangeland and pastureland. Of the 4.5 million acres of net loss of farmland, more than one million acres were converted to development. The 4.5 million acres of net loss account for about 5.34 per cent of total farmland in the region. There were also large conversions between alternative farmland uses in the five western states. For example, between 1982 and 1992, 1.35 million acres of rangeland and pastureland were converted to cropland, but during the same time period 1.37 million acres of cropland were converted to pastureland and rangeland.

Table 12.1 Land-use conversions in five western states of the United States, 1982–1992 (100 acres)

From	Cropland	Pasture/ Range	Forest	To Urban	Water	Federal	Other	Total Loss
Cropland	0	13660	264	3455	288	2273	26659	46599
Pasture/ Range	13511	0	5019	6745	1274	11400	3799	41748
Forest	210	4457	0	3477	291	6575	772	15782
Urban	0	1	4	0	0	0	0	5
Water	271	2690	188	19	0	62	25	3255
Federal	1655	5290	5104	0	0	0	967	13016
Other	1081	691	477	686	150	826	0	3911
Total Gain	16728	26788	11056	14382	2003	21136	32222	124316

Among the five states, Washington lost the most cropland (1.04 million acres), followed by Idaho (0.79 million acres), Oregon (0.58 million acres), California (0.47 million acres), and Nevada (0.07 million acres). However, the total farmland loss was largest in California, where more than one million acres of pastureland and rangeland were converted to non-agricultural uses. The five states also lost 472,600 acres of forestland, with more than 90 per cent of the loss occurring in California and Washington. Total forestland actually increased by 52,700 acres in Idaho. Between 1982 and 1992, total developed area increased by 1.44 million acres in the five western states, with California, Washington. and Oregon accounting for 55, 20, and 11 per cent of the increase, respectively.

Land-Use Regulations

There is a significant variation in the degree of government involvement in land-use planning across the five western states (Tables 12.2–12.7). The most important goal of land-use planning and regulation in Nevada counties was the promotion of industrial and commercial investment, while the most important goal in other states was to conserve open space, farmland, forestland, and natural areas.

A county comprehensive plan had been enacted in almost all of the counties in the five states when the survey was conducted. However, the timing of the initial enactment is different across counties. A county comprehensive plan is a set of development guidelines, which are developed based on population projections and future land-use needs. It is not legally binding. Extra territorial planning and zoning were popular in Idaho, while urban growth boundaries were popular in Oregon and Washington. Agricultural, residential, forestry, conservation, open space, and steep-slope zonings were popular throughout the five states, whereas performance zoning was used only in a limited number of counties in the states. Agricultural zoning is a widely used technique for farmland protection in rural-urban fringes. It is used to separate farming activities from conflicting non-farm land uses and to protect a critical mass of farms and farmland. Forestry zoning is used to protect a critical mass of commercial timberland and to separate forestry operations from conflicting non-forestry land uses (see Tables 12.3 and 12.4). Among land-use regulations, housing caps were rated as least effective by planners in all states except Nevada. Comprehensive plans and urban growth boundaries received comparable effectiveness ratings.

Although minimum parcel size was a popular land-use regulation in many counties, specification of maximum parcel size was not. Developer dedication was the most popular land acquisition technique in many counties. Fee simple purchase and agricultural districts were especially popular in California. Preferential property taxation was the most popular incentive-based policy for preserving farm and forestland. Special assessments to place the cost of certain public facilities on landowners in a specific area were popular in Oregon, Washington, and California. Environmental impact assessments were popular in Washington and California. Regional fair sharing (standards to ensure that all communities get a share of regional growth and affordable housing) was especially popular in California.

Table 12.2 The importance of alternative goals of land-use regulations as perceived by county land-use planners

	Conserve Agricultural Land	Conserve Forestry Land	Promote Industrial Investment	Promote Commercial Investment	Promote Compact Development
Oregon	4.4	4.4	3.3	3.1	3.8
Washington	4.7	3.8	3.8	3.6	3.5
California	4.0	4.0	3.7	3.6	3.5
Idaho	4.7	4.2	3.2	3.1	3.6
Nevada	3.6	2.9	4.6	4.4	4.2

*One being least effective and five being most effective.

Table 12.3 The effectiveness of land-use regulations (per cent of counties enacting policies)

	County Comprehensive Plan	Urban Growth Boundaries	Housing Caps
Oregon	4.0 (100)	4.3 (86)	1.0 (3)
Washington	3.5 (94)	3.6 (91)	2.8 (6)
California	4.0 (100)	3.9 (46)	2.6 (23)
Idaho	3.8 (100)	3.3 (40)	N/A
Nevada	3.2 (100)	3.5 (36)	4.5 (18)

*One being least effective and five being most effective.

Table 12.4 The effectiveness of zoning regulations (per cent of counties enacting policies)

	Agricultural Zoning	Forestry Zoning	Rural Residential Zoning
Oregon	4.4 (96)	4.4 (93)	4.0 (89)
Washington	4.1 (82)	3.9 (65)	3.6 (79)
California	4.1 (94)	4.4 (49)	3.5 (86)
Idaho	4.0 (96)	4.0 (36)	3.9 (80)
Nevada	3.7 (82)	3.3 (27)	3.4 (91)

*One being least effective and five being most effective.

Planners predicted a high possibility of farmland development. This is especially true in Idaho and Nevada (see Table 12.5). Counties in California spent the largest amount of money on planning, while counties in Idaho spent the least. However, the average share of money spent on planning out of county general funds remained fairly close in the five states (see Table 12.6). Thus, while spending to effect the extent and types of land conversions, such as agriculture to development, is more limited in some states, this appears to be a more general funding issue and not specifically a lack of funding for land-use policy. As to questions regarding influential parties over land-use decisions, planners in Oregon and Washington felt strong influences from the state government, while planners in California, Idaho, and Nevada felt strong influences from non-governmental organizations (see Table 12.7).

Table 12.5 The likelihood of alternative land-use conversions as perceived by county land-use planners

	Forestry to Agricultural Land	Agricultural to Forestry Land	Forestry to Residential Land	Agricultural to Residential Land
Oregon	1.7	1.8	1.7	2.3
Washington	1.4	1.8	2.8	3.2
California	1.8	1.2	1.8	3.1
Idaho	1.1	1.6	2.4	3.8
Nevada	1.2	1.5	1.9	3.9

*One being least effective and five being most effective.

Table 12.6 The average number of land-use planners per county, annual expenditure on land-use planning, and percentage of county general funds spent on land-use planning

	Average Number of Planners Per County	Average Annual Expenditure on Planning ($)	Average Share of General Fund (per cent)
Oregon	5.3	494,646	2
Washington	11.8	2,013,928	3
California	18.8	6,773,814	3
Idaho	3.1	199,062	2
Nevada	7.0	1,230,122	2

Table 12.7 The degree of influence of parties in land-use planning

	State Government	Private Business	Average Citizens	Professional Planners	Developers
Oregon	4.2	2.9	3.5	3.1	3.0
Washington	3.6	3.2	3.6	3.8	3.3
California	3.3	3.4	3.7	3.4	3.8
Idaho	3.3	3.2	3.4	3.0	3.1
Nevada	2.5	3.4	3.2	3.4	3.8

*One being least effective and five being most effective.

In addition to county land-use policies, two state land-use programs were also identified. These were state land-use planning and mandatory review of projects involving farmland conversions. State land-use planning programs generally require counties and cities to adopt comprehensive plans that meet state guidelines. California, Oregon, and Washington have a formal state land-use planning program. Washington is the only state that has mandatory review of projects involving farmland conversions.

Interactions Between Land-Use Changes and Regulations

In this section we review several recent studies on interactions between land-use changes and land-use regulations in the five western states. Wu and Cho (2002) use an option value approach to model land development decisions under uncertainty and irreversibility. They apply the model to estimate the effect of land-use regulations and other socioeconomic and spatial variables on farmland development in the five western states. Their empirical results suggest that the relative profits from farming and development significantly affect the likelihood of land development. In addition, the relative magnitude of risks associated with farming and development are also important. The larger the risk associated with land development and the smaller the risk associated with farming, the less likely farmland is to be developed.

Wu and Cho (2002) also estimate the relationship between the intensity of local land-use regulations and the effect of several location and land quality variables on the probability of land development. They find that land development is quite responsive to the intensity of local land-use regulations. In contrast, state land-use regulations such as state planning and mandatory review of projects involving farmland conversions are found to be less effective in reducing land development than local land-use regulations. They also find that a parcel is more likely to be developed if it is located close to a metropolitan center or an urban-type national park. A parcel is less likely to be developed if it is located close to a wilderness or national park. Other things equal, development and farming compete for high quality land. An increase in population and household income also increase the pressure of urbanization of farmland.

To explore land-type/climatic differences, Cho, Wu, and Alig (2001) compare land development and land-use regulations between the west and east sides of the Cascade Range in Oregon, Washington, and California. The Cascades form an important climatic divide, with the western slope receiving abundant precipitation and the eastern slope receiving relatively little. As a result, the western part of the range is heavily wooded and the eastern section is covered mainly by grass and scrub plants. Because of the drastic climatic differences between the west and east sides of the Cascade Range, the two sides have different types of human settlements and land-use patterns.

Cho, Wu, and Alig (2001) find, however, that both sides of the Cascade Range experienced continuous development and farmland loss between 1982 and 1992, although the acreage and the rate of land development were greater on the west side than on the east side. Forestland loss was a continuous phenomenon on the west side, but surprisingly, forestland increased by 140,300 acres between 1987 and 1992 on the east side of the Cascade Range. The increased forestland was converted mainly from farmland and other land.

In the two studies discussed above, land-use regulations are treated as exogenous. Land-use changes during a period are related to land-use regulations at the beginning of the period. However, as Cho, Wu, and Boggess (2002) point out, rapid land development may promote land-use regulations, which may in turn affect land development and public finances. To evaluate the dynamics of land-use changes and regulations and their impacts on public finances, the authors estimate a simultaneous equations system that includes a regulation adoption equation, a land development equation, a housing price equation, and two public financial impact equations. The empirical results suggest that the conversion of farmland and open space to development, along with high public expenditure and property taxes, promote the imposition of more stringent land-use regulations by county governments. More stringent land-use regulations, in turn, reduce land development, long-run public expenditures, and property taxes at the cost of higher housing prices and larger public expenditures and property taxes in the short run. However, in the long run, land-use regulations reduce public expenditures and property taxes. The results also indicate that land-use regulations, land development, public expenditures, and property taxes are all significantly affected by population, geographic location, land quality, housing rent, and risks of land development.

Concluding Remarks

Urban sprawl and the resulting socioeconomic and environmental consequences have become forefront issues in many countries around the world. Controlling urban sprawl has been within the domain of state and local governments, but the federal government may be able to help in such areas as providing financial incentives for channeling growth in desirable directions or coordinating local, regional, and state efforts. To understand the nature of any efficient land-use policy, it is necessary to first understand the interactions between land development, land-use regulations, and their socioeconomic and ecosystem impacts. These interactions, however, are seldom analyzed in a formal and vigorous fashion. Further research is needed to better understand these interactions and the costs and benefits of land development.

References

Brueckner, J.K. 2000. 'Urban Sprawl: Diagnosis and Remedies.' *International Regional Science Review* 23(2): 160–71.

Cho, S., J. Wu, and W.G. Boggess. 2002. 'Measuring Interactions Among Urban Development, Land-use regulations, and Public Finance.' Department of Agricultural and Resource Economics working paper, Oregon State University.

Cho, S., J. Wu, and R. Alig. 2002. 'Land Development Under Uncertainty: A Comparison Between The West And East Sides Of The Cascade Range in Oregon, Washington and California.' Department of Agricultural and Resource Economics working paper, Oregon State University.

Daniels, T. 1999. *When City and County Collides*. Washington, District of Columbia: Island Press.

Daniels, T. 1998. 'The Purchase of Development Rights, Agricultural Preservation and Other Land-use policy Tools: The Pennsylvania Experience.' Proceedings of the 1998 National Public Policy Education Conference. Clackamas, Oregon, September 21–23.

Daniels, T., and D. Bowers. 1997. *Holding Our Ground*. Washington, District of Columbia: Island Press.

Dillman, D.A. 1978. *Mail and Telephone Surveys: The Total Design Method*. New York, New York: John Wiley & Sons.

Henderson, J.V. 1991. 'Optimal Regulation of Land Development through Price and Fiscal Controls.' *Journal of Urban Economics* 30(1): 64–82.

Kline, J.D. and R.J. Alig. 1999. 'Does Land-use planning Slow the Conversion of Forest and Farm Lands?' *Growth and Change* 30: 3–22.

Lang, R.E., S.P. Hornburg. 1997. 'Planning Portland Style: Pitfall and Possibilities.' Housing Policy Debate V8: 1–10.

Libby, L., M. Altobello, T.W. Ilvento, A.D. Sokolow, and B.A. Weber (conference organizers). 1998. Proceedings of a National Conference on the Performance of State Programs for Farmland Retention. Columbus, Ohio, September 10–11.

McMillen, D.P., and J.F. Mcdonald. 1993. 'Could Zoning Have Increased Land Values in Chicago?' *Journal of Urban Economics* 33(2): 167–88.

Mills, D.E. 1981. 'Growth, Speculation and Sprawl in a Monocentric City.' *Journal of Urban Economics* 10: 201–26.

Landis, J.D. 1995. 'Imagining Land Use Futures: Applying the California Urban Futures Model.' *Journal of the American Planning Association* 61(4): 438–57.

Landis, J.D., and M. Zhang. 1998. 'The Second Generation of the California Urban Futures Model. Part 2: Specification and Calibration Results of the Land–Use Change Submodel.' *Environment and Planning A* 25(6): 795–824.

Pfeffer, M.J., and M.B. Lapping. 1994. 'Farmland Preservation, Development Rights and the Theory of the Growth Machine: The Views of Planners.' *Journal of Rural Studies* 10(3): 233–48.

Wu, J., and S. Cho. 2002. 'Urbanization Under Benefit Uncertainty and Government Regulations.' Department of Agricultural and Resource Economics working paper, Oregon State University.

PART IV
VALUATION OF
LAND-USE CHANGE

Chapter 13

Valuation and Land-Use Change

Kevin J. Boyle, Kathleen P. Bell, and Jonathan Rubin

Introduction

Economists evaluate changes in land use by comparing the net return to society from the land before and after the change in use. Employing this perspective, the desirability of a land-use change rests on the extent to which the benefits of the change exceed its costs. In practice, land policy and management decisions depend on the best available measurements of the benefits and costs of alternative uses of lands. As is the case in other areas of environmental economics, the measurement of benefits and costs exhibits tremendous variation in terms of feasibility and difficulty. In many instances, certain benefits and costs are straightforward to measure. Other benefits and costs are less well understood. For example, the private return to a parcel of land in residential use is easier to characterize than the social return to a parcel in an undeveloped use that provides wildlife habitat and aesthetic amenities. This chapter presents an introductory discussion of how economic valuation methods can be used to measure the benefits and costs of alternative uses of land resources. Throughout the chapter, emphasis is given to the role of valuation in elucidating the demand for services provided by rural lands and in conceptualizing the benefits of rural lands.

The demand for services provided by land resources essentially reduces to the demand for different land attributes. Both the study of the demand for land attributes and the management of land resources are complicated by the manner in which the services provided by land resources are produced and consumed. In short, many of these services are public goods. Hence, they are non-rival and non-excludable in consumption and are under-provided by markets. Because of market failure, governments commonly intervene and regulate the management of land resources. Zoning ordinances are a classic example of such interventions. In many cases, these ordinances are written to prevent the overprovision of an undesirable service, such as noise, to encourage the provision of a desirable service, such as wildlife habitat, or to limit the external effects of one land use on another, such as the effects of an industrial plant on nearby residences.

Curiously and perhaps surprisingly, economic valuation has played a limited role in the design of these interventions. Although the economics literature is replete with studies of land transactions and land-use patterns, there are few studies that comprehensively value the services provided by land resources (Santos 1999). As more attention is devoted to land-use change and land-use policy, the urgency to complete such studies increases. There are also administrative reasons to expect further inquiries into the demand for different land services or attributes. Executive Order 12866 (1996), which supersedes Executive Order 12291 (1981), requires federal agencies to undertake benefit-cost analyses of major regulations. Regulations designed to protect and enhance services provided by rural lands fall under the purview of this order. Secondly, because economic values are often used in litigation involving damages to land resources, natural resource damage assessment is also a strong catalyst for valuation.

Economic valuation methods strive to understand the preferences of society for goods and services. When goods and services are bought and sold in markets, price and quantity-demanded information may be used to gauge preferences and to assess the relative values held for different goods and services. However, when goods and services are not traded in formal markets, non-market valuation approaches apply instead of market-based valuation methods. For extensive reviews of market-based and non-market valuation methods, refer to Braden and Kolstad (1991), Champ, Boyle, and Brown (2003), or Freeman (2003). Land resources provide a myriad of services, including views, wildlife habitat, recreation opportunities, and flood prevention. Because there are not formal markets for a significant number of land services, non-market valuation approaches are of great relevance to the study of rural land-use change.

This chapter offers an introduction to five non-market valuation approaches and discusses the general applicability of these approaches to the study of the economics of rural land-use change. Our objective here is to raise awareness of how economic methods may be used to value the services provided by lands. After reading this chapter, readers may better understand what goes into the design of an economic valuation study of land-use change and how to interpret the results of such a study. Designing a credible valuation study requires knowledge and careful implementation procedures. Readers who choose to use the methods identified in this chapter should carefully review the current literature before proceeding with an original study. Our introduction to these methods features empirical applications selected from articles published in *Land Economics* from 1991 through 2000. *Land Economics* is the major outlet for journal articles on the economics of rural land-use issues. Because our review of applications is not comprehensive, readers interested in the full range of applications are advised to conduct a broader search of the literature, including articles from additional journals.

Economic valuation methods are commonly grouped under the headings of 'revealed preference' and 'stated preference' methods. Revealed preference methods gauge preferences based on decisions individuals make in market situations. In contrast, stated preference methods characterize preferences based on decisions stated by individuals. Our discussion of economic valuation methods features approaches falling under both of these headings. This chapter begins with a comparison of hedonic property value, travel cost, and averting behavior approaches, which are revealed preference methods, and concludes with a summary of contingent valuation and conjoint analysis approaches, which are stated preference methods.

Revealed Preference Valuation Methods

Hedonic property value, travel cost, and averting behavior models are commonly applied revealed preference valuation methods. Table 13.1 describes the key features of these methods. Recall that revealed preference methods draw statistical inferences from actual choices individuals make within markets. Hedonic property value models analyze housing transactions to reveal the relative value of different property attributes. Travel cost models examine recreation decisions to obtain the relative value of different site attributes. Averting behavior models explore decisions made by households to avoid specific damages or losses and, in doing so, reveal the relative value of avoiding damages or risks.

Using these methods, economic valuation proceeds by specifying a theoretical framework and then analyzing data from purchase or recreation decisions in a manner consistent with the underlying economic framework. Conceptually, there are strong parallels in the frameworks of these three valuation approaches. Individuals are assumed to search for housing with desirable characteristics, including land services, and to purchase the housing unit with the most desirable set of characteristics. Variation in purchase prices and housing characteristics allows for estimation of the implicit price of individual characteristics. Travel cost and averting behavior models arise from a household purchase and their own time to produce a desired outcome. Individuals combine travel costs and other marginal costs of participating in a recreation activity with their travel time to produce a recreation experience. Travel and time costs serve as an implicit price of participation, and the payment of higher prices is assumed to reflect higher quality recreation experiences. In the case of averting behavior, individuals combine purchased inputs with time to avoid damages and to produce outcomes such as improved health. The purchased inputs comprise the implicit price of improved health.

Table 13.1 Revealed preference valuation methods

Method	Revealed behavior	Conceptual framework	Typical application(s)
Hedonic Property Value	Property purchase	Demand for differentiated goods	Property value
Travel Cost	Participation in recreation activity and choice of site	Household production, weak complements	Recreation demand
Averting Behavior	Expenditures to avoid damages or undesirable outcomes	Household production, perfect substitutes	Morbidity, mortality, material damages, aesthetics

Hedonic Property Value Models

Hedonic models are based on Lancaster's theory of consumer demand, where the price of a differentiated good, such as a parcel of land, is a function of a myriad of attributes (Lancaster 1966). Empirical applications of hedonic models estimate implicit prices for the individual attributes of differentiated goods. These implicit prices are then employed to describe the use values of various attributes. Rosen (1974) develops the basic theory for using hedonic property value models to derive the demand for attributes such as environmental quality or land characteristics. Refer to Palmquist (1991, 2004), Freeman (2003), and Taylor (2003) for comprehensive discussions of this economic valuation approach.

Using a hedonic property value framework, the choice of property arises from a utility maximization problem, where a household maximizes utility by adjusting its consumption of a variety of goods and services. These adjustments in consumption are constrained by household income and the prices of goods and services. Property characteristics are assumed to enter the utility function and to affect the prices of properties. A central part of the empirical estimation of a hedonic property value model is the specification of a hedonic function defining the relationship between property prices (P) and property characteristics. For example, the price of the ith property, P_i, may be assumed a function of land characteristics (LC_i), structural characteristics (SC_i), locational attributes (LA_i), and environmental characteristics (EC_i) of this property. Formally, this may be written as:

(1) $P_i = P(LC_i, SC_i, LA_i, EC_i)$,

where $P(\cdot)$ represents the hedonic function. Examples of land characteristics (LC) include parcel size, slope, soil quality, and land cover. Examples of structural characteristics (SC) include features of housing or other structures, such as total square footage, number of bedrooms, and year built. Examples of locational attributes (LA) include proximity to amenities, such as employment centers or shopping areas, access to and the quality of public services, such as schools or public water, and the attributes of surrounding properties. Examples of environmental characteristics (EC) include air and water quality, landscape characteristics, and proximity to environmental hazards, such as a hazardous waste site. When using the hedonic method to value the services provided by, or the attributes of, rural lands, time and consideration should be given to the measurement of these services or attributes. In many instances, descriptive and numerical representations of service flows are difficult to develop.

An empirical hedonic property analysis begins with collection of data on property sales and property characteristics. Data are collected from a specific market area over a specific time period. Studies generally use political boundaries, such as towns or counties, to define market boundaries and employ data on sales from recent years. Hedonic property value models are based on real estate markets in equilibrium, where buyers and sellers make tradeoffs and engage openly and freely in market transactions. Therefore, periods of rapidly increasing or decreasing prices are not desirable periods from which to sample. Data on sales and property characteristics are available from private firms and local government agencies. Additional data are required to describe land, locational, and environmental characteristics. Researchers are increasingly using geographic information systems (GIS) data and analysis tools to generate these additional data. GIS data and tools are particularly well-suited to characterizing land-use patterns and measures of proximity.

Empirical estimation of Equation (1) involves applying statistical modeling techniques to explain the variation in sales prices as a function of property characteristics. Let X represent the full set of property characteristics (*LC, SC, LA,* and *EC*) included in the empirical model. The empirical representation of the ith housing price is then

(2) $\quad P_i = P(X_i \beta; \varepsilon)$,

where β is a vector of parameters to be estimate and ε is a stochastic residual term. To estimate this model requires assumptions of the functional form of $P(\cdot)$ and the distribution of ε.

The implicit price of any property characteristic is computed by taking the first derivative of the function shown in (2) with respect to that characteristic. Estimated implicit prices may be used to value marginal changes in characteristics. Under certain conditions, estimated implicit prices may also be used to estimate the demand for specific characteristics and to enable welfare estimation for non-marginal changes in characteristics (Palmquist 1991 and 2004; Boyle, Poor, and Taylor 1999; Zabel and Kiel 2000).

The direct linkage between land characteristics and property characteristics substantiates the applicability of the hedonic property value model to examine preferences for land attributes and services. Changes in land use have broad impacts on property characteristics. For example, maintaining open space may be expected to increase the values of adjacent properties (Cheshire and Sheppard 1995; Irwin and Bockstael 2001; Irwin 2002; Geoghegan, Lynch, and Bucholtz 2002), while proximity to a landfill may be expected to decrease property values (Nelson, Genereux, and Genereux 1992; Hite 1998). The breadth of such impacts is manifest in the subset of applications summarized in Table 13.2.

The range of subjects addressed in the applications summarized in Table 13.2 demonstrates both the flexibility of the hedonic property value method and the diversity of land-use services and land attributes affecting property values. Applications are nearly evenly split between services that enhance the value of a property, such as beach proximity, and services that diminish property values, such as proximity to a landfill. Applications are also split between services or attributes associated with biophysical processes (e.g., earthquakes) and anthropocentric sources (e.g., proximity to high voltage lines).

Table 13.2 Recent applications of hedonic property value models

Citation	Subject
Beaton (1991)	growth management programs
Beaton and Pollock (1992)	growth management policies
Beron et al. (1997)	earthquake risk
Colwell, Dehring and Lash (2000)	group homes
Dale et al. (1999)	presence and proximity of a lead smelter facility
Folland and Hough (1991)	presence of nuclear generating facilities
Gatzlaff and Smith (1993)	public transportation
Hamilton and Schwann (1995)	proximity and view of high voltage lines
Hite (1998)	proximity to landfills
Kask and Maani (1992)	risk of being located near a natural gas pipeline
Kiel (1995)	proximity to hazardous waster sites
Mahan, Polasky and Adams (2000)	proximity to wetlands
Michael, Boyle and Bouchard (2000)	lake eutrophication from nonpoint source pollution
Nelson, Genereux and Genereux (1992)	landfills
Palmquist, Roka and Vukina (1997)	proximity to large commercial swine farms
Parsons and Wu (1991)	coastal amenities such as distance to water, water frontage and water view
Taylor and Smith (2000)	proximity to the beach
Xu, Mittlehammer and Barkley (1993)	land characteristics and agricultural land value

The hedonic property value method has numerous advantages and disadvantages. A notable advantage of using the hedonic property value method is the reliance on actual market decisions. In addition, changes in several land services can be evaluated at one time. Four disadvantages of this approach are noteworthy. First, a land-use change is likely to affect a number of services simultaneously and this correlation of effects makes it difficult to statistically identify the values associated with specific services. For example, a reduction in non-point source pollution associated with a land-use change may improve water clarity, reduce odor from algae blooms, and result in changes in fish abundance and species. These effects may be highly correlated, making it difficult to estimate a value for each separate effect with a hedonic model. Second, a proposed land-use change might present a new condition that has not been experienced in the real estate market, making it impossible to use existing sales data to infer implicit prices associated with the new condition. An example might be a pest, such as the hemlock woolly adelgid, which moves into an area and kills all or most of the mature shade trees. Third, the impacts of land-use changes are not limited to surrounding property owners. For example, the U.S. Department of Agriculture's Conservation Reserve Program (CRP) has converted sizable amounts of land from cropland to grassland in various parts of the country. People who live in these areas might enjoy the consequent increases in the population of grassland birds, but if they live in apartment complexes within cities, their rents may not reflect these preferences. Alternatively, people who do not own land or live near CRP lands may hold non-use values for improved populations of grassland birds. Hedonic models can only be used to estimate use values. Lastly, transaction-based samples are samples of convenience. Because the most desirable properties sell first, there may be a sample selection bias and empirical results may not apply to properties within the market area that have not been sold.

Travel Cost Models

Travel cost models use recreation decisions to elucidate the linkages between the demand for recreation sites and the attributes of these sites. When applied to outdoor or natural resource recreation sites, these models permit assessment of the use value of access to specific sites, the use values of environmental attributes, and changes in use values associated with changes in environmental attributes. Under this modeling framework, the costs incurred to visit recreation sites comprise the implicit prices of visitation. Without this assumption, estimation of demand for recreation sites proves difficult because access is frequently not priced or priced uniformly, resulting in little to no variation in price. Refer to Bockstael, McConnell, and Strand (1991), Herriges and Kling (1999), Freeman (2003), and Parsons (2003) for comprehensive discussions of this economic valuation approach.

Using a travel cost modeling framework, recreation trips arise from a utility maximization problem, where a household maximizes utility by adjusting its consumption of a variety of goods and services. These adjustments in consumption are constrained by household income and the prices of the goods and services. The quantity and quality of recreation trips are assumed to enter the utility function directly. In turn, recreation trip prices are assumed to represent the full marginal costs of participation, including purchased inputs and travel costs. Empirical applications focus on estimating demand functions for particular sites or estimating the parameters of the indirect utility function. A variety of empirical estimation approaches are used to model recreation demand. Recent advances in travel cost models are summarized in Herriges and Kling (1999).

Two aspects of the intuition of this modeling framework are noteworthy. First, site attributes, which may include land attributes, influence the quality of a recreation trip. Examples of site attributes include measures of infrastructure, such as parking, bathrooms, and trails, and measures describing natural resources, such as water or air quality, wave height, tree health, and fish abundance. Travel cost models enable researchers to learn about the relative values held for different site attributes. Second, travel costs are a major determinant of the price of a recreation trip. In practice, travel costs are estimated using measures of trip distance and time. If expressed in monetary terms, these time measures are weighted by wage rates to represent the opportunity cost of time. It is assumed households will travel further to visit a higher quality recreation site as long as the increase in utility is sufficient to offset the increased travel cost.

Surveys of potential and actual users of recreation sites are one means of data collection for empirical studies of recreation demand. Household surveys collect information to compute travel costs and visitation rates to different sites. Additional data from primary or secondary sources are required to describe the attributes of the recreation sites. GIS data and analysis tools have been employed by researchers to estimate travel costs and to describe site attributes.

Changes in land use or land attributes may influence the price and quality of recreation trips. For example, changes in land use may affect the environmental quality of a recreational experience. A change in land use may reduce erosion and other forms of non-point source pollution and consequently may improve water quality and, in turn, may improve the quality of fishing and swimming sites. Similarly, land attributes may be associated with habitat quality, and a change in land use may influence the quality of hunting or wildlife viewing at a site. Moreover, travel costs may be influenced by changes in land use that affect travel routes and times. For example, improved highways in rural areas may reduce travel costs and increase demand for recreation in rural areas.

We are not aware of any studies that have used a travel cost model to estimate values for land-use changes directly. However, a number of travel cost studies have estimated recreational use values that indirectly relate to changes in land services. For example, Hicks and Strand (2000) estimated the demand for beach use; Milon and Clemmons (1991) estimated the demand for species variety by hunters; Montgomery and Needleman (1997) estimated the value of fish consumption advisories due to toxic contamination; Parsons and Hauber (1998) estimated the value of cleaning up fresh water lakes and rivers for fishing and for selected species; and Rockel and Kealy (1991) estimated the demand for nonconsumptive recreation such as wildlife viewing. These studies represent a sampling of the travel cost models estimated in recent years that have estimated values that might be induced by a land-use change, likely in rural areas.

By altering habitat quality and pollution flows, land-use change can affect beach use, species availability for hunting, and water quality for fishing and swimming. To evaluate the welfare effects of such land-use impacts using travel cost models requires the development of a dose-response relationship linking the change in land use with the attributes of a recreation site. In many instances, these relationships are unknown. Land-use changes resulting in new sites may prove easier to value than those resulting in a marginal change in the quality of a site. For example, a travel cost model may be more appropriate to value the hunting benefits of purchasing land for a new public hunting area than to value the hunting benefits of increased hunter success due to a minor change in land cover.

Travel cost models have several advantages and disadvantages. Like hedonic property value models, they are based on actual behavior or decisions and therefore lend themselves well to characterizing human behavior and preferences. In addition, the design of such models allows for considerable flexibility in terms of incorporating site attributes and estimating the welfare effects of changes in site attributes and access to sites. A notable disadvantage of travel cost models is that they can only be used to estimate use values. A second issue relates to the change in environmental quality being studied. For example, when evaluating a change in land use, the before and after land-use states must be represented at the set of recreation sites visited by the sample. Otherwise, the travel cost model will not be able to address this particular change in land use. Lastly, travel cost models typically focus on day trips and overlook multiple-day trips and multiple-purpose trips. In recent years, greater attention has been given to changing the design of models to account for these different types of trips.

Land-use changes often only indirectly alter the quality of recreation sites, making it difficult to link changes in land-use services to changes in value. As the population of the United States becomes more concentrated in urban areas and people view rural areas as sources of recreation opportunities, more and more land-use decisions may be motivated by concerns to protect or enhance the quality of recreation opportunities. For this reason, applications of travel cost models may be used more commonly in the future to address issues related to the study of land-use change.

Averting Behavior Models

Models of averting behavior relate defensive expenditures and actions to preferences for environmental quality and personal health. Averting behavior typically occurs when individuals spend time and money to avoid an undesirable outcome. For example, an individual may put up a fence or plant a hedge to avoid a view of an undesirable land use, or, conversely, build a deck on their house to enhance a desirable view. Environmental economists have mainly applied these models of defensive behavior related to the morbidity and mortality outcomes associated with environmental pollution. Employing this approach to study rural lands requires positing that individuals will spend money and time to avoid (access) undesirable (desirable) land services.

The household production framework provides the theoretical basis for averting behavior models. Households are assumed to combine purchased inputs with time to produce service flows. In the case of averting behavior applications, these service flows typically depend on measures of environmental quality or health and the purchased input is viewed as a perfect substitute for environmental quality or health. Under these assumptions, expenditures on these inputs can be used to estimate the implicit price of improved environmental quality or health. Refer to Smith (1991), Dickie (2003), and Freeman (2003) for comprehensive discussions of this economic valuation approach.

Analogous to the hedonic property value and travel cost modeling frameworks, a constrained utility maximization problem provides the foundation of the averting behavior modeling framework. Households maximize utility by adjusting their consumption and production of a variety of goods and services. These adjustments in consumption and production are constrained by household income, prices of goods and services, and prices of purchased inputs. In averting behavior models, purchased inputs (n) and land attributes (q) are assumed to be substitutes in the production of a good (z) that enters the utility function directly along with the consumption of other goods and services (X). The utility function takes the form of $U(X, z)$ and the production function of the good, z, takes the form of $z=f(n,q)$.

Consider the case of a house located near a landfill. The landfill is an undesirable land use and results in an unsightly view. The view from the household's yard, z, enters the household's utility function and is produced by the household as a function of attributes of the yard and the view, q, and purchased inputs, n, such as fencing. The household's increased expenditure on fencing due to the landfill becomes a lower bound estimate of the marginal value of improving the view. These defensive expenditures are a lower bound estimate because the household may not be able to fully avert the undesirable view or there may be an inconvenience or cost associated with the fencing that is not captured in its price.

As noted above, the majority of averting behavior applications relate to health outcomes and do not relate to land attributes or land services. A notable exception is Jakus (1994), which applies an averting behavior model to study household responses to gypsy moth infestations. Gypsy moths are a nuisance pest and reduce the health of trees in residential settings. Jakus (1994) examines the mitigation behavior of households in response to this pest. In this case, defensive expenditures are aimed at maintaining the services provided by a household's yard and its neighborhood landscape. No studies that utilized averting behavior to estimate values for positive or negative land-use changes directly were found in our review of the literature from 1990 to 2001 in *Land Economics*.

Averting behavior models have several advantages and disadvantages. On the positive side, they are based on actual behavior or decisions and therefore lend themselves to characterizing human behavior and preferences. However, averting behavior studies rely on the assumption of perfect substitutability, an assumption that is, in many instances, tenuous. Moreover, averting behavior models require knowledge of the household production function. In some cases, discrete choice methods have been applied to overcome these knowledge requirements. Overall, the potential of using averting behavior methods to value the effects of land-use changes appears limited.

Stated Preference Methods

Stated preference methods characterize preferences based on decisions made by individuals, or intentions stated by individuals, in hypothetical market situations. Contingent valuation and conjoint analysis are stated preference valuation methods. Both of these methods are survey-based approaches for eliciting preferences. They share a common conceptual basis and utilize similar statistical procedures to derive valuation estimates. For these reasons, these methods are summarized jointly.

Contingent Valuation and Conjoint Analysis

Contingent valuation methods are more commonly employed by economists to study the demand for environmental quality (Mitchell and Carson 1989; Boyle 2003). Contingent valuation focuses on deriving total values for goods, services, and policy changes rather than concentrating on the values of specific attributes of those goods, services, or policies. Conjoint analysis is well-established in the marketing literature (Green and Roa 1971; Green and Wind 1975; Green and Srinivasan 1978; Louviere 1988), but has not been widely applied in the environmental economics literature (Louviere, Hensher, and Swait 2000; Holmes and Adamowicz 2003). In the marketing literature, conjoint analysis is used to measure consumer purchase intentions for new products or to evaluate consumer responses to changes in existing products. Market researchers are interested in predicting how changes in product attributes will change the prices consumers are willing to pay for market goods. The extension of conjoint analysis to study land-use change is straightforward and relies on viewing land-use characteristics as product attributes.

Despite their differences in purpose, contingent and conjoint valuation studies are implemented in a similar manner. In addition, they share a common theoretical basis. Similar to revealed preference methods, stated preference approaches start with a household utility maximization problem. Stated preference approaches motivate this problem using a random utility modeling framework. Both methods rely on survey questionnaires to collect data. Stated preference surveys describe the change in land services to be valued using a scenario and then follow this description with a valuation question.

Consider a valuation study of a farmland protection program. A contingent valuation survey begins with a statement describing the full extent of changes in land services and then asks individuals to reveal how much they would be willing to pay for these changes. For the farmland protection program, a stylized contingent-valuation scenario and valuation question might look as in Figure 13.1.

The protection program will apply conservation easements to 80,000 acres of prime farmland near urban areas in New England. All six New England states have agreed to participate in this program. The program will be funded by a one-time increase in your 2003 household state income taxes of $100.

Would you vote to approve this program if it cost your household $100 for the conservation easement program?

YES
NO

Figure 13.1 Example of a contingent-valuation scenario

By design, the cost amounts vary over different respondents in the sample. Analysis of the response data uses discrete choice modeling to estimate the probability of a YES response as a function of its cost. A YES response is consistent with an increase in utility or welfare. The 'with program' utility is based on consumption of the conservation program at a specified cost. The 'without program' utility assumes no program and no cost to the household.

A conjoint survey begins with a statement describing changes in land-use services and then summarizes these changes using an attribute-based scenario. Survey questions then prompt respondents to compare multiple scenarios. By asking individuals to consider two or more scenarios that differ in terms of their component attributes, the relative value of different attributes can be inferred. Conjoint analysis scenarios vary all attributes of the program, not just the cost. This variation makes it possible to identify what attributes significantly affect the desirability of the program and the relative values of these attributes. Empirical estimation focuses on describing the probability of program selection as a function of program attributes and household characteristics. A conjoint analysis scenario is shown describing two alternative farmland protection programs in Figure 13.2.

The conceptual framework for analyzing contingent valuation and conjoint data is based on a random utility framework, where indirect utility is defined over the conservation easement program and other goods and services. In the analysis of the data from the stylized contingent-valuation question, the cost or bid amount is the only attribute that varies. An estimate of the value that people place on the entire program is derived by analyzing how the response data varies with the bid amount. The value (willingness to pay [WTP]) that someone places on the conservation easement program is defined as: $V(X, Z=1, I-WTP) = V(X, Z=0, I)$, where V represents the indirect utility function; X is the consumption of private goods and services; Z is an indicator variable indicating the presence or absence of the conservation easement program; and I represents income. Based on the farmland protection example, WTP estimates are related to payments for a program that purchases and applies conservation easement to 80,000 acres of prime farmland near urban areas in New England. In the analysis of the conjoint data, four attributes vary, one of which is the cost, C. The indirect utility function

CONSERVATION EASEMENT PROGRAM

Program Attributes	Program A	Program B
Prime farmland	Targeted	Not targeted
Farmland location	Near urban areas	Not targeted
Acres of easements	80,000	100,000
One-time cost (2003 state income taxes)	$80.00	$100.00

If you were able to vote on the conservation easement program, how would you vote?

I WOULD CHOOSE PROGRAM A.
I WOULD CHOOSE PROGRAM B.
I WOULD NOT CHOOSE PROGRAM A OR B.

Figure 13.2 Example of a conjoint analysis scenario

changes to accommodate the additional variation, $V(X,Z,I-C)$, where Z is now a vector of attributes (z_1, z_2, z_3) and the program cost becomes a deduction from income. Conjoint analysis follows the Lancaster (1966) conceptual framework, the same framework underlying hedonic models. Estimates of WTP for each of the levels of the attributes are possible. Continuing with the farmland protection example, WTP estimates could be derived for the following attribute levels: prime farmland or not, near urban areas or not, and different acreages of conservation easements. It is also possible to compute value estimates for programs with different combinations of these attributes.

Table 13.3 summarizes recent contingent-valuation applications related to the valuation of land services. Only one example of a conjoint application occurred in *Land Economics* from 1990 to 2001. Johnston and Swallow (1999) used conjoint analysis to estimate the values of various watershed management options.

Two important advantages of stated preference methods are the ability to estimate values for conditions that have not been experienced and the capacity to describe non-use values. Yet these advantages come at a cost and there are several issues that must be considered when using stated preference methods. Valuation estimates are based on stated preferences, not revealed preferences, and there is evidence that this leads to overestimates of value. Furthermore, although stated preference methods have the potential to estimate values for conditions that have not been experienced, it may be difficult to design valuation scenarios that people understand or believe. Another disadvantage relates to sampling. It is not always possible to obtain a representative sample of the population of people whose values are to be estimated. Even when a representative sample is obtained, non-response bias or item non-response to survey questions may compromise the usefulness of

Table 13.3 Recent applications of contingent valuation approaches

Citation	Subject
Bateman et al. (2000).	reducing road congestion
Bergstrom and Stoll (1993)	wetland recreation
Blamey, Bennett and Morrison (1999)	protecting agricultural lands from salinity due to high ground water levels and flooding
Boyle et al. (1996) Boyle et al. (1998)	access to moose hunting
Brown et al. (1996)	removing abandoned and unpaved roads from the Grand Canyon National Park
Kramer and Mercer (1997)	tropical rain forests
Langford et al. (1998) (see also Scarpa and Bateman, 2000)	protecting a freshwater wetland from saline flooding
Loomis, Gonzalez-Caban, and Gregory (1994)	forest fire control in a habitat area for an endangered species
Loomis (2000)	endangered species
Park, Loomis, and Creel (1991)	elk hunting in Montana under current conditions and reduced crowding
Silberman, Gerlowski, and Williams (1992)	New Jersey beaches
Stevens et al. (1991)	existence values for bald eagles, coyote control and wild turkeys

value estimates. To minimize these problems, the NOAA Blue Ribbon Panel (1993) advocated using a conservative approach to survey design and data analyses. The Panel also concluded that stated preference studies provide useful information to support policy decisions and court cases.

The attribute-based approach of conjoint analysis has two advantages over contingent valuation. First, at the time that many valuation studies are conducted, it is not known exactly what form a policy will take. The attribute-based approach allows value estimates to be customized to the final design of a policy. Second, land-use changes affect multiple services. Having information on the values people associate with different services enables decision-makers to select the attributes and attribute levels that will maximize the value of the change to affected individuals.

Other Valuation Methods

Paired comparisons, production function, and benefits transfer approaches are other valuation methods used by economists to examine changes in services flows and natural resource attributes. The method of paired comparisons (Peterson and Brown 1998; Brown and Peterson 2003) is a stated preference approach that asks people to choose between combinations of goods and combinations of goods and money. Although it has not been demonstrated how to derive value estimates from paired comparison response data, this approach can be useful for identifying public priorities for land use with a fixed budget. For example, a town may have a fixed budget for land preservation and be interested in setting priorities in terms of which parcels to target.

The production function approach recognizes that natural resources are a factor input in the production of marketed goods and services that yield utility (Barbier 1994). If changes in land services affect the costs or quantity supplied of marketed goods, or the returns to other factor inputs, this approach can be used to value changes in land services. Applying the production function approach requires modeling the behavior of firms and their response to changes in land services. Therefore, a dose-response relationship is required to understand how a change in land use might affect the production of market goods.

Finally, many economic analyses completed to support government decisions and legal damage settlements are based on benefits transfer analysis. Benefit transfer analyses take estimates previously derived and transfer these estimates to a new situation or area. Given the small number of valuation studies related to land use, the promise of this approach to support land-policy decisions is limited at this time. However, it may become more relevant in the future, especially if the economic valuation of land attributes increases.

Conclusions

Increased use of economic valuation methods to assess changes in land attributes and land services will follow from increased knowledge of the services provided by land resources. Understanding the relationships between changes in land use and changes in goods and services is essential to the expansion of research in this area. Many of these relationships have spatial aspects. Spatial correlation of the effects of land-use change on land services complicates the statistical estimation of revealed preference models and the design of stated preference valuation scenarios. Respondents often have difficulty understanding the spatial aspects of land-use changes in stated preference scenarios. Modeling the spatial aspects of land-use changes may prove to be a major hurdle to developing credible benefit estimates.

Because multiple services are typically affected by a land-use change, hedonic property value models and conjoint analysis are better suited than some of the other approaches reviewed in this chapter to value changes in rural land use. In the subsequent chapters of this text, empirical applications of these two methods illustrate the utility of these approaches. In Chapter 14, conjoint analysis methods are used to investigate the influence of different land-management attributes on values held for public forestland protection programs. In Chapter 15, a hedonic property value model is estimated to examine the impact of large, industrial hog farms on residential properties in North Carolina.

In closing, many policy decisions warrant estimates derived from multiple valuation methods. Moreover, there is a rarely an absolutely preferred valuation method. Indeed, there is much to be gained by comparing and contrasting results based on different economic valuation methods to investigate the validity of value estimates.

References

Barbier, E.B. 1994. 'Valuing Environmental Functions: Tropical Wetlands.' *Land Economics* 70(2): 155–73.

Bateman, I.J., I.H. Langford, A. Munro, C. Starmer, and R. Sugden. 2000. 'Estimating Four Hicksian Welfare Measures for a Public Good: A Contingent Valuation Investigation.' *Land Economics* 76(3): 355–73.

Beaton, W.P. 1991. 'The Impact of regional Land-Use Controls on Property Values: The Case of the New Jersey Pinelands.' *Land Economics* 67(2): 172–94.

Beaton, W.P., and M. Pollock. 1992. 'Economic Impact of growth Management Policies Surrounding the Chesapeake Bay.' *Land Economics* 68(4): 434–53.

Bergstrom, J.C., and J.R. Stoll. 1993. 'Value Estimator Models for Wetlands-Based Recreational Use Values.' *Land Economics* 69(2): 132–7.

Beron, K.J., J.C. Murdoch, M.A. Thayer, and W.P.M. Vijverberg. 1997. 'An Analysis of the Housing Market Before and After the 1989 Loma Prieta Earthquake.' *Land Economics* 73(1): 101–13.

Blamey, R.K., J.W. Bennett, and M.D. Morrison. 1999. 'Yea-Saying in Contingent Valuation Surveys.' *Land Economics* 75(1): 126–41.

Boyle, K.J. 2003. 'Contingent Valuation in Practice,' in *A Primer on Nonmarket Valuation*, eds. P. Champ, K.J. Boyle, and T.C. Brown. Dordrecht, Netherlands: Kluwer Academic Publishers.

Boyle, K.J., F.R. Johnson, D.W. McCollum, W.H. Desvousges, R.W. Dunford, and S.P. Hudson. 1996. Valuing Public Goods: Discrete versus Continuous Contingent-Valuation Responses.' *Land Economics* 72(3): 381–96.

Boyle, K.J., H.F. MacDonald, H. Cheng, and D.W. McCollum. 1998. 'Bid Design and Yea Saying in Single-Bounded, Dichotomous-Choice Questions.' *Land Economics* 74(1): 49–64.

Boyle, K.J., J. Poor, and L.O. Taylor. 1999. 'Estimating the Demand for Protecting Freshwater Lakes from Eutrophication.' *American Journal of Agricultural Economics* 81(5): 1118–22.

Braden, J.B., and C.D. Kolstad, eds. 1991. *Measuring the Demand for Environmental Quality*. Amsterdam, The Netherlands: Elsevier Science Publishers.

Brown, T.C., P.A. Champ, R.C. Bishop, and D.W. McCollum. 1996. 'Which Response Format Reveals the Truth about Donations to a Public Good?' *Land Economics* 72(2): 152–66.

Brown, T.C., and G.L. Peterson. 2003. 'Multiple Good Valuation,' in *A Primer on Nonmarket Valuation*, eds. P. Champ, K.J. Boyle, and T.C. Brown. Dordrecht, Netherlands: Kluwer Academic Publishers.

Champ, P., K.J. Boyle, and T.C. Brown, eds. 2003. *A Primer on Nonmarket Valuation*. Dordrecht, Netherlands: Kluwer Academic Publishers.

Cheshire, P., and S. Sheppard. 1995. 'On the Price of Land and the Value of Amenities.' *Economica*. 62(246): 247–67.

Colwell, P.F., C.A. Dehring, and N.A. Lash. 2000. 'The Effect of group Homes on Neighborhood Property Values.' *Land Economics* 76(4): 615–37.

Dale, L., J.C. Murdock, M.A. Thayer, and P.A. Waddell. 1999. 'Do Property Values Rebound from Environmental Stigmas? Evidence from Dallas.' *Land Economics* 75(2): 311–26.

Dickie, M. 2003. 'Defensive Behavior and Damage Cost Methods,' in *A Primer on Nonmarket Valuation*, eds. P. Champ, K.J. Boyle, and T.C. Brown. Dordrecht, Netherlands: Kluwer Academic Publishers.

Freeman, A.M. 1993. *The Measurement of Environmental and Resource Values: Theory and Practice*. Washington, District of Columbia: Resources for the Future.

Folland, S.T., and R.R. Hough. 1991. 'Nuclear Power Plants and the Value of Agricultural Land.' *Land Economics* 67(1): 30–36.

Gatzlaff, D.J., and M.T. Smith. 1993. 'The Impact of the Miami Metrorail: An Application of Cooperative decision-Making Theory.' *Land Economics* 69(1): 54–66.

Geoghegan, J., L. Lynch, and S.C. Bucholtz. 2002. 'Capitalization of Open Spaces into Housing Values and the Residential Property Tax Revenue Impacts of Agricultural Easement Programs.' *Agricultural and Resource Economics Review* 32(1): 33–45.

Green, P.E., and V.R. Rao. 1971. 'Conjoint Measurement for Quantifying Judgemental Data.' *Journal of Marketing Research* 8: 355–63.

Green, P.E., and V. Srinivasan. 1978. 'Conjoint Analysis in Consumer Research: Issues and Outlook.' *Journal of Consumer Research* 5: 103–23.

Green, P.E., and Y. Wind. 1975. 'New Way to Measure Consumers' Judgements.' *Harvard Business Review* 53: 107–17.

Hamilton, S., and G.M. Schwann. 1995. 'Do High Voltage Electric Transmission Lines Affect Property Values?' *Land Economics* 71(4): 436–44.

Herriges, J.A., and C.L. Kling, eds. 1999. *Valuing Recreation and the Environment*. Northampton, Massachusetts: Edward Elgar.

Hicks, R.L., and I.E. Strand. 2000. 'The Extent of Information: Its Relevance for Random Utility Models.' *Land Economics* 76(3): 374–85.

Hite, D. 1998. 'Information and Bargaining in Markets for Environmental Quality.' *Land Economics* 74(3): 303–16.

Holmes, T.P., and W.L. Adamowicz. 2003. 'Attribute-Based Methods,' in *A Primer on Nonmarket Valuation*, eds. P. Champ, K.J. Boyle, and T.C. Brown. Dordrecht, Netherlands: Kluwer Academic Publishers.

Irwin, E.G. 2002. 'The Effects of Open Space on Residential Property Values.' *Land Economics* 78(4): 465–80.

Irwin, E.G., and N.E. Bockstael. 2001. 'The Problem of Identifying Land Use Spillovers: Measuring the Effects of Open Space on Residential Property Values.' *American Journal of Agricultural Economics* 83(3): 698–704.

Jakus, P.M. 1994. 'Averting Behavior in the Presence of Public Spillovers: Household Control of Nuisance Pests.' *Land Economics* 70(3): 273–85.

Johnston, R.J., and S.K. Swallow. 1999. 'Asymmetries in Ordered Strength of Preference Models: Implications of Focus Shift for Discrete-Choice Preference Estimation.' *Land Economics* 75(2): 295–310.

Kask, S.B., and S.A. Maani. 1992. 'Uncertainty, Information and Hedonic Pricing.' *Land Economics* 68(2): 170–84.

Kiel, K.A. 1995. 'Measuring the Impact of the Discovery and Cleaning of Identified Hazardous Waste Sites on House Values.' *Land Economics* 71(4): 428–35.

Kramer, R.A., and D.E. Mercer. 1997. 'Valuing a Global Environmental Good: U.S. Residents' Willingness to Pay to Protect Tropical Rain Forests.' *Land Economics* 73(2): 196–210.

Lancaster, K.J. 1966. 'A New Approach to Consumer Theory.' *Journal of Political Economy* 74: 132–57.

Langford, I.H., I.J. Bateman, A.P. Jones, H.D. Langford, and S. Georgiou. 1998. 'Improved Estimation of Willingness to Pay in Dichotomous Choice Contingent Valuation Studies.' *Land Economics* 74(1): 65–75.

Loomis, J.B. 2000. 'Vertically Summing Public Goods Demand Curves: An Empirical Comparison of Economic versus Political Jurisdictions.' *Land Economics* 76(2): 312–21.

Loomis, J., A. Gonzalez-Caban, and R. Gregory. 1994. 'Do Reminders of Substitutes and Budget Constraints Influence Contingent Valuation Estimates.' *Land Economics* 70(4): 499–506.

Louviere, J.J. 1988. 'Conjoint Analysis Modelling of Stated Preferences.' *Journal of Transport Economics and Policy* 22(1): 93–119.

Louviere, J.J., Hensher, D.A., and D.J. Swait. 2000. *Stated Choice Methods: Analysis and Applications.* New York, New York: Cambridge University Press.

Mahan, B.L., S. Polasky, and R.M. Adams. 2000. Valuing Urban Wetlands: A Property Price Approach.' *Land Economics* 76(1): 100–113.

Maler, K., and J.R Vincent, eds. 2004. *Handbook of Environmental Economics: Volume 2 – Valuing Environmental Changes.* Amsterdam, The Netherlands: Elsevier Science Ltd.

Michael, H.J., K.J. Boyle, and R. Bouchard. 2000. 'Does the Measurement of Environmental Quality Affect Implicit Prices Estimated from Hedonic Models.' *Land Economics* 76(2): 283–98.

Milon, J.W., and R.Clemmons. 1991. 'Hunters' Demand for Species Variety.' *Land Economics* 67(4): 401–12.

Mitchell, R.C., and R.T. Carson. 1989 *Using Surveys to Value Public Goods: The Contingent Valuation Method.* Washington, District of Columbia: Resources for the Future.

Montgomery, M., and M. Needleman. 1997. 'The Welfare Effects of Toxic Contamination in Freshwater Fish.' *Land Economics* 73(2): 211–23.

Nelson, A.C., J. Genereux, and M. Genereux. 1992. 'Price Effects of Landfills on House Values.' *Land Economics* 68(4): 359–65.

Palmquist, R.B. 1991. 'Hedonic Methods,' in *Measuring the Demand for Environmental Quality*, eds. J.B. Braden and C.D. Kolstad. Amsterdam, The Netherlands: Elsevier Science Publishers.

Palmquist, R.B. 2004. 'Property Value Models,' in *Handbook of Environmental Economics: Volume 2 – Valuing Environmental Changes,* eds. K.G. Maler and J.R. Vincent. Amsterdam, The Netherlands: Elsevier Science Ltd.

Palmquist, R.B., F.M. Roka, and T. Vukina. 1997. 'Hog Operations, Environmental Effects, and Residential Property Values.' *Land Economics* 73(1): 114–24.

Park, T., J.B. Loomis, and M. Creel. 1991. 'Confidence Intervals for Evaluating Benefits Estimates from Dichotomous Choice Contingent Valuation Studies.' *Land Economics* 67(1): 64–73.

Parsons, G.R. 2003. 'The Travel Cost Model,' in *A Primer on Nonmarket Valuation*, eds. P. Champ, K.J. Boyle, and T.C. Brown. Dordrecht, Netherlands: Kluwer Academic Publishers.

Parsons, G.R., and A.B. Hauber. 1998. 'Spatial Boundaries and Choice Set Definition in a Random Utility Model of Recreation Demand.' *Land Economics* 74(1): 32–48.

Parsons, G.R., and Y. Wu. 1991. 'The Opportunity Cost of Coastal Land-Use Controls: An Empirical Analysis.' *Land Economics* 67(3): 308–16.

Peterson, G.L., and T.C. Brown. 1998. 'Economic Valuation by the Method of Paired Comparisons, with Emphasis on Evaluation of the Transitivity Axiom.' *Land Economics* 74(2): 240–61.

Rockel, M.L., and M.J. Kealy. 1991. 'The Value of Nonconsumptive Wildlife Recreation in the United States.' *Land Economics* 67(4): 422–34.

Rosen, S. 1974. 'Hedonic Prices and Implicit Markets – Product Differentiation in Pure Competition.' *Journal of Political Economy* 82: 34–55.

Santos, J.L. 1999. *The Economic Valuation of Landscape Change.* Northampton, Massachusetts: Edward Elgar.

Scarpa, R., and I. Bateman. 2000. 'Efficiency Gains Afforded by Improved Bid designs versus Follow-up Valuation Questions in Discrete-Choice CV Studies.' *Land Economics* 76(2): 299–311.

Silberman, J., D.A. Gerlowski, and N.A. Williams. 1992. 'Estimating Existence Values for Users and Nonusers of New Jersey Beaches.' *Land Economics* 68(2): 225–36.

Smith, V.K. 1991. 'Household Production Functions and Environmental Benefit Estimation,' in *Measuring the Demand for Environmental Quality,* eds. J.B. Braden and C.D. Kolstad. Amsterdam, The Netherlands: Elsevier Science Publishers.

Stevens, T.H., J. Echeverria, R. Glass, T. Hagar, and T.A. Moore. 1991. 'Measuring the Existence Value of Wildlife: What do CVM Estimates Really Show?' *Land Economics* 67(4): 390–400.

Taylor, L.O. 2003. 'Hedonic Method,' in *A Primer on Nonmarket Valuation*, eds. P. Champ, K.J. Boyle, and T.C. Brown. Dordrecht, Netherlands: Kluwer Academic Publishers.

Taylor, L.O., and V.K. Smith. 2000. 'Environmental Amenities as a Source of Market Power.' *Land Economics* 76(4): 550–68.

Xu, F., R.C. Mittlehammer, and P.W. Barkley. 1993. 'Measuring the Contributions of Site Characteristics to the Value of Agricultural Land.' *Land Economics* 69(4): 356–69.

Zabel, J.E., and K.A. Kiel. 2000. 'Estimating the Demand for Air Quality in Four U.S. Cities.' *Land Economics* 76(2): 174–94.

Chapter 14

Valuing Changes in Rural Land Uses: Measuring the Willingness to Pay for Changes in Forest Management Practices

Mario F. Teisl and Kevin J. Boyle

Introduction

Concerns about rural land-use change have primarily focused on losses of agricultural lands, with the associated losses in amenities (see e.g., Kline and Wichelns 1996; Ready, Berger, and Blomquist 1997; Mcleod et al. 1998). Policy approaches, such as conservation easements and property tax reductions, have been public attempts to reduce some of these losses. However, concerns about rural land-use change encompass more than simply slowing the loss of a specific type of land use. A broader definition of land-use change also includes issues surrounding changes in management approaches for a particular type of land use. For example, although there may be no net loss of agricultural land, the public is increasingly concerned about changes in livestock management (i.e., the conversion of small livestock operations to large-scale animal feeding operations).

During the last two decades, public concern over the use, management, and protection of rural forestland in the United States has grown rapidly. During the 1970s, public participation in forest management decisions on public lands was legislatively integrated into U.S. Forest Service planning decisions (Rosenberger, Smith, and Gonzalez-Caban 1997), and during 1992 the public's participatory role in public forest management decisions was expanded (Schaberg, Homes, and Abt 1997). More recently, the public has also been asking for the right to influence forest management decisions made on privately held forestlands. For example, in 2000, Maine voters were asked to vote on a forestry referendum that would have limited cutting levels and the ability to use clear cutting techniques on privately held forestland (Forestry Ecology Network 2000). Decisions regarding where, when, and how to cut timber are no longer purely silvicultural decisions made by forest managers, but are increasingly subject to public scrutiny, debate, regulation, and litigation.

The debates surrounding the loss of agricultural land often focus on losses of agricultural amenities, such as scenic beauty. Similarly, recent efforts to influence forest management decisions appear to go beyond preventing obvious environmental degradation, such as soil erosion and nutrient loadings in streams and lakes; the public is now demanding that forestlands also be managed for aesthetic and less-apparent ecological goals. For example, many individuals are against forest management techniques, such as clearcutting (Welsh 2002) or prescribed burning (Taylor and Daniel 1984), solely for aesthetic reasons.

Preferences for forestland amenities and for landscape attributes imply underlying preferences for the way these lands are managed. The growing public interest in the management of public and private forestland in the U.S. has presented forest managers and policy makers with the need to better understand these preferences. One approach to doing this is to use conjoint analysis in a survey setting to elicit the public's preferences.[1] Conjoint analysis is a method whereby differentiated goods are described in terms of their attributes and survey respondents are asked to evaluate the assigned combinations of attributes. Timber harvesting can be thought of as a differentiated good where the attributes may include, for example, the size of the land area where harvesting occurs, the number of live tress left in the area after harvesting, and the size of protection zones for wetlands. The primary objective of this research is to use a conjoint survey to elicit the values individuals hold for specific timber harvesting practices on publicly owned forestland in Maine.

Previous Research

Until recently, there has been little economic research investigating the values individuals may have for different forest management practices. However, in the field of forestry there has been a large body of work conducted on public preferences for forest landscapes and forest conditions. The majority of these studies measure aesthetic preferences using scenic beauty estimation methods where participants are shown photographs and then administered surveys to determine their preferences for specific forest attributes. This research highlights that people have preferences for stands of tall trees (Hull and Buhyoff 1986; Brown 1987; Rudis et al. 1988; Mattsson 1994); small trees are only appreciated when they comprise a lower canopy layer (Schroeder and Daniel 1981; Ribe 1990); tree density should not be so high so as to hamper within-forest visibility (Hull and Buhyoff 1986; Brown 1987; Rudis et al. 1988; Ribe 1990); and slash (the bark, limbs, and other wood debris left in the forest after a logging operation) has a negative impact on scenic beauty (Rosenberger and Smith 1997).

Three studies have used a stated preference approach to investigate individuals' willingness to pay (WTP) for altered forest practices in Europe. Hanley and Ruffell (1993) indicate that individuals in the United Kingdom value improvements in specific forest attributes. Specifically, they find that U.K. forest visitors prefer forests with taller trees, the presence of views, and deciduous (as opposed to coniferous) trees. Although not significant, they also seem to prefer increased species diversity, more open space and the presence of water features.

Garrod and Willis (1997) indicate that U.K. residents value forest management standards that promote increased forest diversity. Specifically, residents prefer management standards that increase the native woodland characteristics of the forest (e.g., increased diversity of tree species and age classes, variation in open spaces, more dead and dying trees, and more plant and animal biodiversity). However, they also find that the forest management plan with the highest level of biodiversity (natural woodland) received the lowest rating. Apparently, there may be a non-linear valuation response toward biodiversity. Mattsson and Li (1994) find that Swedish residents place higher values on forests with more diverse tree characteristics. They also find that the non-timber value of the forests increases with a change in forest policy that decreases clear-cutting and replaces artificial regeneration with natural regeneration.

In the U.S., Lippke and Bare (1999) find that Washington State residents value increased forest biodiversity and more mature forests; and that urban dwellers have higher values for these attributes than rural inhabitants. However, they also obtain a finding similar to Garrod and Willis: individuals value increases in forest biodiversity only up to a point. Past that point, values decline, and in some cases, become negative. In addition, New Hampshire residents value forestland conservation programs to protect wildlife habitat and water resources (Cooksey and Howard 1995). Finally, O'Brien (2001) indicates that U.S. residents value forest management practices that protect fish and wildlife resources.

In general, the above studies find that forestland preservation seems to be driven by a desire to protect the environment (preserve ponds and woodlands, ensure clean water and abundant wildlife) and to preserve scenic amenities, not a preference for a particular land use, *per se*. In addition, these studies indicate that the public is able to distinguish between different forest management practices, that they value more environmentally benign approaches to forest management, and that substantial non-use values can be generated by specific forest management practices.

Conceptual Framework

In attempting to model individuals' values for specific types of forest management attributes, we begin by assuming that individuals are able to distinguish, and have preferences for different forest management practices. We assume that individuals know their preferences with certainty, and that with the information provided in the survey instrument, they can form a complete preference ordering of the alternatives presented to them. We assume that respondents have linear preferences over the forest attributes in the experimental design such that:

(1) $V(X, M) = \beta X + \alpha M + \varepsilon$,

where $V(X,M)$ is an indirect utility function, β is a row vector of coefficients to be estimated that reveal the effect of the levels of individual forest management practices, X is a column vector of variables that represent the levels of the individual practices, α is a parameter to be estimated that represents the marginal utility of money, M is the monetary incentive included in the experimental design, and ε is the random econometric error.

The estimated coefficients from a conjoint experiment can be used to calculate the willingness to pay for a change in attribute levels (see Roe, Boyle, and Teisl 1996). Here the willingness to pay (WTP) for a change in forest management practices is defined as:

$$(2) \quad WTP_{i-j} = \frac{\beta(X_i - X_j)}{\alpha},$$

where the subscripts i and j denote variables set at different levels of forest management practices, and at least one $x_i \neq y_i$ for WTP greater than zero.

Data

Sampling Frame and Survey Administration

The sample was composed of 730 randomly selected individuals, 18 years of age or older, from records of Maine driver's licenses and state identification cards.[2] The survey was administered by mail in early 1997; of the initial sample, 70 had addresses that were undeliverable by the U.S. Post Office. A total of 297 surveys were completed and returned for a usable response rate of 45 per cent.

Survey Design

Within the questionnaire, a scenario for evaluating forest management practices was described in the context of the state purchasing a 23,000 acre parcel of forestland.[3] The forest practices described the management of timber harvesting on this land. Respondents were told that the land would be purchased from a large forestland management company, were given a brief description of the parcel (Figure 14.1), and were provided with a map that identified the general geographic location of the parcel. The intent was for the parcel to be a generic piece of industrial forestland that was located in an area where people would believe that it contained many of the common features of forestland in Maine.

Respondents were asked to consider seven timber harvesting/land management practices, including the density of forest roads, the number of dead and dying trees left in the harvest area, the number of live trees left after harvesting, the maximum size of harvest openings, the percentage of forestland available for timber harvesting, the size of watershed protection zones, and how slash is to be disposed (Table 14.1). Respondents were also told that dispersed recreation would continue to occur on the land. While this is not a comprehensive list of timber harvesting attributes, with issues such as separation zones between

This piece of forestland has been offered for sale by a large forestland management company.

This forestland is in northwestern Maine and is within LURC (Land Use Regulation Commission) jurisdiction.

This forestland is the size of a township and is approximately 6 miles long and 6 miles wide.

This forestland contains one lake that is the headwaters of a small stream.

The lake and the stream are used for fishing and canoeing.

The property has about 23,000 forested acres of spruce, fir and pine.

Trees have been harvested in the southern half of this forestland within the last 5 years.

A map of the location of this piece of forestland is on the next page.

This study has nothing to do with the clearcutting referendum that was on the November 5, 1996 Maine ballot.

Figure 14.1 Hypothetical purchase proposal

harvest areas not addressed, we chose these practices as key features in beginning to develop a general understanding of public preferences. Information regarding the forest practices was presented by enclosing an information booklet that accompanied the questionnaire (the booklet was designed with the assistance of a silviculturalist and a wildlife biologist).[4]

Each forest practice was allocated two facing pages in the information booklet. The page on the left portrayed two black and white drawings representing alternative levels of the respective forest practice. Drawings were used instead of photographs to maintain consistency across attributes and levels of individual attributes, and to avoid the possibility that some pictures may be relatively more aesthetically appealing to respondents than other pictures. The facing page provided written descriptions of each practice and the levels of each attribute that respondents were asked to evaluate.

Respondents were presented with four management plans to consider (Figure 14.2 presents one example of a management plan); each management plan was composed of randomly assigned levels of each of the forest practices (Table 14.1).[5] An eighth attribute, a one-time increase in state income taxes to pay for the proposed purchase of forestland, was included. The conjoint question used to elicit values for forest management attributes used a ranking format:

How would you rank the desirability to you of each of the proposed forest management plans for this piece of forest land with one (1) being most desirable and 4 being least desirable?

Respondents fill in a blank for each of four management plans with the ranks 1, 2, 3, and 4.

Empirical Model

The responses to the valuation question were used to estimate the following empirical model:

$$
\begin{aligned}
\beta X + \alpha M = \ & \beta_0 + \beta_1(PER50) + \beta_2(PER80) + \beta_3(ROADS) + \\
& \beta_4(DEAD5) + \beta_5(DEAD10) + \beta_6(LIVE153) + \beta_7(LIVE459) + \\
& \beta_8(HOPEN35) + \beta_9(HOPEN125) + \beta_{10}(ZONE500) + \\
& \beta_{11}(DISTSL) + \beta_{12}(REMSL) + \alpha(TAX)
\end{aligned}
$$

(3)

Variable definitions and codings are listed in Table 14.1.

The coefficients β_1 and β_2 indicate respondent preferences for leaving 50 per cent and 80 per cent of the land available for harvesting relative to the omitted category of 20 per cent. If β_1 and/or β_2 are significantly different from zero, then 50 per cent and/or 80 per cent is preferred (positive effect) or not preferred (negative effect) to 20 per cent. β_3 indicates respondent preferences for having roads every mile relative to every half mile. β_4 (β_5) indicates respondent preferences for leaving five (ten) dead or dying trees per acre relative to removing all such trees. β_6 (β_7) indicates respondent preferences for leaving 153 (459) live trees per acre relative to removing all such trees. β_8 (β_9) indicates respondent preferences for having the maximum size of the harvest opening limited to under 35 (125) acres relative to having the maximum size of the harvest opening limited to under five acres. β_{10} indicates respondent preferences for having a watershed protection zone of 500 feet relative to the current practice of 250 feet. β_{11} (β_{12}) indicates respondent preferences for distributing slash along skid trails (removing it all) relative to leaving slash on the ground where it fell.

Equation (3) is estimated using an ordered probit model. In addition, the equation is estimated, following Garrod and Willis (1996) and Layton and Lee (1998), using a rank-ordered logit model. Rank-order estimation exploits all rank information by implicitly assuming that each rank is made as part of a sequential random utility selection process. The alternative ranked first is assumed chosen because it yields higher utility than the other three alternatives. It is assumed that respondents repeat this random utility maximization with the remaining three commodities. Another datum is created to represent that the second-ranked alternative is chosen over the other two alternatives. A last datum represents that

Table 14.1 Forest practices and levels

Practices	Levels	Variable name	Variable coding
Percent of land available for timber harvesting	80% for timber harvesting and 20% as a natural area	PERH80	1 if 80%; 0 otherwise
	50% for timber harvesting and 50% as a natural area	PERH50	1 if 50%; 0 otherwise
	20% for timber harvesting and 80% as a natural area		
Road density	One road every mile	ROADS	1 if every mile; 0 otherwise
	One road every half mile		
Dead/ dying trees standing after harvest	Leave one dead or dying tree about every 93 feet (five trees per acre)	DEAD5	1 if five; 0 otherwise
	Leave one dead or dying tree about every 66 feet (ten trees per acre)	DEAD10	1 if ten; 0 otherwise
	Remove all		
Live trees standing after harvest	One tree six inches thick about every 17 feet (153 trees per acre)	LIVE153	1 if 153; 0 otherwise
	One tree six inches thick about five feet (459 trees per acre)	LIVE459	1 if 459; 0 otherwise
	No trees greater than six inches left standing		
Maximum size of harvest openings	Five to 35 acres	HOPEN35	1 if 5–35; 0 otherwise
	36 to 125 acres	HOPEN125	1 if 36–125; 0 otherwise
	Less than five acres		
Size of watershed protection zones	At least a 500-foot zone	ZONE500	1 if 500-foot; 0 otherwise
	At least a 250-foot zone		
Slash disposal	Distribute along skid trails	DISTL	1 if distributed; 0 otherwise
	Remove all	REMSL	1 if removed; 0 otherwise
	Leave where it falls on the ground		

the third-ranked alternative is chosen over the alternative ranked last. All three data points (or more generally, K–1 data points are exploded from K commodity ranks) are used to estimate the rank-order logit model. The choose-one data are analyzed using a probit model. This model includes four observations per respondent, with the chosen alternative coded as one and the other three alternatives coded as zero. We use the estimated models to calculate the compensating variation of moving from the status quo forest practices to more environmentally benign timber harvesting (see Table 14.2).

Bootstrapping from the original data derives 90 per cent confidence intervals for welfare estimates. For each model, N observations are randomly sampled with replacement from the original data set of size N. The model coefficients are estimated from the re-sampled data and the compensating variation measure is calculated from these coefficients. This procedure is repeated 1,000 times for each model.

Table 14.2 Variable specifications for calculating average willingness to pay

Variable	Assume Current Harvesting Practices Prior to Purchase	Proposed Harvesting Practices After Purchase
Percentage of land available for timber harvesting	80%	50%
Road density	1 every ½ mile	1 every mile
Dead and dying trees left	None	5/acre
Live trees greater than 6" diameter at basal height left	153	153
Harvest opening sizes	5–35 acres	5–35 acres
Size of wetland protection zones	250 feet	500 feet
Slash	Remove all	Leave where it falls

Results

Sample Characteristics

The majority of respondents were male (56 per cent). The average respondent was 48 years of age, had a high school education or some education beyond high school (64 per cent), and had an annual household income of $42,388. The U.S. Bureau of the Census reports that 49 per cent of Maine adults are male, and that the average household income, converted to 1997 dollars, is $36,634. Thus males and individuals with higher incomes were more likely to respond to the survey than other Maine residents. 27 per cent of respondents own forestland in Maine, with an average ownership of 55 acres and a high of 1,000 acres. Only 20 per cent of these landowners harvest wood from their land. Ten per cent of the respondents belong to an environmental group, with Maine Audubon (32 per cent), The Nature Conservancy (27 per cent), and The Sportsman's Alliance of Maine (24 per cent) being cited most frequently. Eight per cent were employed in Maine's timber industry (primarily logging and papermaking). These results indicate people who have a vested interest in the timber industry, forestland owners, or people with strong environmental leanings do not dominate the sample.

Evaluations of Management Plans

Analyses of the conjoint data result in the same variables, except one, being significant with the same signs in both statistical models (Table 14.3). Overall, we find that respondents preferred management plans that include setting some land aside from timber harvesting. However, respondents disliked having 80 per cent of the land available for harvesting. Respondents also preferred management plans that include less dense roads, leaving dead and dying trees in harvest areas, leaving live trees larger than six inches diameter at basal height left in harvest areas, and leaving slash distributed in the forest. Neither the size of harvest openings nor moving from 250-foot to 500-foot wetland protection zones were significant. These results suggest that respondents are more concerned with the timber harvesting practices that are implemented on the land than they are with the actual size of the harvest area, as long as the area is less than 125 acres (the maximum size evaluated in the study). Likewise, once a 250-wetland protection zone is established, respondents again appear to be more concerned with the actual timber harvesting practices rather than expanding the wetland protection zone. For the practices the public is concerned about, they appear to prefer the middle levels rather than choosing the extremes. The mean compensating-variation estimates for a change from the status quo to the more benign harvesting practices listed in Table 14.2 is about $1,500 per household. The overlapping confidence intervals across the mean compensating-variation estimates from the two equations indicate that the estimates are statistically identical.

Table 14.3 Estimated equations with willingness to pay estimates[a, b]

Variable	Ordered probit	Rank-ordered logit
INTERCEPT	−0.9208*	N/A
	(0.1476)	
PERH50	−0.1732*	−0.1940
	(0.0936)	(0.1285)
PERH80	−0.3573*	−0.4703*
	(0.0919)	(0.1296)
ROADS	0.1557*	0.2124*
	(0.0756)	(0.1049)
DEAD5	0.3056*	0.3867*
	(0.0928)	(0.1329)
DEAD10	0.2776*	0.4212*
	(0.0918)	(0.1332)
LIVE153	0.3950*	0.5151*
	(0.0917)	(0.1274)
LIVE459	0.3539*	0.4407*
	(0.0926)	(0.1284)
HOPEN35	0.0966	0.1504
	(0.0925)	(0.1282)
HOPEN125	0.0872	0.0629
	(0.0909)	(0.1290)
ZONE500	0.0519	0.0608
	(0.0751)	(0.1045)
DISTSL	0.0374	0.0154
	(0.0923)	(0.1312)
REMSL	−0.2757*	−0.3512*
	(0.0913)	(0.1300)
TAX	−0.0006*	−0.0009*
	(0.0001)	(0.0001)
INTERCEPT 2	0.7298*	
	(0.0445)	
INTERCEPT 3	1.4522*	
	(0.0578)	
Mean CV[c]	$1,603	$1,317
	($981 – $2,389)	($749 – $2,078)

[a] * denotes significance at the ten per cent level.

[b] Standard errors are reported in parentheses.

[c] Compensating variation estimates for a change from the status quo to more benign harvesting practices as denoted in Table 14.2 (90 per cent confidence intervals in parentheses).

Discussion

Expanding the lowest estimate of $1,317 to the population of Maine, while assuming that survey non-respondents have a value of zero dollars and that respondents stated values associated with the household, yields an aggregate willingness to pay estimate of $273.6 million ($273,643,099 = [461,728 households x 0.45 x $1,317). This willingness to pay calculation suggests that the public's willingness to pay likely exceeds the cost of purchasing commercial forestland. Given that the sample tends to have more high-income individuals than the general population of Maine, the average willingness to pay estimates may be somewhat high. However, the qualitative finding of a strong preference for more benign timber harvesting practices, and a willingness to back up this preference with tax dollars, may be generalized to the population of Maine.

Although it is difficult to determine the amount of money used to purchase land for conservation and preservation purposes, the above result seems to be substantiated by actual land purchases. Within the last 10–15 years, there have been several significant land purchases, or conservation easements, made to preserve the rural Maine landscape. In 1989 and again in 1999, state voters passed two bond issues (for a total of $85 million) dedicated to purchasing land for preservation. In 1998, The Nature Conservancy took the lead in raising $50 million for land purchases; in 1999 the New England Forestry Foundation announced a land purchase of $28 million; and recently, the Forest Society of Maine, along with other groups, announced their intention to purchase a conservation easement worth over $35 million. In addition to these larger purchases there are at least 80 active local land trusts operating within the state. The bottom line is that the survey results, and actual behavior, indicate that there is substantial support for public purchases of commercial forestland in Maine that will be used for multiple uses including timber harvesting, dispersed recreation, and ecosystem protection.

Notes

1   There are other approaches available to measure these values (e.g., contingent valuation, travel cost, and hedonic pricing). See Chapters 13 and 15 of this volume.
2   People who do not hold a driver's license generally posses a state identification card for purposes of check cashing and other occasions when official identification is required. These records cover over 89 per cent of the adult residents of Maine.
3   The survey instrument and an accompanying information booklet were pre-tested in focus groups held in Bangor, Maine (n=5) and Portland, Maine (n=7). Focus group participants were solicited by telephone using random selection from local telephone directories. No major problems were identified in the questionnaire design, but respondents did make a number of suggestions that helped to clarify the content of the information booklet.
4   A prior concern was that respondents would focus on the maximum size of the harvest opening given the media attention of the clear-cut controversy in the state. We did not find that this was a problem in the pre-tests. One item that was clear from the focus

groups was that the public was not likely to favor allowing timber harvesting on all of the land once it was conveyed to state ownership, nor were they likely to approve precluding any timber harvesting. Thus, when considering the amount of land for timber harvesting, respondents were asked to evaluate options that allowed timber harvesting on a portion of the land area and set some land aside from timber harvesting.

5   Many researchers use orthogonal designs whereby the combinations of the practices/levels are reduced to an independent, parsimonious group. This implies that the effects of the practices are linearly additive. We did not wish to impose this assumption because there may be combinations of the attributes that respondents find to be particularly undesirable or particularly desirable. We do not investigate this issue here, but it is certainly an issue of concern for future research initiatives.

References

Cooksey, R.A., and T.E. Howard. 1995. 'Willingness to Pay to Protect Forest Benefits with Conservation Easements.' Presented at the International Union of Forestry Research Organizations (IUFRO) World Congress. Tampere, Finland, August 6–12.

Forest Ecology Network. 2000. 'An Act Regarding Forest Practices.' *The Maine Woods* 4(1).

Garrod, G.D., and K.G. Willis. 1996. 'The Non-Use Benefits of Enhancing Forest Biodiversity: A Contingent Rank Study.' *Ecological Economics* 21: 45–61.

Hanley, N.D., and R.J. Ruffell. 1993. 'The Contingent Valuation of Forest Characteristics: Two Experiments.' *Journal of Agricultural Economics* 44: 218–29.

Hull, B., and G. Buhyoff. 1986. 'The Scenic Beauty Temporal Distribution Method: An Attempt to Make Scenic Beauty Assessment Compatible with Forest Planning Efforts.' *Forest Science* 32: 271–86.

Kline, J., and D. Wichelns. 1996. 'Public Preferences Regarding the Goals of Farmland Preservation Programs.' *Land Economics* 724: 538–49.

Layton, D.F., and S.T. Lee. 1998. 'From Ratings to Rankings: The Econometric Analysis of Stated Preference Ratings Data.' Selected paper, World Congress of Environmental Economists. Venice, Italy, June 25–27.

Lippke, B., and B. Bare. 1999. 'Cost and Compromise: Determining the Public's Willingness to Pay for Values Received from Forests.' University of Washington, College of Forest Resources, Center for International Trade in Forest Products.

Mattsson, L., and C.Z. Li. 1994. 'How do Different Forest Management Practices affect the Non-Timber Value of Forests? An Economic Analysis.' *Journal of Environmental Management* 41: 79–88.

McLeod, D., J. Woirhaye, C. Krause, and D. Menkhaus. 1998. 'Private Open Space and Public Concerns.' *Review of Agricultural Economics*. 202: 644–53.

O'Brien, K. 2001. 'Factors Affecting Consumer Valuation of Environmentally Labeled Forest Products.' Masters Thesis, University of Maine. Orono, Maine.

Ready, R.C., M.C. Berger, and G.C. Blomquist. 1997. 'Measuring Amenity Benefits from Farmland: Hedonic Pricing vs. Contingent Valuation.' *Growth and Change* 28(4): 438–58.

Ribe, R. 1990. 'A General Model for Understanding the Perception of Scenic Beauty in Northern Hardwood Forests.' *Landscape Journal* 92: 86–101.

Ribe, R.D. 1989. 'The Aesthetics of Forestry: What has Empirical Preference Research Taught Us?' *Environmental Management* 13(1): 55–7.

Roe, B., K.J. Boyle, and M.F. Teisl. 1996. 'Using Conjoint Analysis to Derive Estimates of Compensating Variation.' *Journal of Environmental Economics and Management* 31: 145–59.

Rosenberger, R.S., and E.L. Smith. 1997. 'Nonmarket Economic Impacts of Forest Insect Pests: A Review of the Literature.' U.S. Department of Agriculture, Forest Service General Technical Report PSW-GTR-164. Albany, Canada: Pacific Southwest Research Station.

Rosenberger, R.S., E.L. Smith, and A. Gonzalez-Caban. 1997. 'Using Multiple Valuation Methods for Public Involvement in Management Decisions. Valuing Non-Timber Forest Resources: Timber Primacy is Passe.' Proceedings of the Southern Forest Economics Workers Meeting. Little Rock, Arkansas, March 19–21.

Rudis , V., J. Gramann, E. Ruddell, and J. Westphal. 1988. 'Forest Inventory and Management-Based Visual Preference Models of Southern Pine Stands.' *Forest Science* 34: 846–63.

Schaberg, R.H., T.K. Holmes, and R.C. Abt. 1997. 'A Comparison of Stakeholder Preferences for Market and Non-Market Goods and Services from Two Forests in Western North Carolina. Valuing Non-Timber Forest Resources: Timber Primacy is Passe.' Proceedings of the Southern Forest Economics Workers Meeting. Little Rock, Arkansas, March 19–21.

Schroeder, H., and Daniel, T. 1981. 'Progress in Predicting the Perceived Scenic Beauty of Forest Landscapes.' *Forest Science*. 27: 71–80.

Taylor, J.G, and T.C. Daniel. 1984. 'Prescribed Fire: Public Education and Perception.' *Journal of Forestry* 82: 361–5.

U.S. Department of Commerce, Bureau of the Census. Retrieved online from http://www.census.gov.

Welsh, C. 2002. 'Experiment in Harvesting Seeks Clear-Cut Answer to Logging Eyesores.' *The Seattle Times*, April 8.

Chapter 15

Using Hedonic Techniques to Estimate the Effects of Rural Land-Use Change on Property Values: An Example

Raymond B. Palmquist

Introduction

There have been many different types of rural land-use change in recent years as populations grow and technologies change. The causes and effects of these changes are discussed throughout this book. One of the useful techniques for valuation is to study the effects of changes on land values or property values. This chapter presents an example using the conversion to large-scale, concentrated hog feed operations in southeastern North Carolina. While this example is a single case study, in the process of describing it, the various modeling and estimation decisions that will be present in any rural land value or property value study are highlighted.

Studies of rural land values have been around for many years and became quite common in the 1980s. Many, but not all of these, have used the characteristics of agricultural land to explain land prices. In recent years, hedonic techniques developed within the context of urban housing markets have been applied to agricultural land. However, it is important to be aware that agricultural land is a differentiated factor of production, whereas residential land is a differentiated consumer good; the later case is what was described in Chapter 13. This means that the hedonic models for the two types of land are different.[1] It is important to consider the underlying model in choosing an appropriate specification for a hedonic equation.

Many hedonic studies of rural land have focused on land in agricultural use that will be likely to stay in that use in the future (at least over the short term). The important characteristics of such land include the productivity of the land, as well as considerations, such as how susceptible it is to erosion or the need for drainage. Examples of such studies include Miranowski and Hammes (1984), Ervin and Mill (1985), Gardner and Barrows (1985), King and Sinden (1988), and Palmquist and Danielson (1989). Other studies have concentrated on the effects of urban proximity on farmland values. The potential future conversion of agricultural land to urban uses is more closely related to the topic of this current book. Examples of this research include Chicoine (1981), Dunford, Marti, and Mittelhammer (1985), Pardew, Shane, and Yanagida (1986), and Shonkwiler and Reynolds (1986). Recently Bockstael and colleagues applied spatial econometrics to land-use conversion issues using hedonic, discrete choice, and duration models (for example, see Bockstael 1996; Geohegan et al. 1997; Bell and Bockstael 2000; and Irwin and Bockstael, forthcoming).

There have been fewer studies that focus on rural residential land and consider the effects of changes in the land use on surrounding agricultural lands. If technological innovations make agricultural lands more productive, surrounding lands may also appreciate in value because of the productivity improvements. Even if the surrounding lands stay in residential use, the value may appreciate because of the increased employment opportunities or the improved tax base in the county. However, it is also possible that the new uses of agricultural land will have negative spillover effects on the surrounding residential land, which may adversely affects property values. This is the type of effect studied in the current research.

Swine Production

There was a rapid transformation in the swine production industry during the 1990s. Earlier, most swine were produced in relatively small herds and the animals were not as concentrated as they are today. North Carolina was a leader in moving toward production in concentrated feeding operations. While North Carolina was second to Iowa in hog production, North Carolina production was predominantly in concentrated feed lots, while most Iowa production was more dispersed. In North Carolina it was estimated that 95 per cent of the swine output was produced on just 13 per cent of the farms with hogs.

This rapid movement to concentrated feeding operations represented a major shift in rural land use in the southeastern counties of North Carolina. This change resulted in increases in income and employment in these areas. However, it also resulted in concerns about the odor from hog barns and from the field application of hog manure. There were, as well, concerns about the effects on ground and surface waters. Vigorous political debates about these environmental issues followed. Some people who lived near large hog operations claimed that they could not sell their houses at any price because of the stench. Hog producers contended that the odor was barely perceptible, or at least not bothersome, so they maintained that housing prices were unaffected. Multiple bills were introduced in the North Carolina General Assembly to regulate swine production starting in 1993, but only a bill funding further research passed.

A Rural Property Value Study

Because of this divisive debate with little real evidence, we undertook a study of the effect of hog operations on neighboring rural residential property values. The price for which a house sells is hypothesized to depend on the characteristics of the structure, lot, neighborhood, location, and, perhaps, environment. The functional relationship between housing prices and the characteristics they contain is called the hedonic price function.[2] It is an equilibrium schedule of prices and results from the interaction of potential purchasers and the stock of houses in a location. In the hedonic function, if an environmental characteristic has a significant coefficient, this is evidence of the importance of that characteristic to consumers.

However, can the results be used to infer the willingness to pay for environmental quality? That depends on the nature of the environmental change, the valuation questions asked, and the data availability. If the change in the rural market only affects a relatively small number of properties within the market, the price of those properties are affected, but the equilibrium hedonic price schedule will not change. This is the case of a localized externality. In this case, non-marginal changes can be evaluated using only the hedonic schedule. If the change is large enough to affect the equilibrium price schedule, then the hedonic is insufficient for this valuation and the demands for the characteristics must be estimated. The shift to large-scale hog operations was so significant that one would anticipate that the equilibrium prices were changed by the transformation. However, one can still evaluate the impact of one new hog operation moving into an area by studying the market equilibrium hedonic schedule. That is the purpose of the study described here.

Data Collection

In doing a hedonic study, a separate hedonic price schedule should be estimated for each market. That requires that the researcher determine the extent of the market. In urban areas the consensus seems to be that the urban area defines the market, although not all would agree. It is hard to explain what would segment markets within an urban area in such a way that the segments are the same for all individuals, and each consumer considers only a single segment. In a rural context the lines are less clear. Is a single county a market? Do several counties form an integrated market? These become empirical questions.

In North Carolina the nine counties in the southeastern part of the state are where almost all of the large-scale hog operations are located.[3] Because we restricted our sample to rural residential properties, we excluded houses where the surrounding jurisdiction contained more than 2,500 people in order to avoid urban influences, and we limited the acreage associated with the house to under ten acres (most were under three acres), in order to avoid considering properties that were used primarily for agriculture or timber, rather than residential use. Because of changes in the area, we only collected sales during a relatively short time period (January 1992 to July 1993). We also only used 'arms-length' sales and excluded sales between relatives or sales that involved other considerations. These factors resulted in a relatively small number of valid sales (n=237). For this reason, it is helpful to consider the entire area as a single market. This is not implausible since the counties are all in the southern Coastal Plain and are relatively homogeneous. While a given individual might only consider one or a few of the counties, there is probably a great deal of overlap in the potential areas considered by different consumers in different areas. Thus, the markets might be integrated even if each consumer only considered part of the market. Later, the method used to check the assumption of a single market is explained.

Obtaining the sales data was more involved than in an urban area. Instead of a single source, we used a variety of sources, including three district offices of the Farm Credit Association. The Sampson County Assessor's records were also used, although other counties' databases were less complete. Finally, we used data from two private real estate companies that were active in the rural markets in the study area. The variables obtained from these sources were sale price and date, heated square feet, lot size, number of bathrooms, adjusted age, presence of decks, patios, garages, wood floors, fireplace, and whether the house was located within a platted subdivision. The legal description of the property was also obtained in order to determine the geographic location of the house and to link it to other variables. These data on houses were supplemented with data on the neighborhoods from the 1990 Census of Population and Housing (U.S. Department of Commerce, Bureau of the Census 1990). The Census variables used were population density by township, and income and commute time by census tract.

Obtaining data on the locations and sizes of the hog operations would be easier today because the North Carolina Department of Environment and Natural Resources now maintains an inventory of the operations. However, at the time the data was collected, the only centralized list of the locations and sizes of the hog operations was the State Veterinarian's office. They collected the information because of concerns about an animal disease (psuedorabies), but the information was confidential by law. An agreement was negotiated whereby confidentiality was maintained, while allowing access to some of the data. The location of each of our houses was supplied, and the State Veterinarian's office used geographical information system (GIS) programs to provide a summary of the number of herds and the head capacities for breeding, finishing, and nursery stock within one half, one, and two miles of the house.[4] A summary of the data is given in Table 15.1.

Specifying the Hedonic Equation

The basic specification of a hedonic equation is often straightforward, and the literature is filled with examples. The selling price of a property (or some transformation of that price) is explained by the contributions of the various structural and neighborhood characteristics of the house to its value. Table 15.1 defines the characteristics used in this study. In many cases ordinary least squares regression has been used for the estimation. However, there are various situations

Table 15.1 Variables of the hedonic model and their descriptive statistics (n=237)

Variable	Description	Units	Min	Max	Mean	Std Dev
PRICE	market price	$	15,000.0	320,000.0	73,132.0	36,601.0
HTD	heated area	sq ft	792.0	3,817.0	1,678.0	540.0
LOT	lot size	ac	0.2	8.5	1.2	1.1
BATH	bathrooms	no	1.0	4.0	1.8	0.6
AGE	effective age	yrs	0.0	100.0	18.0	16.0
DATE	date of sale	yr/mo	90.1	94.1	92.1	0.9
GAR2	2-car garage	y/n	0.0	1.0	0.3	N/A
DECK	deck/patio	y/n	0.0	1.0	0.5	N/A
FIRE	fireplace	y/n	0.0	1.0	0.6	N/A
POPDTW	township population density	no/m^2	9.0	1,992.0	342.0	466.0
INC90CT	income by census tract (1990)	$/fam	19,945.0	41,145.0	27,846.0	4,780.0
TRAVCT	commute time by census tract	min	15.4	28.9	21.7	3.1
NMAN0	manure 0–½ mile	tons/yr	0.0	11,016.0	331.0	1,329.0
NMAN1	manure ½–1 mile	tons/yr	0.0	48,152.0	1,780.0	4,761.0
NMAN2	manure 1–2 mile	tons/yr	0.0	40,467.0	6,104.0	9,210.0

that can make the estimation more complex. One of these, which is discussed below, is the form in which an environmental variable enters the equation. In the example discussed here, the complexity of combining hog operations at various distances from the houses into a nonlinear aggregate measure required the use of nonlinear least squares to simultaneously estimate the hedonic equation and the weights given to hog operations at various distances.

Often in hedonic studies one has a variety of objective measures of the characteristic of interest. However, it is people's perceptions of the characteristic that are important in determining property values, so some judgment is necessary in selecting the variables to use. In our case, we have the number of head measured at three different distances (concentric rings), but the variable we are interested in was odor, which comes from the manure.[5] The volume of manure produced depends on the number of head. We generate predictions for the volume of manure in tons generated within one half of a mile, between one half and one mile, and between one and two miles of a house. The odor at a house depends on the manure generated in each of the three distance rings, but the relative contribution of the manure in each of the rings to the overall perceived odor has to be determined in the estimation. This is where the weights in the manure index have to be estimated in the hedonic regression.

The number of herds near the house may also be important to the residents. The issue is that the same amount of manure might be of more concern to the residents if it is generated on one concentrated operation, rather than a number of smaller operations. Of course, one has to hold the amount of manure constant for the number of operations to have meaning, and zero operations may be desirable. We create a herd index using the reciprocal of the number of herds in each ring and set the value equal to zero in any ring where there are no herds. The value of this variable varies from zero to one, with one representing the most concentrated and zero being the least concentrated. The value for each ring is multiplied by the amount of manure produced in the ring to control for the number of animals in the ring. A weighted sum of the three rings is used, where the weights are estimated using nonlinear least squares.

Another issue with the variable(s) of interest is the form in which they enter the hedonic regression. Consider, for example, an environmental variable. The textbook example has the marginal effect of a pollutant increasing at an increasing rate. However, there are other patterns that may be equally plausible. It is not unusual to have a marginal effect of zero (or very low) with low levels of the pollutant. It is also plausible that some pollutants' marginal effects may be increasing at a decreasing rate at high levels. For hog odor, it seems reasonable that the effect is almost negligible at very low levels of hog numbers and then increases rapidly with additional hogs. However, once the odor is well established, it may be that adding to the source causes the damages to increase, but at a decreasing rate, as residents take averting actions or their senses become saturated. For these reasons we experiment with nonlinear forms for the environmental variable in this study. These forms include the more familiar logistic and the more general Gompertz and Richards.[6] We also experimented with thresholds, below which the hog odor has no effect.

Functional form also plays a more general role in hedonic studies. The functional form for the hedonic equation cannot be determined theoretically, it must be determined empirically. However, what appear to be the most general functional forms, for example the quadratic Box-Cox, may turn out to be more restrictive than they appear. This is because the Box-Cox coefficients on the independent variables are almost always restricted to be identical.[7] The coefficient is primarily determined by the most important explanatory variables, such as square feet of living space, yet the estimated coefficient is imposed on the environmental variable as well. As computing power increases, this restriction will likely be removed.

In the research described here, we find that a semi-log functional form performs significantly better than other simple forms, such as linear and log-linear. The linear Box-Cox was quite close to the semi-log, so we use the semi-log and devote our effort to the environmental variable.

Estimation Results

The impact of hog populations at different distances from a house may have different impacts on property values. However, the cumulative odor at a house is expected to determine the property value. It is necessary to estimate the contribution of the hogs in each distance ring to an index of odor at the house, and to simultaneously estimate the effect of this index on the property value. For this reason, nonlinear least squares is used for the hedonic regressions. The chosen specification for the regressions is:

$$(1) \quad \ln P = \alpha + \sum_{1}^{n} \beta_i x_i + \beta_M \ln(M_0 + \gamma_1 M_1 + \gamma_2 M_2) + \varepsilon,$$

where P is the price of the house, the x_i are n non-environmental characteristics and interaction terms, and M_j is the manure in the jth ring. The parameters estimated are α, β_i, and γ_j.

These regression results are reported in the first column of Table 15.2. The hedonic equation is semi-log, with the natural logarithm of price determined by the characteristics, most of which enter the estimated function linearly. With this specification, the coefficient of continuous variables is a close approximation to the relative change in the price of the house for a one unit change in the characteristic.[8] Thus, the value of an additional unit of a particular characteristic in a house equals almost exactly the coefficient multiplied by the price of that house. For example, the number of square feet of living space is a continuous variable. A one square foot difference at the mean (1,678) is effectively marginal. The value of a square foot of living space in the average house is a little over $29 ($73,132 x .0004). For variables that are discrete (count variables and dummy variables), this approximation is often quite inaccurate. The relative change is better estimated by

Table 15.2 Estimation results for two alternative specifications[a, b]

Variable	Base Model Coefficient	Std. Error	Model with Market Area Effects Coefficient	Std. Error
Intercept	9.9056*	0.166	10.1513*	0.162
Heated Area	0.0004*	0.000	0.0004*	0.000
Lot size	0.0414*	0.013	0.0263*	0.013
Bath rooms	0.0994*	0.032	0.1087*	0.030
Effective age	−0.0119*	0.001	−0.0117*	0.001
Pre 1992	−0.1068*	0.037	−0.0851*	0.035
Post 1992	0.0329	0.031	0.0259	0.030
2-car garage	0.1413*	0.032	0.1364*	0.030
Deck/Patio	0.0894*	0.027	0.0801*	0.026
Fireplace	0.0365	0.030	0.0232	0.028
Pop. density	0.0000	0.000	0.0000	0.000
Commute time	−0.0022	0.005	−0.0088	0.005
Family income	0.0000*	0.000	0.0000*	0.000
Ln manure index	−0.0089*	0.004	−0.0104*	0.004
γ_1	0.0054	0.026	0.0068	0.029
γ_2	0.0023	0.009	0.0066	0.020
Lenoir County			−0.1231*	0.046
Wayne x income			0.0000	0.000
Wayne x h.area			0.0002*	0.000
Johnston x lot			0.0449*	0.018
Adjusted R^2	0.8484		0.8692	

[a] Dependent variable is the natural log of price. All independent variables are linear except the natural log of manure index.
[b] * indicates that the estimate is statistically significant at the five per cent level.

taking the exponential of the coefficient and subtracting one. For example, the value of an additional bathroom in the average house (a discrete variable) would be over $7,500 [$73,132 x (e^.0994−1)].

The weights in the manure (or odor) index deserve explanation. The weights for all three distance rings and the coefficient for the index are not independent. One of the weights must be normalized. We normalize the weight in the closest ring to one. Thus, the coefficients γ_1 and γ_2 represent the lower weights that homeowners place on hog operations that are farther away. As one would expect, the impacts decline with distance.

Herd size does not have a statistically significant effect on property values, either when interacted with the number of hogs in the distance ring or when entered alone.[9] It appears that the property value effects are based on the odor and are not affected by perceptions about the herd size generating that odor.

As mentioned earlier, determining the size of the market is more difficult for rural areas than is it is for urban areas. To examine whether there are significant differences between the counties, dummy variables are included for the counties and are also interacted with all of the variables in the hedonic equation, to determine whether significant differences between the counties exist. For a total of 36 dummy variables and interaction terms, only four were significantly different than zero. This indicates that the assumption that the real estate market crossed county lines is reasonable. The results with the four new terms that are significant are reported in the second set of columns in Table 15.2. The significantly positive coefficient on the interaction between Johnson County and lot area is important to include. Johnson County is close to the thriving Raleigh-Durham metropolitan area and Research Triangle Park. Thus, it is expected that land values there are higher because of urban pressure. Indeed, including this interaction term significantly lowers the estimated coefficient on lot area in the remaining counties. The coefficients on the structural characteristics are not affected much by adding these new variables. The coefficients for the manure index are increased slightly, particularly γ_2. The three counties in the interaction terms have the most urban pressure of the counties in the study area. If we do not control for this influence, the effect of the index is slightly underestimated.

It is important to check how robust the results of interest are to minor changes in the empirical specification or data set. To do so, additional variables are included to see if they have an effect on the coefficients for the manure index. They did not. There are seven influential observations (outliers) that may drive the results. However, including or omitting them had little effect on the manure coefficients. Thus, our results are relatively stable.

Presenting Results

While the regression results seem quite satisfactory, it is hard to get an impression of the actual impacts from them. The effect of hog odor on the price of a house depends on a wide variety of considerations. The manure index shows that distance between the house and hog location has a major effect on the impact. The manure index enters nonlinearly, so the effect of a change in the hog population depends on the number of hogs already in the area. Also, the effect on the price of a house depends on its initial value, which in turn depends on the characteristics of the house. It would be possible to develop a wide range of scenarios for both the baseline situation and any change in the hog population near the house. If it were anticipated that there would be a specific change in the hog population at a specific location, it would be possible to forecast the change in property values for each house near the change in hog population. Of course, since the estimates of the parameters in the regression model have a statistical distribution, the transformation to the forecast change also generates a random variable with a distribution. It is important to provide not only a point estimate of the change but also a confidence interval for the forecast.

Table 15.3 Predicted values for the median price house with alternative levels of odor

Manure index	Location in Distribution	Predicted House Value	Range ($)*
0.725	1/8	$63,272	
2.309	1/4	$62,517	61,948–63,086
13.563	3/8	$61,381	60,029–62,733
33.107	1/2	$60,816	59,078–62,554
50.025	5/8	$60,557	58,642–62,472
118.82	3/4	$60,016	57,736–62,296
311.47	7/8	$59,420	56,742–62,098
11016.0	1	$57,266	53,182–61,350

*Range is based on the 95 per cent confidence interval for the change in the predicted price resulting from a change in the manure index where the base value is 0.725.

To provide examples of this use of regression results, we follow Palmquist, Roka, and Vukina (1997). We take the observed distribution of values for the manure index and divide it into eight parts. The values of the index at the dividing point between each of these octiles are then used in the examples. A given value of the index could be generated by various distributions of the hog operations between the three distance rings. For our examples, we assume that the number of hogs per acre is constant across the three distance rings. The values of the manure index at the octiles of the distribution of manure observations are given in the first column of Table 15.3.

We use the characteristics of the median priced house in our sample for generating the predicted price changes. This house had 2,034 square feet of living space, two baths, one fireplace, and was 40 years old. It did not have a deck or garage. The lot size was 2.4 acres, located in Johnston County. The neighborhood had 260.2 people per square mile, and the median annual family income was $25,671. The average commute time to work was 22 minutes. We then vary the number of hogs near the house. The predicted price of a house with these characteristics and no hogs within two miles is $63,365. The predicted house values with hogs in proximity are given in Table 15.3. The mean predicted price and the 95 per cent confidence interval for the forecast are given for different levels of hog concentration.[10]

It is also possible to predict the change in property value that will result if there is a change in the hog population near a house with these characteristics. The new operation is assumed to be a 2,400-head finishing floor. The new operation will have a different effect depending on how far from the house it is located, so

Table 15.4 Predicted changes in value for the median price house with a new hog operation

Manure index	Location in Distribution	Predicted change in house value* when a new operation locates within:		
		½ mile	1 mile	2 mile
0.725	1/8	−5,339 (8.44)	−2,279 (3.60)	−2,266 (3.58)
2.309	1/4	−4,585 (7.33)	−1,563 (2.50)	−1,551 (2.48)
13.563	3/8	−3,450 (5.62)	−649 (1.06)	−641 (1.04)
33.107	1/2	−2,889 (4.75)	−346 (0.57)	−340 (0.56)
50.025	5/8	−2,632 (4.35)	−248 (0.41)	−244 (0.40)
118.820	3/4	−2,103 (3.50)	−116 (0.19)	−113 (0.19)
311.470	7/8	−1,537 (2.59)	−46 (0.08)	−45 (0.08)
11,016.000	1	−167 (0.29)	−1 (0.00)	−1 (0.00)

* Predicted change in house value reported in dollars (per cent change)

the results are given for locating it in each of the three rings. The results also depend on the existing hog concentrations in the neighborhood. If there are almost no hogs near the house, the impact of this new operation is substantial. However, if the hog concentrations in the area were already at a very high level, the additional operation would have a lesser effect. These results are shown in Table 15.4.

Conclusions

This chapter has demonstrated the types of decisions that must be made in doing a hedonic study of rural land-use change. There are significant differences in the data collection process in rural areas, compared with the more typical hedonic studies done in urban areas. The determination of the relevant real estate market areas is not as simple as in urban areas. This chapter also emphasized the decisions that must be made in selecting an appropriate measure for the variables of interest (in this case, an environmental variable), and how that variable should enter the hedonic regression. The decisions that must be made in specifying and estimating the hedonic equation were discussed, and the results were interpreted. Finally, alternative ways of presenting the hedonic results so that they are more easily interpreted were presented. Overall, this analysis demonstrated that hedonic techniques are useful in studying rural land-use change.

Are the results plausible? The hog industry contends there is no effect, while an extreme environmentalist might say that nearby houses would lose all value. However, most economists would expect some effect but not a total loss in value because there is self-sorting in the presence of an environmental disamenity. For example, people who are less bothered by noise choose to live closer to highways than people who find noise annoying. Because of this sorting, prices are not necessarily reduced as much near a highway as they would be if occupants were randomly assigned to houses. Similarly, houses that are subject to odor and that sold with the odor present would be expected to be occupied by people who are less bothered by the odor. Thus, the discounts seems plausible. Nonetheless, as more precise geographical data become available, the issue should be revisited.

Notes

1   The seminal article by Rosen (1974) provides the model for hedonic studies of consumer products. Palmquist (1989) modified that model for use with factors of production such as agricultural land.

2   Hedonic techniques were discussed in Chapter 13. More detailed surveys are available in Bartik and Smith (1987), Palmquist (1991), Freeman (1993), and Palmquist (2000).

3   The counties are Bladen, Duplin, Greene, Johnson, Lenoir, Pender, Pitt, Sampson, and Wayne. Sampson and Duplin counties have the highest concentrations, but the surrounding counties also have substantial hog operations. In 1993, hog concentrations ranged from almost 1,300 hogs per square mile in Sampson to just over 100 per square mile in Pender.

4   These data were the best available to us at that time, but there were some shortcomings. Since we did not know the exact locations of the operations, we could not incorporate data on prevailing wind directions, etc. We also were unable to incorporate information on differences in management practices that might affect odor generation.

5   It is difficult to get objective measures for odor. While it is possible to detect and measure the volume of specific molecules in the air, odors can be formed from complex mixtures of the molecules. Also, human perception determines the difference between an objectionable odor and a pleasant odor. The only direct objective measure of odor uses a trained panel of individuals. The cost of taking such a panel to each house in the study for an extended period of time (to allow for varying wind direction, etc.) would been prohibitive.

6   All three forms have inflection points. Before the inflection point, the function is increasing at an increasing rate. After the inflection point, the function is increasing at a decreasing rate. With the logistic function, the inflection point is in the middle of the range of the function. With the Gompertz, the location of the inflection point is estimated. That is also true of the Richards, but the Richards also allows the function to have a threshold before it becomes positive. The logistic and Gompertz functions are nested within the Richards. Details on the functions are available in, for example, Schnute (1981).

7   With the quadratic Box-Cox, the Box-Cox coefficient for the linear terms may differ from that for the second-order terms, but each coefficient is still forced to be the same for every variable.

8   For the percentage change, multiply the coefficient by 100.

9   These regressions are not reported here.

10 For the details of calculating the confidences intervals, see Palmquist, Roka, and Vukina (1997).

References

Bartik, T.J., and V.K Smith. 1987. 'Urban Amenities and Public Policy,' in *Handbook of Regional and Urban Economics vol. 2*, ed. E.S. Mills. Amsterdam, The Netherlands: North-Holland.

Bell, K.P., and N.E. Bockstael. 2000. 'Applying the Generalized Method of Moments Approach to Spatial Problems Involving Micro-level Data.' *Review of Economics and Statistics* 82: 72–82.

Bockstael, N.E. 1996. 'Modeling Economics and Ecology: The Importance of a Spatial Perspective.' *American Journal of Agricultural Economics* 78: 1168–80.

Chicoine, D.L. 1981. 'Farmland Values at the Urban Fringe: An Analysis of Sale Prices.' *Land Economics* 57: 353–62.

Dunford, R.W., C.E. Marti, and R.C. Mittelhammer. 1985. 'A Case Study of Rural Land Prices at the Urban Fringe Including Subjective Buyer Expectations.' *Land Economics* 61: 10–16.

Ervin, D.E., and J.W. Mill. 1985. 'Agricultural Land Markets and Soil Erosion.' *American Journal of Agricultural Economics* 67: 938–42.

Freeman, A.M. III. 1993. *The Measurement of Environmental and Resource Values*. Washington, District of Columbia: Resources for the Future.

Gardner, K., and R. Barrows. 1985. 'The Impact of Soil Conservation Investments on Land Prices.' *American Journal of Agricultural Economics* 67: 943–47.

Geohegan, J., L.A. Wainger, and N.E. Bockstael. 1997. 'Spatial Landscape Indices in a Hedonic Framework: An Ecological Economics Analysis Using GIS.' *Ecological Economics* 23: 251–64.

Irwin, E.G., and N.E. Bockstael. Forthcoming. 'Interacting Agents, Spatial Externalities and the Evolution of Residential Land Use Patterns.' *Journal of Economic Geography*.

King, D.A., and J.A. Sinden. 1988. 'Influence of Soil Conservation on Farmland Values.' *Land Economics* 64: 242–55.

Miranowski, J.A., and B.D. Hammes. 1984. 'Implicit Prices of Soil Characteristics for Farmlands in Iowa.' *American Journal of Agricultural Economics* 66: 745–49.

Palmquist, R.B. 1989. 'Land as a Differentiated Factor of Production: A Hedonic Model and its Implications for Welfare Measurement.' *Land Economics* 65: 23–8.

Palmquist, R.B. 1991. 'Hedonic methods,' in *Measuring the Demand for Environmental Quality*, eds. J.B.Braden and C.D. Kolstad. Amsterdam, The Netherlands: North-Holland.

Palmquist, R.B., 2000. 'Property Value Models.' In Handbook of Environmental Economics, eds. , K.G. Mäler and J. Vincent. North Holland, Amsterdam.

Palmquist, R.B., and L.E. Danielson. 1989. 'A Hedonic Study of the Effects of Erosion Control and Drainage on Farmland Values.' *American Journal of Agricultural Economics* 71: 55–62.

Palmquist, R.B., F.M. Roka, and T. Vukina. 1997. 'Hog Operations, Environmental Effects, and Residential Property Values.' *Land Economics* 73: 114–24.

Pardew, J.B., R.L. Shane, and J.F. Yanagida. 1986. 'Structural Hedonic Prices of Land Parcels in Transition From Agriculture in a Western Community.' *Western Journal of Agricultural Economics* 11: 50–57.

Shonkwiler, J.S., and J.E. Reynolds. 1986. 'A Note on the Use of Hedonic Price Models in the Analysis of Land Prices at the Urban Fringe.' *Land Economics* 62: 58–63.

Schnute, J. 1981. 'A Versatile Growth Model with Statistically Stable Parameters.' *Canadian Journal of Fisheries and Aquatic Sciences* 38: 1128–40.

U.S. Department of Commerce, Bureau of the Census. 1990. *Census of Population and Housing*. Retrieved online from http://www.census.gov/main/www/cen1990.html.

PART V
CONCLUSIONS

Chapter 16

Summary and Conclusions

Kathleen P. Bell, Kevin J. Boyle, and Jonathan Rubin

Introduction

The economics of rural land-use change encompass numerous tradeoffs involving the allocation of land resources. From an economics perspective, rural land-use change is a bountiful research area because it involves, among other factors, market and non-market services, private and public goods, uncertainty, and temporal and spatial dependence. Moreover, the modeling of preferences and production decisions related to land necessitates a diverse range of theoretical and empirical methods. In editing this volume, we hope to inspire an appreciation of this research area and to foster future advancements in the economics of rural land-use change.

Divergent private and social interests make the use and management of rural lands compelling public policy and economic issues. In turn, the persistence and the variation of these interests over time and space account for the endurance of public policy issues related to rural land-use change. Conflicts over the use of public and private rural lands are bolstered by diverse values and worldviews over our rural landscape, as well as by government and market failure. Recent examples of such conflicts include the national discussions of oil drilling in the Arctic National Wildlife Refuge, the removal of the Hetch-Hetchy Dam, the regulation of snowmobiling at Yellowstone National Park, and the construction and maintenance of roads on national forestlands. Local land-use discussions throughout the U.S. share common threads, as rural communities ponder the advantages and disadvantages of hosting 'big-box' retail outlets, gambling casinos, waste disposal facilities, and various forms of new development.

Rural land-use change presents complex and challenging issues for economists, planners, and policymakers interested in evaluating outcomes and making suggestions for future land management. Many of these issues follow from the uniqueness of land as both a form of property and a broader natural resource that provides important ecological and social services. Although considerable advancements have been made in modeling the private market returns from lands (and hence the demand for land as a private input by firms and households), there is less of a clear understanding of the demand (and supply) for private non-market services associated with land resources. Moreover, numerous questions remain regarding how to assess the efficiency of aggregate land-use decisions. Said differently, economists have made significant advances modeling individual land-use decisions but struggle when making broad welfare statements regarding land-use patterns, which are the collective result of many individual decisions. In addition, the local dimensions of land as a policy issue necessitate tailored analytical methods and policy prescriptions. While certain rural communities are presently overwhelmed with intense growth and development pressures, others are threatened by opposite pressures and are experiencing concentrated losses of population and employment opportunities. These distinct settings are likely to raise strikingly different research questions regarding land management and land-use policy.

Objectives of this Book

Building on the momentum of earlier books on the economics of land use rooted in the traditions of Ricardo and von Thünen (e.g., Barlowe 1958, Found 1971, Van Kooten 1993), the primary objective of this book is to feature contemporary land-use change models and cost-benefit analyses of land-use policies. As noted previously, we perceive land use as an active research area for economists and are excited by recent advances in modeling, such as explicit consideration of the dynamic and irreversible nature and spatial aspects of land-use decisions, as well as recent advances in valuation methods to estimate the demand for non-market services and the external costs and benefits associated with rural land-use change. A second objective of this volume is to make a case for using economic thinking to evaluate, understand, and manage rural land-use change. We believe economists have much to contribute to future discussions of rural land-use change. Moreover, the strength and value of these contributions rest on the continued development of theoretical and empirical frameworks for addressing policy issues related to land use. It is our intention that this volume plays a role in supporting such developments.

Direction of Future Research

The writings of the various contributors to this volume raise several interesting research questions to guide future research. Part I of this volume evokes several research questions related to land-use trends. Chapters 1 and 2 raise questions related to the underlying determinants of recent increases in developed land uses. Although developed uses are still a small share of the total land base, land was converted to developed uses at the rate of 2.2 million acres per year from 1992 to 1997. Chapter 3 emphasizes the significance of anticipating future conditions, especially accounting for technological advances, when simulating impacts of future proposed policies and highlights the need for future work on measurable indicators of long-term ecological, economic, and social well being as it relates to alternative uses of land. The connections between land-use and transportation outlined in Chapter 4 underscore the importance of future research accounting for the interdependencies between land-use change and the demand for travel. Chapter 5 calls for future research to decipher two forms of rural land-use change: urban peripheral expansion and green field development in areas far from urban centers. Chapter 5 also emphasizes the joint significance of demographic and regional economic characteristics in determining the type of settlement patterns observed in response to growth pressures. A common theme throughout Part I is the dynamic aspects of land-use trends. Land-use trends are inextricably linked with other social, economic, and ecological trends.

In response to the trends outlined in Part I of this volume, the chapters comprising Part II offer examples of how economic thinking is employed to characterize land-use decisions and to model changes in land use. Chapter 6 provides guidance for future theoretical advances that involve further consideration of heterogeneous land qualities, alternative formations of expectations of returns to land, and spatial attributes of lands. Chapter 6 also calls for theoretical research on policy instruments aimed at the external costs and benefits of land use, especially comparisons of market-based and regulatory (standard) approaches. In the review of empirical models, Chapter 7 makes several suggestions for future research, including the value of studying the influences of private non-market benefits, option values, and uncertainty on land-use decisions. This chapter also stresses the design of models that allow for direct simulation of policies and the advantages and disadvantages of modeling land-use change at different spatial scales. Current examples of modeling land-use change at macro and micro scales make up the final two chapters of Part II. Based on a study of Wisconsin land-use policy, Chapter 8 emphasizes the utility of research on how policies influence different types of land-use conversions. The implications that some land-use shares are less responsive to policies will have major consequences for the design of land-policy programs, such as those that target carbon sequestration. Emphasis is also given to better understanding the broader effects of land quality changes on aggregate land-use patterns. The empirical work summarized in Chapter 9 employs parcel-level data to describe residential development in rural Maryland. Chapter 9 emphasizes the need for research on the spatial aspects of rural land-use change, the usefulness of incorporating spatial data and modeling tools into economic models of land-use decisions, the value of directly integrating policies into such models, and the relative appropriateness of different policy tools for achieving spatial land management objectives. As a whole, the chapters of Part II offer insights into why the use of rural lands change over time and where future changes in the use of these lands are more or less likely to occur. The chapters making up Part III assess the implications of these changes.

The chapters comprising Part III of this volume stimulate questions regarding the ecological and social consequences of rural-land use change. Chapter 10 illustrates the interplay of public values, scientific information, and private property rights in contemporary land-use decisions in South Florida. Similar case studies are likely to improve our understanding of land-use management processes. Chapter 11 calls attention to the role of rural areas in achieving biodiversity objectives and the need for research on balancing economic and ecological objectives in designing land-use plans. Chapter 12 stresses balance by calling for an improved understanding of the interactions between land development, land-use regulations, and their socioeconomic and ecosystem impacts.

The chapters of Part IV of this volume continue the discussion of the consequences of rural land-use change and focus on the development of economic valuation methods and empirical studies to support benefit-cost analysis of land-use changes. Chapter 13 thoughtfully discusses the relative appropriateness of different valuation methods for evaluating land-use change and points out several gaps in the empirical literature. Chapter 14 illustrates how conjoint methods can be used to examine public preferences for multiple-use lands. Similar work in other regions of the U.S. is likely to produce valuable information for policymakers. Chapter 15 demonstrates how hedonic techniques can be useful in studying rural land-use change and hints at future refinements of hedonic modeling to incorporate sorting effects and micro-scale spatial data. Conjoint and hedonic property valuation methods explicitly account for the heterogeneous attributes of land and land uses. As a result, these two valuation methods are likely to be employed by researchers in future studies of rural land-use change.

Final Remarks

As colleagues at the University of Maine, we do not have to look far to observe indications of rural land-use change. The predominantly rural landscape of Maine is undergoing notable transitions. The spatial distributions of population and employers are increasingly clustered in southern and coastal areas. As traditional manufacturing industries, such as paper mills and shoe manufacturers close, rural communities are reaching out to industries such as biotechnology and tourism with mixed success. The uneven results of such efforts support a range of pressures in rural areas, spanning high-growth to no-growth pressures. Ownership of the largely forested landscape, which is over 95 per cent private land, is diversifying markedly and tenure of ownership is falling. Residential development is occurring throughout the state and tends to be increasing at a faster rate in non-established service or employment center communities. This latter trend is influenced by, among other factors, the sale of numerous lands by the forest industry and the appeal of coastal, lake, and mountain communities. In turn, the northern portion of the landscape is rife with uncertainty. A patchwork of conservation easements and outright purchases of land for conservation is growing with time. Heated debates arise with even the mention of a new national park in northern Maine. Discussions of issues such as loss of farmlands are rivaled by parallel discussions of the siting of new landfills and rural industrial parks. A citizen referendum calling for increased purchase of land for open space, recreation, and habitat appears on the same ballot as a second referendum calling for the siting of multiple gambling facilities. These trends in development and policy discussions are not unique to Maine. Similar discussions are being held in rural areas throughout the United States. From an economic perspective, the changing rural landscape raises numerous interesting and challenging questions. Our expectation is that the compelling nature of these questions and the pervasiveness of rural land-use change will support further refinements in the economic modeling of land-use change and the economic valuation of the benefits and costs of land-use change.

References

Barlowe, R. 1958. *Land Resource Economics.* Englewood Cliffs, New Jersey: Prentice-Hall.

Found, W.C. 1971. *A Theoretical Approach to Rural Land-Use Patterns.* New York, New York: St. Martin's Press.

Van Kooten, G.C. 1993. *Land Resource Economics and Sustainable Development: Economic Policies and the Common Good.* Vancouver: University of British Columbia Press.

Index

For Product Safety Concerns and Information please contact our
EU representative GPSR@taylorandfrancis.com Taylor & Francis
Verlag GmbH, Kaufingerstraße 24, 80331 München, Germany